About the Author

Glyn Ford has been the European Member for Manchester East since 1984. He was a Local Councillor in Tameside for a number of years. Between 1979 and 1980 he was the Chair of the Environmental Health and Control Committee and then, between 1980 and 1985, he was the Chair of Tameside Education Services Committee. He was a founder member, in 1973, of the Socialist Environmental Resources Association, an organisation that "looks back to the socialism of William Morris rather than to the sterile Crosslandite corporatism of the 1950s".

With a degree in geology from Reading University and a Masters Degree in Marine Earth Science from University College London, Glyn Ford worked as a student and then as a staff member in Manchester University's Department of Science and Technology Policy, finishing in 1984 as a Senior Research Fellow. In 1983 he spent six months as a visiting professor teaching science and technology policy in the Department of Systems Science at the University of Tokyo. He is currently the Vice Chair of the European Parliament's Japanese delegation. Whilst at Manchester University he worked on the Programme of Policy Research in Engineering Science and Technology, co-ordinating the Marine Resources Project. In 1987, he published a book with Chris Liblett and Lindsay Walker entitled *The Future of Ocean Technology*.[1]

Glyn Ford was re-elected to the European Parliament in 1989. From 1989 to 1993 he was the Leader of the European Parliamentary Labour Party (EPLP) and, consequently, a member of the National Executive Committee of the Labour Party. He has been, since 1989, a member of the Bureau of the Socialist Group. As a Socialist Group Bureau Member he is responsible for relations with the Parties of the Party of European Socialists. He was also responsible for the Socialist Group input into the common manifesto in preparation for the June 1994 European Elections.

Glyn Ford is an active member on a number of Parliamentary committees. For the last ten years he has been a member of the Energy Research and Technology Committee. He is also a member of the Institutional Affairs Committee, and a substitute member on the Foreign Affairs and Security Committee, and the Security and Disarmament Sub-Committee. Between 1984 and 1986 Glyn Ford was the Chair of the Parliament's Committee of Inquiry into the Rise of Racism and Fascism and then, in 1990, he was the rapporteur for the second Committee of Inquiry into Racism and Xenophobia. From this came his recent book, *Fascist Europe*.[2]

Glyn Ford has also been responsible for a number of other reports submitted to the Parliament. In October 1986 he was the rapporteur on the Committee on External Economic Relations, which submitted a report to the Parliament on counter trade. In 1987, he submitted a report on Star Wars and Eureka, calling for 'non participation' in the Star Wars programme. This was lost in the Parliament by two votes (176 votes to 174). Glyn Ford has also been the rapporteur on two further reports submitted to the Parliament on the arms trade. He is currently working on a third report.

Glyn Ford has four main areas of interest: science and technology policy, Japan, the rising tide of racism, and Europe. He has campaigned against racism both within his constituency, which has a large immigrant population, and at the European level. He has attended rallies across Europe to speak out against racist violence and the electoral victories of the Far Right groups in the European Elections of 1989. He has consistently argued for Europe to establish its own technological trajectory and for science and technology to be placed high on the political agenda in order to combat American and Japanese technological advances.

References
1. Glyn Ford, Lindsay Walker and Chris Liblett, *The Future of Ocean Technology* (London: Frances Pinter, 1987).
2. Glyn Ford, *Fascist Europe: The Rise of Racism and Xenophobia* (London: Pluto Press, 1992).

THE EVOLUTION OF A EUROPEAN

Socialism, Science and Europe

GLYN FORD MEP

SPOKESMAN
for
EUROPEAN LABOUR FORUM

*To the windsurfers and
chess players in my life*

First published in Great Britain in 1993 by
Spokesman
Bertrand Russell House
Gamble Street
Nottingham, England
Tel. 0602 708318
Fax 0602 420433

Copyright © Glyn Ford, 1993

Permission to reproduce these articles and pictures is gratefully acknowledged. Every effort was made to trace copyright ownership. In the few cases where this proved impossible, we apologise for any possible infringement of copyright.

All rights reserved.
Enquiries should be addressed to the publishers.

British Library Cataloguing in Publication Data available on request
ISBN 0-85124-560-9 cloth
ISBN 0-85124-561-7 paper

Printed by the Russell Press Ltd, Nottingham
(Tel. 0602 784505)

CONTENTS

Part 1
1975-1979

1. Environmentalism and Reaction	3
2. Lebanon and the Next Few Months	6
3. Galileo's Tidal Theory: A Partial Vindication	8
4. Libya — Land of Lost Opportunities	13
5. Review of *Islamic Science: An Illustrated Study* by Seyyed Hossein Nasr	17
6. Science in Society: Even the Truth is Relative plus correspondence	20
7. Letter to *Socialist Challenge*	28
8. Demolising a Whale	29
9. All at Sea with the Third World	31
10. Tameside: The Score Labour Has to Settle	33

Part 2
1980-1982

11. Letter to the *London Review of Books*	37
12. Review of *The Visible College* by Gary Werskey	37
13. Review of *The Heyday of Natural History* by Lynn Barber and *Science and Colonial Expansion: The Role of British Royal Botanic Gardens* by Lucile H. Brockway	41
14. Science for All	45
15. Review of *Science and Sexual Oppression* by Brian Easlea	48
16. Review of *The Baroque Arsenal* by Mary Kaldor	49
17. Japan Stakes its Industrial Future in the Sea	50
18. The Costs of Good Intentions	52
19. Review of *Kew: Gardens for Science and Pleasure* edited by F. Nigel Hepper	56
20. Independence for Gib	57
21. Energy: The Hot and Cold Solution	58

Part 3
1983-1985

22. Letter from Port Blair	63
23. Manga Mania in Japan	66
24. Review of *Geophysics in the Affairs of Man* by C. Bates, T. Gaskell and R. Rice	69

25. Revealing Illness: Radical Science in Japan	70
26. Review of *Betrayers of the Truth: Fraud and Deceit in the Halls of Science* by William Broad and Nicholas Wade	76
27. Review of *The Japanese Mind* by Robert C. Christopher	77
28. The Tide of Racism Sweeps over Europe	78

Part 4
1986

29. Star Wars Secret Could Cost us Dear	83
30. An Appeal to the People of Japan — Don't Play Star Wars	86
31. Review of *Aborted Discovery* by Susantha Goonatilake	88
32. Kamikaze Politics or the Collective Madness that Grips Labour in Europe	90
33. Rebirth of Islamic Science	93

Part 5
1987

34. Letter from Urumqi	111
35. Top Gun — Designer Death	113
36. Japan Bids for a Corner in the World Power Triad	115
37. Le Pen: This Racist Menace Should be Banned from Britain	117
38. Review of *James Maxton* by William Knox, *J. Ramsay MacDonald* by Austen Morgan, *Philip Snowden* edited by Keith Laybourn and David James	119

Part 6
1988

39. Review of *Europe without America?* by John Palmer	125
40. Review of *The Enchanted Glass: Britain and its Monarchy* by Tom Nairn	126

Part 7
1989

41. Review of *Unit 731* by Peter Williams and David Wallace	133
42. European Arms Exports	134
43. Europe — The Lost Agenda	158

44. Labour in Europe	161
45. We Can Open a Second Front in Europe	164
46. Testimony to the House of Commons Foreign Affairs Committee on the Single European Act	166

Part 8
1990

47. The New Europe: A Socialist Vision	187
48. Our Common European Future	193

Part 9
1991

49. The European Parliament and Democracy	201
50. Europe, the Gulf and the New World Order	203
51. Nietzsche was Right; Twice	207
52. Review of *Neo-Fascism in Europe* edited by Luciano Cheler, Ronnie Ferguson and Michalina Vaughan	209
53. Interview on Racism in Europe	210
54. Europe's Baltic Dilemma	217
55. Review of *European Union: Fortress or Democracy?* by Michael Barratt Brown	220

Part 10
1992

56. Maastricht: The Lost Opportunity	225
57. Review of *Paradigms Lost* edited by Chester Hartman and Pedro Vilanova	227
58. The EC and Japan: The New Agenda	229
59. European Socialisms in Crisis: The Rise of Radical Right Populism	236
60. Jamboree Starts Race for the White House	239
61. The Choice is Stark: Maastricht or Nothing	241

Part 11
1993

62. Part of or apart from Europe?	247
63. Images of Science and Progress	248
64. One More Heave for South Africa	257
65. Review of *Head to Head* by Lestor Thurow	258
66. Review of *Science, Technology and Society in Postwar Japan* by Shigeru Nakayama	260
67. Our Europe, Not Theirs	262

68. Review of *Europe and America in the 1990s* by   264
    John Peterson
69. Review of *Hope Dies Last* by Alexander Dubcek   265
70. Sheron Gags Swales Boo-boys   267

Contributors

Christine Crawley is the Labour MEP for Birmingham East. She was first elected to the European Parliament in 1984. She is now Chair of the Women's Rights Committee and EPLP spokesperson on civil liberties.

Luke Georghiou is now a PREST Professor at Manchester University.

Duncan Hallas has been an active socialist since the 1940s and is a leading member of the Socialist Workers' Party.

Nakajima Keiko worked at the University of Tokyo in the Department of System Science.

David Martin is the Labour MEP for Lothians. He has been an MEP since 1984. Between 1987 and 1988 he was the Leader of the EPLP. He is now a Vice-President of the European Parliament.

David Morris is the Labour MEP for Mid and West Wales. He has been an MEP since 1984. He is a founding member of CND and a Presbyterian Minister.

Chris Pienning is Head of Divisions of Inter-Parliamentary Delegations in the European Parliament.

Julian Priestley is the Secretary General of the Group of the Party of European Socialists, the largest group within the European Parliament. He has previously stood in Westminster elections as a Labour candidate in Plymouth in 1974, 1979 and 1983.

Gary Titley is the Labour MEP for Greater Manchester West. He was first elected to the Parliament in 1989. He is currently the Chair of the European Parliament's delegation to the European Economic Area Joint Parliamentary Committee.

Carole Tongue is the Labour MEP for London East. She has been a member of the European Parliament since 1984. She was the rapporteur on the future of the European car industry and is currently a member of the European Parliament's delegation for relations with the Commonwealth of Independent States.

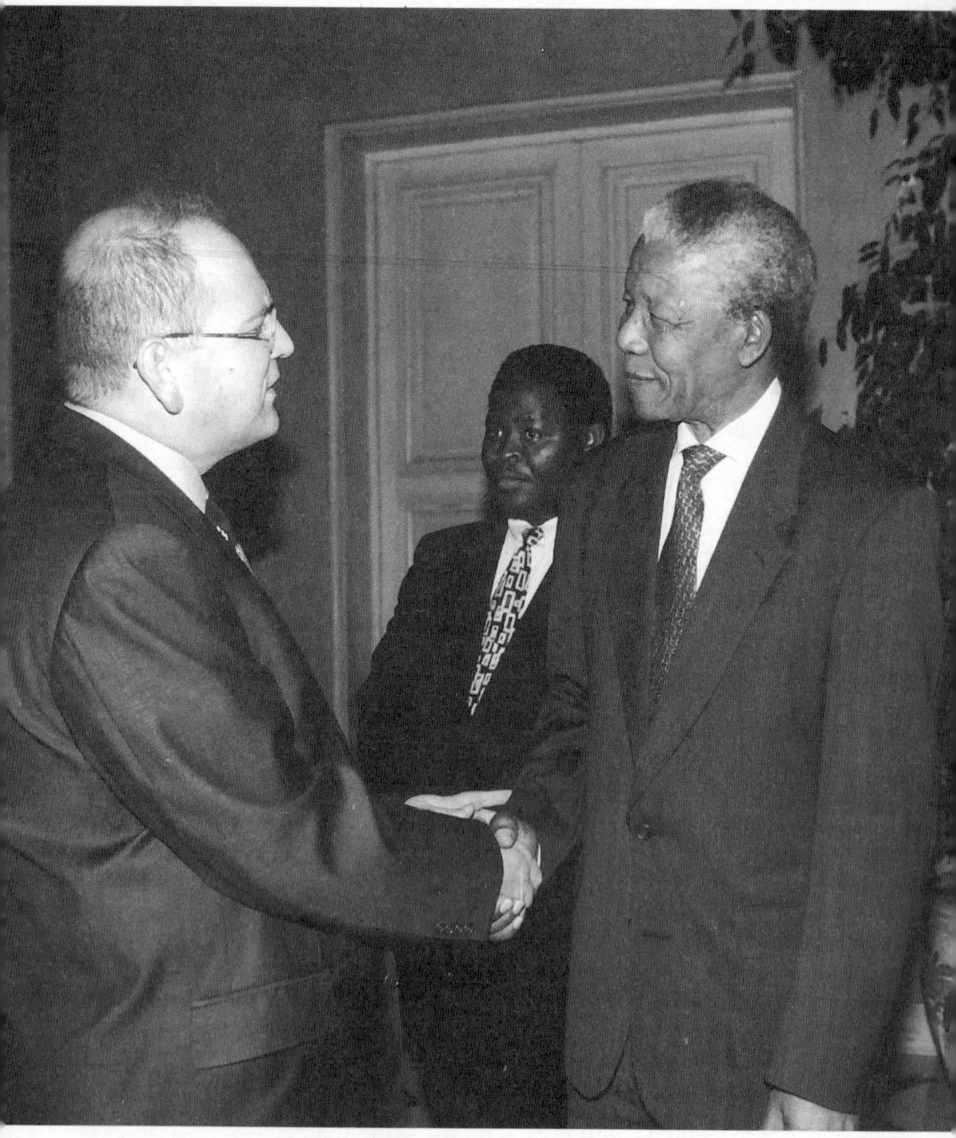

Introduction

My childhood was spent in an exclusively labour environment. My parents were both Labour and my extended family, in the Forest of Dean, had all the men working as miners, with the politics that flowed automatically from that in the 1950s. In my extended family there were members who wouldn't buy a blue second hand bike — although I have managed to overcome the colour bar with my football team! (See page 267.)

Not that these family members held key positions in the Labour movement. There was only a thin scatter of local councillors and trade union branch officers. Yet, for them their politics were a central part of their lives. It was not something they put on at election times, but something that affected them at work, at home, and at play. The family went on holiday in a 49 seater coach. In consequence, I never consciously became a socialist; I was born one.

Becoming a European was not so easy. In 1975, I was actively involved in the 'No Campaign' around the referendum. I believed socialism in one country was possible and desirable. I campaigned and voted accordingly. In 1979, for the first direct elections to the European Parliament, I was put forward as an Anti-Common Market candidate within the Labour Party. I lost the selection in Greater Manchester North to Barbara Castle.

By 1984 I was starting to have doubts. Socialism had not proved itself a success between 1974 and 1979 in the United Kingdom, and in France the Mitterrand Government had just blown up before take off. My own career had started in the Wilsonian white hot heat of the technological revolution. It peaked with Maths, Physics, and Chemistry at A-Level, and then began a long slow retreat via Geology and Marine Earth Science to Science and Technology Policy. It was the latter that took me to Japan and the University of Tokyo in 1983. In the spring and summer of that year I suppose, to paraphrase Sydney and Beatrice Webb, "I saw the future and it worked". The vibrance of the Japanese economy and its clear successes were astounding.

Yet it did not strike me immediately that, if we were to compete, Europe was the only way to do it. It was a gradual dawning. The first time it really struck home was at a socialist conference on Science and Technology Policy in London in the autumn of 1983 when clear arguments for the European option came forward. As Huxley said of Darwin's *On the Origin of Species*, "How stupid not to have thought of it before". It was now self evidently true. That

◄ *October 1993: Nelson Mandela visits the European Parliament in Brussels (photo: Serge Weinber).*

would not have been the case twelve months earlier, pre-Japan. Going from the technological imperative to the economic, social and political consequences took more time. In this collection are the peregrinations on the road to Europe and the evolution of a European. Where possible, the original versions of articles have been used, so that they may vary slightly from what was published in the various journals.

Seventy-five years to the day after the end of the First World War is a fitting time to complete the text. I give my grateful thanks to all those who have shared the journey with me. Some are mentioned, others remain anonymous. I would like to thank all my staff over this period: Kay Baxter, Andy Rowe, Oona King and, in particular, Sarah Chilton who helped organise the unorganisable, and gave me breathing space to complete this book.

Glyn Ford
Mossley
11 November 1993

Part 1

1975-1979

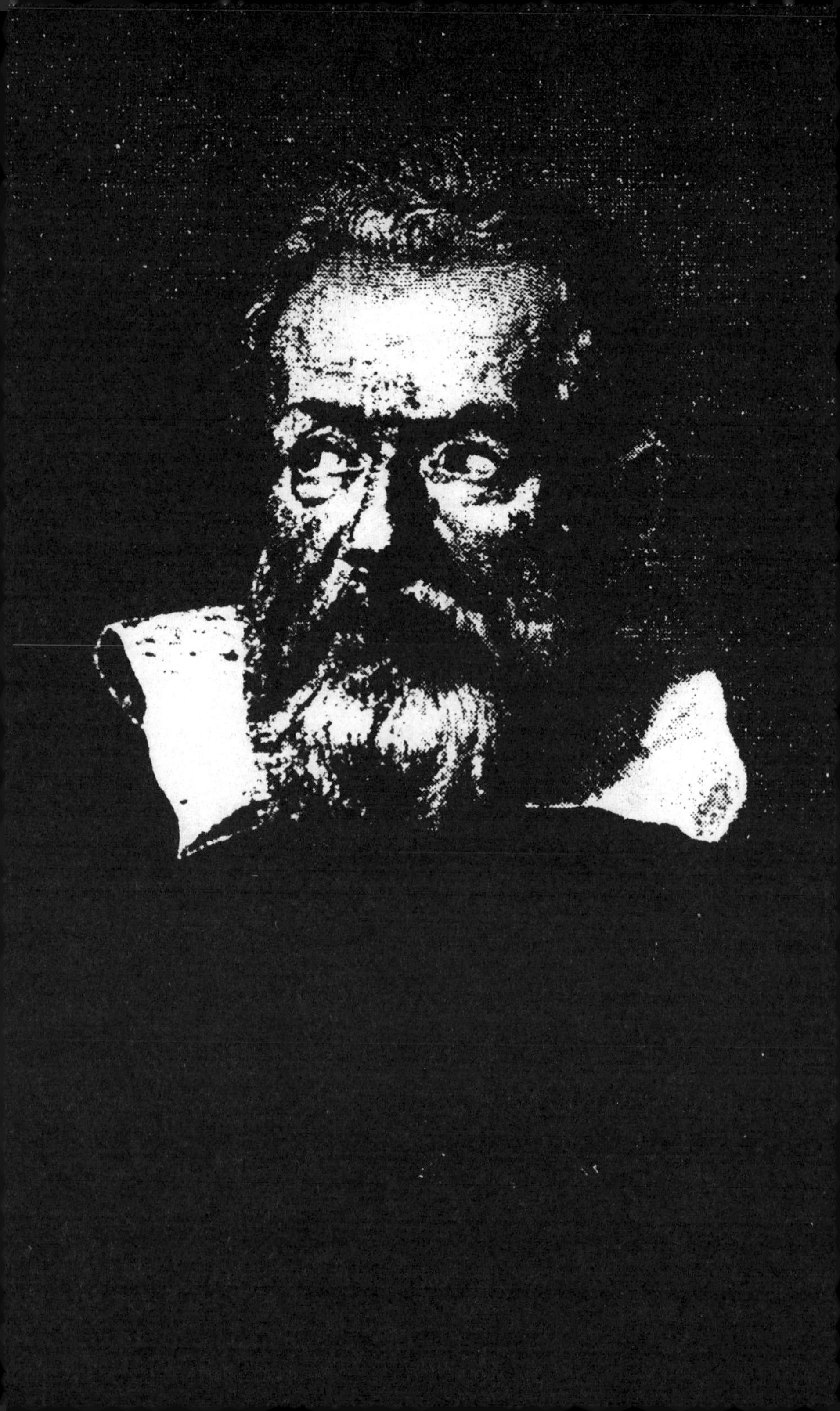

1. Environmentalism and Reaction

Environmental considerations today evoke a positive response from people who until recently would have dismissed the Conservation Movement as a merely middle-class pressure group out to protect their own living standards. This conversion has been particularly prolific amongst members of the Labour Movement. Like all neophytes these members still have a very unsophisticated view of the movement which they have so recently clasped to their bosoms. The Labour Movement as yet still sees environmentalists as members of a monolithic movement who have so recently been transformed *en masse* from being a middle-class coalition in league with the devil, to an affiliated organisation of the angels, with honourary worker status. Both the former and latter views are naive.

The environmentalists are part of a movement which is as rent asunder by ideological divisions as the Christian Church or the Left-wing groups in Britain. To use the all embracing word 'movement' with respect to this phenomena is to conceal much of the reality of the situation. The positions adopted by environmentalists range from the Technocrats of the Club of Rome, initiators of the study which led to the book *Limits to Growth* (Pan, 1972), to Libertarian Communists at the other end. The only features common to all these groups are their condemnations of Economism, and Industrial society, plus a marked ambivalence, at least, towards modern science.

If an undue simplification of the situation is allowed, two main forms of this rejection of industrial society exist, firstly the Puritan/Technocratic and secondly the Libertarian strain. The former is epitomised in the writings contained in *The Ecologist*. Here the 19th Century notion of 'station and duties in life' is justified by reference to the need for Order, Hierarchy, and Inequality for the sake of Mankind's continual survival on this planet. Whereas the libertarians are identified by an antipathy to all these, and an inherent sense of romanticism. It should be unnecessary to say, but not all conservation groups or individuals fall neatly into one of these two opposing camps; a whole spectrum of positions between them exist. But this dualism does lead to socialists being in danger of falling into one of two traps. If the relentless authoritarian type of thinking is discovered, this critique of Capitalist society may be rejected as a whole, while equally if this is not found 'Ecological consciousness' may, like the Trojan horse, bring into socialist thought a hidden and unsuspected danger. This is that the elitist

◄ *Galileo: born on about the day on which Michelangelo died, he died in the year in which Newton was born (see item 3).*

and intolerant portions of ecological thought may distort humanitarian considerations in socialism.

Firmly set on the elitist limb of ecological thought is Edward Goldsmith, who is currently editor of *The Ecologist*. Much of Goldsmith's thought is incorporated in his recent book *The Epistemological and Behavioral Basis of Culturalism; A General Systems Approach*, which consists of rewritten material first published in *The Ecologist*, and his thinking is typical of this elitist strain of ecologists. The book is a mess of semi-comprehensible verbiage about such entities as cybernismic order, heterotelic responses and the teleonomic principle; but the book is still important, being one of the first attempts to produce a comprehensive philosophical basis for the right-wing of the movement. Reading it one is reminded in every paragraph of Rhodes Boyson and the recent Black Paper on Education. The assumptions are the same and often the rhetoric.

> "Nor can it (The family unit-JGF) survive when the father's normal functions have been usurped by an all-pervading welfare state that takes over the education of his children, the care of his family's health, and even their very substance when he is unemployed or otherwise incapacitated." (p.15)

The quote above came from Edward Goldsmith's book, but it could so easily have been Rhodes Boyson. But Goldsmith cannot be so easily dismissed for he is busily erecting a set of philosophical crutches for the middle classes; ones similar to those erected by Malthus one hundred and seventy years ago when he published his *Essay on the Principle of Population*, which enabled the middle-class for so long to banish from their sight and mind the evils of industrial civilisation, as these deprivations were essential propitiations to the God of Progress. For Karl Marx the justification of the suffering was to be born out in generations to come. Those who suffered were hostages to the future. Malthus had concluded that the population increased more rapidly than food supplies and that wages should accordingly sink to subsistence level, to check the natural prolificacy of the labouring classes. This theme was used as late as the 1880's by the Charity Organisation Society to justify their belief that the mass misery of great cities arose mainly from indiscriminate doles.

Goldsmith's position is that of one who wishes to justify, whether consciously or not is immaterial, the abandonment of two groups in society. Firstly on a worldwide scale he desires the desertion by the Northern Stockade of Developed Countries of the impoverished Southern Third World, and secondly, internal to Britain he wants to jettison the welfare state, hence allowing those marginal groups in our society to go to the wall. This is a revamped version of the late 19th century Social Darwinism of Herbert Spencer. In the present climate of crumbling institutions and false optimism it is more liable to influence groups on the British radical right than the rather outmoded visions of World Domination espoused by Hitler. It is a philosophy which will appeal to ratepayers' action groups and other middle class pressure groups.

But Goldsmith's philosophy is by no means totally composed of themes played on *a priori* tunes. If it was it would be less dangerous than it is, for Goldsmith claims to have the solutions to some problems of society which are as yet unsolved. Also some of his criticisms are profound. His claim that society now spends most of its time suppressing manifestations rather than remedying the underlying causes is patently true. You only have to look around. Bigger, stronger and more fool-proof locks, chains, bars, grills and alarms substitute for a transformation of society which would change those aspects which breed vandalism, slum housing, dead-end jobs of infinite monotony, and no prospects of change. He also trenchantly criticises modern Empiricist philosophy for leading society into an evolutionary cul-de-sac. The total domination of scientific modes of thought has created a society where adaptability is at a premium, and this must be remedied for the long-term survival of the human race, though it is a pity that no glimpse of the millennium is given by Goldsmith.

To finish the best thing is to quote from the man himself,

"The notion of the Universal brotherhood of Man is therefore totally incompatible with the systemic approach to human cultural systems." (p.19)

This quote reflects exactly the position adopted by some environmentalists, and it contains a forthrightness of language as yet missing from the utterances of the more overtly political far right, and the dangers of the future spread of such an ideology must not be underestimated. But equally the small number of environmentalists who think in this way must not cause the rejection of all environmental principles. The best form of defence against these dangers is to acknowledge the existence of, and find alternative solutions to, the problems posed.

Tribune, 14 May 1975

2. Lebanon and The Next Few Months

The streets of Beirut have ceased to echo to the sound of gunfire and a calm has descended over the city like a fog, removing all trace of it from the front pages of Britain's newspapers. Now the only events which protrude themselves above this calm are the political manoeuvres of the various leaders which make short paragraphs on the inside pages of the quality press, but beneath the apparent calm the tension is high and activity furious.

Has anything fundamentally changed in Beirut this time, or is this yet another brief respite between bouts of fighting? The latter appears more likely. The present cease-fire appears to be no more than another interlude between periods of conflict each more bloody, prolonged and extensive than the last. The whole struggle has the appearance of steadily increasing violence punctuated by brief intervals for regrouping.

The three factions involved, the Christians, the Muslims and the Palestinians are all using the opportunity to bring in fresh supplies of men and arms. The latter two groups are bringing in weapons from Syria whilst the Phalangists are being supplied by sources which are close to both Israel and America.

The Phalangists in particular seem to be intent on intensifying the struggle. They have in the past round of fighting been using more powerful weapons, but now they are preparing to escalate the conflict still further. They, or rather an Armenian on their behalf, has started to manufacture armoured cars near Beirut. Constructed from landrover chassis at the rate of six a month these will enter into the next round of fighting. The situation seems to be leading inexorably towards civil war.

What's more from the mere fact of the escalation itself the Phalangists have become pawns in the hands of those supplying the arms. Control of events in Lebanon is slipping out of the country to those who interests are not entirely coincident with those of either side. That they have obtained these weapons has led them to be used to hold positions untenable without them. This increased technical sophistication has given rise to a situation common to all cases where reliance is placed on outsiders; their freedom of action has been constrained, as without continual fresh supplies of ammunition these weapons become useless. This tendency has been exacerbated by their secret suppliers who have deliberately supplied weapons which use a multitude of different types of ammunition meaning that adequate alternative supplies are impossible to obtain.

The Muslims and Palestinians with their reliance on weapons more traditionally employed in guerrilla warfare do not as yet suffer from this problem.

Politically the Lebanon is polarising to a remarkable degree. One reason for this is the past history of the country. The religious divisions have been such that they caused a total lack of contact between the various sectarian groupings within society and mutual understanding between for example a Maronite Christian and a Shiite Muslim is non-existent. This aids the polarisation coupled to the sectarian divisions running almost parallel to those of class interest.

The only people who today are calling for moderation are those in groups whose economic interests are at one. The march which took place through the streets of Beirut on October 11th in support of a ceasefire was led by both prominent Muslims and Christians; people like Raymonde Edde of the moderate christian National Block Party, and the Muslim ex-Premier Saed Salam, who are trying to establish non-sectarian groupings. What is most in common about these men is their prominence and wealth. The danger is that they are in the process of becoming leaders without followers, and like has happened so often amongst Unionist politicians in Northern Ireland in recent years will be disregarded.

What happens next will be dictated by people other than these, who have other interests at heart. Israel and America would both like to see the fighting continue in order to distract the eyes of the Arab World from Palestine, although the former might benefit materially from a Civil War. But the risk is as they well know that events controlled from outside and above can develop a dynamic of their own which can take them out of the control of those who are merely manipulating them in their own best interests.

That a continuing unresolved conflict in Lebanon serves the interests of both America and Israel is the reason why the Palestinians in Lebanon, who did so much directly and indirectly to spark off the initial conflict, are now becoming a force for moderation because consisting of both Christians and Muslims they are unenthusiastic about the more sectarian aspects of the conflict and are deeply concerned that the case of Palestine may be lost by default.

Tribune, 14 November 1975

3. Galileo's Tidal Theory: A Partial Vindication

Galileo's Tidal Theory has normally been treated by historians of science as an aberration within the context of his work. It is generally thought of as nothing more than a hasty attempt to supply an answer to one of the demands of the Anti-Copernicans, who wished for proof of the earth's motion. However, when looked at from the point of view of an empirical oceanographer it turns out to be a sophisticated theory which explains to a high degree of accuracy the complex tidal movements of the Adriatic, from where it is known Galileo obtained his data. His theory was in this respect of far greater explanatory value than the later Newtonian theory, although less theoretically satisfying. Hence this theory was an attempt by a scientist in the true Baconian spirit to make the theory fit the facts, and set in the scientific context of the time was a creditable attempt to solve a problem which is still causing difficulties today.

Galileo's theory runs roughly thus: Any point on the Earth's surface has a two-fold motion. Firstly a daily rotation around the Earth's axis and secondly an annual revolution around the sun. As a result these two motions alternate between reinforcing each other and opposing each other for twelve hour periods. The former occurs at night with the two clockwise motions reinforcing whilst the latter occurs during the day. Thus Galileo considered that the water is left behind at night and rushes ahead of the land during the day.

Such then is the theory glossed over normally by historians of science when dealing with Galileo's contributions to Renaissance science. When it does receive notice it is of a highly unsympathetic kind. Aiton (*Annals of Science*, Vol. 10, p.44), for example states, "Galileo's theory of tides, based on the earth's motion, is amongst the least successful of his investigations, and completely misrepresents the phenomena it is supposed to explain". Nor is this quote from Aiton the worst treatment it receives. Koestler (*The Sleepwalkers*, Penguin, p.471) goes so far as to use it as evidence for Galileo's mind being unbalanced, and when comparing it to Kepler's monomania concerning perfect solids considers the latter at least "was a creative obsession: a mystic chimera whose pursuit bore a rich and unexpected harvest; Galileo's mania was of the sterile kind".

Yet Galileo himself thought his tidal theory was, if not the crowning achievement of his scientific career, one of his major contributions to science, and its exposition takes up the whole of the fourth and final day's dialogue in *Dialogue concerning the Two Chief World Systems*, a book which at one time he had intended to entitle *Dialogue on the Flux and Reflux of the Tides*. The theory was no sudden inspiration, but the articulation of ideas that had been years maturing. As early as 1597 Galileo was considering it, writing in a letter to Kepler that he had been an adherent to the Copernican theory for several years and by means of this theory had been able to discover the causes of several physical effects which could not perhaps be satisfactorily explained under the geostatic theory. The identification of the causative factor in tide generation with terrestrial motion was not one unique to Galileo. He himself mentions the similar theory of tides of Seleucus, and it is known that Cesalpinus of Pisa, in Galileo's own student days advanced a tidal theory whose mechanism was the motion of the earth.

The first time Galileo committed his theory to paper, as far as is known, was in 1616 when he wrote to Cardinal Orsini explaining his tidal theory in an attempt to influence the Copernican-Anti-Copernican debate of that year within the Catholic church. This letter was probably written as one result of another letter written by Cardinal Bellarmine to one of Galileo's allies, Foscarini, that stated, "I say that if there were a true demonstration that the sun was in the centre of the universe and the earth in the third sphere, and that the sun did not go around the earth but the earth went around the sun, then it would be necessary to use careful consideration in explaining the Scriptures that seem contrary, and we should rather have to say that we do not understand them than to say something is false which has been proven. But I do not think there is any such demonstration since none has been shown to me".

Galileo's letter was unsuccessful in influencing the debate, the Holy Office declaring the Copernican system false. But Galileo continued to circulate manuscript copies of his theory to his scientific correspondents and in 1618 sent a copy to Archduke Leopold of Austria. What the response of these correspondents was is unknown, but there is no evidence that they considered the theory as ludicrous as think the modern commentators. It was in 1632 that the theory appeared in an expanded form in the *Dialogue*. So no less than thirty-five years passed between the theory's inception and its publication in its final form, a length of time comparable with that taken by Copernicus in having *Revolutions of the Heavenly Spheres* published, despite Galileo's impetuous nature.

Yet despite this inordinately long gestation period, the theory is treated today as an over-hasty bulwark erected to quiet the shrill cries for proof coming from the less bigoted members of the Catholic hierarchy. Far from being an impetuous idea which Galileo promulgated for such a purpose it had an independent life long before these demands were made. That Galileo attempted to use it as a stick to assault the scientific infidels is undeniable, but it was far more than just a stick.

In view of the above, the reasons for the present carping attitude towards the theory are interesting. At the time of its conception it was far in advance of its time, both in that its acceptance necessarily depended upon an acceptance of the heliocentric universe — a belief at this time with few adherents, — and secondly being a detailed explanation of phenomena apparently unknown to many scholars. When the Newtonian solution to the problem of tidal causation was produced, it was readily accepted as the scientific climate had changed markedly in favour of heliocentrism and its theoretical basis was much sounder. But compared to Galileo's theory its explanatory power was of a much lower order, plus the fact that it had Aristotelian overtones of the separation of theory from practice. Although it must be admitted that both Kepler and Newton managed to leap the intellectual hurdle of accepting action at a distance, a hurdle at which Galileo refused.

Yet Galileo, contrary to the impression given by many historians, was — unlike Newton and Kepler — true to the facts. Mach's view of Galileo as an experimentally minded positivist seems particularly apt as regards his tidal theory. Kepler's theory arose from his idea that the moon was kept on its orbit by two forces, one a mutual radial attraction with the earth and the other the motive power of the *anima motrix* impelling it laterally. That this attraction extended to the earth Kepler concluded from the ebb and flow of the tides which he supposed to be caused by the moon pulling the water of the seas towards itself. There is no indication that Kepler had any more evidence than hearsay in support of his theory. The sum total of Kepler's factual information contained in his *Somnium* seems to be the statement 'Experienced sailors say that the ocean tides are higher when the luminaries are in syzygy than when they are in quadrature', and this very statement was inexplicable on the basis of his theory.

Much play is made by Koestler (*op cit.*, p.343), and others concerning the superiority of Kepler's ideas. But his theory would have resulted in only one tide every twenty-five hours, and Kepler was forced to explain some tides as rebounds from the American coast. All in all, Kepler's ideas using non-mechanical causal agents had too much of an occult quality for hard-headed scientists like Galileo, even if in retrospect these ideas of mutual attraction seemed to presage those of Newton. Newton, like Kepler, directed his tidal theory from theoretical considerations rather than observation, collecting little in the way of data.

Galileo in contrast seems to have arrived at his theory on the basis of observation. Fulgenzio Micanzio undertook at Galileo's request the collection of data on the tides of Venice and despite the difficult problems of observation — all work being based on visual recording until the development of automatic tide gauges in 1850 — Galileo's data was surprisingly accurate. And his analysis leading to his theory in *Dialogues* is liberally sprinkled with observations culled from other sources. As to how he analysed his data here we are left in the dark and one can only imagine it must have been semi-quantitative for all the tools of modern wave theory were then lacking.

When re-evaluating Galileo's contribution to tidal theory one thing which must be emphasised is how little tides in practice resemble the idealised theoretical tides of Newton. This incompatibility has recently been commented on by Michelson (*Science and Public Affairs*, Vol.30, No.3) and Ford (*Mercian Geologist*, Vol.5). The tide-causing forces can in fact be separated into numerous components of different periods and magnitudes. Species of components exhibit periodicities of semi-diurnal, diurnal and longer periods. The strength of the various components exhibit variations with geographical position and one result of this is that in different regions of the world different species predominate, although rarely one other than diurnal or semi-diurnal.

Newton was lucky in that the tides around the coast of England are dominated by the semi-diurnal species, and as a result, for English waters, the tides do correspond fairly closely qualitatively with the popular conception of Newton's tidal theory. Galileo however, was forced to base his theory mainly on data obtained from the Adriatic, where the tides have only the most superficial resemblance to those around the English coast. The phases of the semi-diurnal tides vary very greatly in different sections of the Adriatic, while those of diurnal tides differ only slightly resulting in a great variety of tidal form in the Adriatic. The northern section shows mixed diurnal-semidiurnal tides, while in the central section the tides are almost exclusively diurnal. The Adriatic also shows a tide which is not synchronous around its coasts but which is progressive, slowly working its way around the coastline (Defant, *Physical Oceanography*, Vol.2 pp.339-401).

It is when these factors are taken into account that Galileo's theory comes to look much less like the work of a deranged mind and more like the work of an empiricist attempting to unravel a highly complex collection of observations. Galileo distinguished three periodicities in the tidal record, diurnal, monthly and annual and recorded a six-hour alternation in flow direction. As a model for his tides he used the water-barge which brought fresh water from the nearby mainland to Venice. The water in this barge shows two kinds of motion, a standing wave motion and a progressive wave motion, which seems to indicate Galileo's recognition of the progressive nature of Adriatic tides.

Galileo also provided explanations for other noted features of Mediterranean surface water movements which have stood the test of time. For example, the fact that the current direction of surface water in the Bosphorus is always out of the Black Sea into the Mediterranean was explained by him as the result of excess river run-off into the Black Sea. Today's oceanographers explain the situation in the Bosphorus as an anti-lagoonal flow regime, with a constant subsurface current of water flowing into the Black Sea — not noted by Galileo — and a constant surface current of water flowing out. The cause is an excess of precipitation over evaporation in the Black Sea.

Despite such prescient theorising and his valiant attempt to assimilate within his theory the complex tidal rhythm of the Adriatic, Galileo is not vindicated. Detractors attack him on the grounds that his understanding of celestial mechanics was faulty and it has been suggested that the effect used by Galileo as the tidal mechanism is illusory and that Galileo either blundered into an absurd contradiction of his own principles of mechanics out of a fondness for his tidal theory, or saw the contradiction and deliberately played on the ignorance of his readers.

As Koestler says the fallacy of Galileo's argument is that motion can only be defined relative to some point of reference, and Galileo in his theory refers the motion of the water to the earth's axis, but the motion of the land to the fixed stars. Thus Koestler identifies the underlying fallacy in Galileo's theory yet what he ignores along with most other commentators is the scientific context of the time in which Galileo was writing. Galileo was the foremost physicist in Europe at the time and he had a good understanding of the difference between motion on a stationary Earth and motion on a rotating Earth, but this understanding was not a perfect one. It was superior to that of any of his contemporaries, but by no means completely faultless. The crime of his detractors is to attack him for this less than perfect understanding, which would be paralleled by upbraiding Columbus for failing to realise when he discovered America that it was not the Indies. Koestler's critique is thus without doubt unfair. Drake (*Galileo Studies*) and Burstyn (*Isis*, Vol.53), have both recently contended that the theory contains profound insights both into the basis and complications of tidal motion and Drake attempts to show by means of a model that the theory would have worked. But Galileo's major contribution to tidal theory was the clarity with which he investigated the complications of the subject, an aspect ignored by Newton. Galileo attributed tidal variations to meteorologic factors, length of sea basins, orientation of sea basins, and depth of water. Galileo's account might be that of today if 'primary' causes are identified with gravitational attraction, as his 'secondary and particular' causes are those of today.

The current explanation of the tides sees them not as Newton did, i.e. worldwide constant phenomena, but as local phenomena. As the response of ocean basins of various sizes, shapes, depths and orientations to the tide-generating forces of the sun and the moon, and which are modified by meteorologic conditions. In this modern oceanographers concur with Galileo. The reason that he is deprived of the credit for this work is that historians fail to consider the true complexity of tidal regimes, treating his theory only in terms of the Newtonian tide, which in reality was nothing more than a chimera. Why Newton's theory found such ready acceptance amongst late seventeenth century scientists when it failed to fit the facts is one that cannot be answered here. But Galileo's crime was no more than to be too faithful a scientists in the empirical mould, rather than being like Newton and Kepler, who having done nothing in the way of data collection, had few facts to constrain their wilder flights of fancy. Galileo's tidal theory is really one monument to the failure of the Baconian programme in science.

New Scientist, 23/30 December 1976

4. Libya — Land of Lost Opportunities

To enter Libya is to enter a land of profound contradictions. The technology of the jet-age deposits you upon acres of black glistening tarmac with its accompanying flock of clustered white thoroughly modern airport buildings. Yet despite an immediately evident degree of organisation and efficiency remarkable outside of the industrialised world the onward journey is fraught with difficulties.

Passport control, with the stubborn insistence of all officials concerned, makes an attempt to conduct all formalities in Arabic. When the amalgam of hesitant and uncertain Arabic, the assistance of fellow passengers and demonstrative arm and hand waving finally drew the proceedings to a close all concerned are physically and mentally exhausted. But one more hurdle remains, for customs officials then instigate a search of the nooks and crannies of one's baggage for the 'demon-drink' as rigorous and thorough as any that the most zealous members of the Band of Hope could or would conduct.

Similar procedures operate in the airport terminals of Saudi Arabia and the Gulf States. The difference is that whilst the latter glory in their political backwardness Libya claims to be a socialist state. Such are the kinds of contradictions which so confuse Europeans when they attempt to analyse the Libyan situation. For Libya's socialism is structured around the Nasserite cry of Arab Nationalism which transforms the socialist message into one almost unrecognisable to Western ears. How did this arise?

Before the mid-fifties Libya was perceived in British and American eyes as a desert wasteland suitable only for locating military bases. An assessment echoing that contained in the fourteenth century book, *Mandeville's Travels* which thought Libya 'a full dry land and little of fruit, for it is overmuch plenty of heat'. But the subsistence economy of Libya was transformed by the discovery of vast quantities of oil in the late 1950's. Today Libya, with a population of two and a quarter million, is in the process of turning into the Kuwait of North Africa. Nationals are assured of well-paid jobs within the overcrowded and underemployed state-sector of the Libyan economy, whilst large numbers of Tunisian and Egyptian 'guest-workers' provide the manpower to fill the places in the lowly-paid service sector of the economy. The standard of living is high and the latest consumer goods are freely available.

The onset of this economic transformation revealed the ineffectiveness of the particularly inept regime of King Idris who ran Libya very much as a tribal sheikdom until his overthrow. The seizure of power by the Revolutionary Command Council (RCC) — a group of middle-ranking army officers with little or no civilian support — on the 1st September 1969 was a negative act. It was a response to the failure of King Idris' regime to come to terms with both the new oil-wealth and its own endemic corruption, and as such deserved success. But over and above the toppling of the regime the coup's aims were nebulous, and the very swiftness of its success left the RCC uncertain of their next steps. It was twelve days before the new government announced the name of the new head of government and four full months passed before the full membership of the RCC was revealed, while no systematic programme of the revolution was ever announced.

It was during this period of uncertainty that Colonel Ghadaffi rose to undisputed leadership of the RCC when he was able to supply them with both an ideology and a programme of action based on a

Nasserite mixture of Pan Arabism and Socialism. Because his was the leading light in the RCC his greater Muslim faith was allowed to vent itself in such measures as the banning of alcohol and demands for recognition of Arabic as an international language. In terms of foreign policy the atheistic nature of communism was sufficient to inure him against the countries of the Eastern Block. For the hinge between thought and action for Ghadaffi was his belief in the possibility of establishing a modern state whose basis was to be a kind of paternal socialism rooted in a millenniarism derived from the Quranic conception of Muhammed. Libyan society was to be monolithic, classless and above all Islamic. For Ghadaffi socialism was the way to close gaps between the classes, but a pluralistic approach was not to be countenanced, for he said in one of his public speeches in 1970, "he who engaged in party activities commits treason".

But for the fulfilment of this dream Ghadaffi concluded that Libya must be isolated from the potentially contaminating cultural influences of Western society. His view of religion as politics meant that success was assured if faith could be retained, and its retention was not to be put at risk by exposure to the West.

It was internally that Ghadaffi initially had most impact. Despite initial promises to the contrary the exploitive nature of the Oil Companies led him to increasingly pressurise them for terms more heavily weighted in Libya's favour. The result was that while output fell by over 30% between 1969 and 1972, Libya's oil revenue leapt by 55% (Ruth First, *Libya; the Elusive Revolution*, Penguin, 1974). But it was in the use of this new wealth, the product of his greatest success, that Ghadaffi's failure was most dismal. Instead of vigorous planning to lead Libya along a path of development consistent with his future vision, with a concentration upon the improvement of techniques within subsistence farming, and the establishment of indigenous industries, he was dazzled by the glittering toys western society offered. Instead of drawing from the West only those technologies appropriate to his and Libya's requirements an attempt was made to swallow the package eagerly offered in one gulp. Subsistence agriculture languished whilst lavish sums were spent on highways leading from nowhere to nowhere, and upon highly intensive high technology agricultural projects in the middle of the desert.

The latter is typified by the scheme at Kufra Oasis, which set out to turn the desert green. The importation of skilled techniques and large quantities of fertilizer plus the use of water from an immense underground natural reservoir, discovered in the early 1960's by accident, enabled the growth of hundreds of acres of alfalfa. This however was more an exercise in hydroponics than farming, and it was to be this scheme that was to form the basis for the establishment of lamb breeding for meat in this area. The scheme had two drawbacks. Firstly the water supply on which its viability was dependent is one which is thought to owe its existence to connate water, i.e. water which has been retained in the rocks since their formation, and which is not being replenished. Secondly, the project is both economically unsound and heavily reliant on Western expertise. Libya's attempt to break its dependence on food imports has in this case tied it instead even more firmly to the Industrialised World.

Since Nasser's death, Ghadaffi's path through the political firmament of the Arab World has become an increasingly eccentric and lonely one. Recently the Egyptian press were calling upon the Libyan people to overthrow him, whilst another of his neighbours Tunisia have been fighting shy of him since the abortive attempt at a shotgun marriage between the two states engineered by Ghadaffi. But internally his support amongst the people appears to be as widespread as it has ever been, although shallow — for after all he has at least delivered the goods. Unfortunately the source of any danger to Ghadaffi lies not with the people but rather in the army, and it is here that enthusiasm has been waning. In August 1975 the regime was shaken by the attempted coup of Major Omar Miheishy, a member of the RCC. This was symptomatic of developments in the RCC. Once twelve strong it has now been reduced by death and disagreement to a hard core of four.

But the Libyan leader's error has not been his failure to start Libyan development along a line parallel with his future vision, nor that of failing even to get Libya started upon the normal development path of Third World countries. After all the first has never really been attempted, apart possibly from in China, and the second has suffered from a singular lack of success. Rather his delusion has been one of thinking it possible to have the artifacts of Industrial Society without its cultural and societal manifestations. The younger Libyans certainly resent the patina of Islamic fundamentalism which appears to shape their society on the surface, for this is in sharp contradiction to those westernising forces moulding the kernel.

Libya is in danger of falling between two stools. It will neither come to resemble Ghadaffi's dream, nor become fully industrialised in the western mode, but rather will become on the of 'new rentier' states. Of course Libya's options will remain open for years yet, the vast financial resources at its disposal will ensure that. But eventually if nothing changes it will become one of the 'new rentier' states whose wealth is dependent not upon rent or profit, but upon the rapidly receding ocean of oil beneath its feet, and which will have no economic superstructure capable of sustaining itself once the last drops of oil have been sucked along the pipelines to the West.

Socialist Commentary, June 1977

5. Review

Islamic Science: An Illustrated Study by Seyyed Hossein Nasr

The fate of Islamic science has been one in common with many aspects of foreign thought alien to our forefathers. In general it has been damned with faint praise. Its achievements have been written down to a mere footnoting of the classics. Its prime function has been presented as that of preserving a medium in which was stored the science of antiquity during those unfortunate centuries when Europe forgot its destiny.

Thus when Europe's temporary insanity ended with the Renaissance Islamic Science fulfilled its preordained mission of temporary custodianship and passed the baton of the texts and techniques of Greek Science back to their rightful owners. Such was the myth.

Seyyed Hossein Nasr a decade and more ago commenced the task of correcting this, at best, part truth. For while the solid details of Islamic Science's achievements have been available since the publication of George Sarton's *An Introduction to the History of Science* (3 volumes, 1927-1948) no-one has before attempted such a re-evaluation.

This particular book is in fact two books in one. The first is a manifest of those Muslim scientists who contributed to the enlargement of the corpus of scientific knowledge within the *dar al-islam* from its birth, and the second is the skeleton of such a reappraisal. While the former is full of fascinating little asides, like *Muhammad's* use of the tooth brush, the fact that syphilis was known as *atishak-i farangi* (Frankish fire), and that *Abu Ali-ibn Sina* — or Avicenna as he is known in the West — like Erasmus Darwin wrote some of his scientific works in verse, it is the latter which is of greatest interest here.

What broadly is the case Prof. Nasr makes? He maintains that there was an Islamic science that was distinct from but related to its origins. All ideas entering the citadel of Islamic thought were transposed into a new spiritual and intellectual form capable of assimilation and integration into the Islamic world picture.

The structure of this worldview was predetermined by its theory of knowledge, and it was this theory of knowledge which set its science apart. For Muslims there were a number of kinds of knowledge. There was 'acquired' knowledge in its twin forms of the transmitted and intellectual sciences and the 'presential' knowledge of vision and experience. In the West today's prevailing rationalism would maintain that the form of knowledge termed the intellectual sciences is — if not the only form of knowledge — that against which all others must be shaped. Whereas for the Muslim these different knowledges were all of equal standing locked within a metaphysical hierarchy whose source was the *Quran* and whose totality was a unity. Thus the quest for all knowledge was impregnated with a religious aura. This determined both the problems the Muslim scientist tried to solve and the types of solutions he offered.

This linkage between science and culture operated at a number of levels. At its most mundane, religious rites with their concern with the *qiblah* direction and the timing of the rising of the sun and moon created a pragmatic interest in geodesy and astronomy. At a higher level the Muslim belief that science as we know it reveals only one aspect of a multidimensional reality tempered their science itself. They posed answers not in the unilateral manner of analytical and quantitative science, but rather as an art form of qualities and symbols. Alchemy was hence firmly within the realm of science. To imagine such a 'science' is difficult for us, but some feel for its distinctiveness can be gained by looking at the technology it produced.

This science coupled with an Islamic cosmology emphasising harmony, equilibrium and balance led Muslims to adopt a technology which utilised natural forces within the environment style which made *maximum* use of human skills and caused the *minimum* amount of disturbance to the human environment. Thus technical change in itself was not welcomed. Any possible innovation was evaluated on the above criteria. Like the Chinese who had gunpowder but never made guns, Muslims accepted no change which would have meant the creation of a technology out of harmony with the natural environment.

For similar reasons, those technical artifacts which were produced were expected to have both a beauty and utility. This was particularly true of those for liturgical use. This emphasis on beauty and utility is particularly interesting in that it predates by a millennium the similar ideas of William Morris and the Victorian 'Arts and Crafts' movement in England.

The above precis fails to do justice to Prof. Nasr's sophisticated treatment, but it must suffice. How valuable is this account of Islamic Science? Certainly it draws out an all but ignored side of this science. Yet this treatment here does have the drawback of being rather too deferentially orthodox. Like the historical interpretation it seeks to replace it too has its lacunae. For Prof. Nasr allows no stains to show which might mar the perfection of his closely woven argument.

Yet the *dar al-islam* could be at times as intolerant of its philosopher-scientists as its Christian counterpart. Catholicism burnt Giordano Bruno at the stake in 1600 for his too advanced ideas. The source of many of these ideas had been the Islamic Hermetic corpus. One of the major contributors to this corpus had been the sufi mystic *Suhrawardi*. He had met his death in 578/1191 in Aleppo at the hands of the intolerant of his own religion. But apart from the omission of this one event Prof. Nasr could be charged more generally with making a virtue of necessity. This charge has in fact been laid against some of his earlier writings on Islamic science aimed more narrowly at professional historians of science.

One example is that in this book Prof. Nasr lauds the wisdom of Muslim astronomers who held with their geocentric view of the universe after Copernicus had swept the Earth from the centre to the periphery of the solar system in Europe. They realised, he claims, that the choice to be made was more of a metaphysical and theological one than scientific and made it accordingly. The question is were they free to make such a choice?

Leaving aside the philosophical problem that lies implicit in this statement for the moment, the event it describes needs setting in context. By the time this choice was put before Muslim astronomers the ideas of the late eleventh century philosopher *Al-Ghazzali* had so worked their way into the body of Muslim thought that its open structure so capable of absorbing new ideas had been turned to a hard crystalline pedantry. This shift even made itself felt in Muslim jurisprudence where the door of *Ijtihad* was firmly closed. *Ijtihad* was the system that had allowed noted jurists to give independent judgements derived from general principles. After the tenth century instances of such judgements became vanishingly rare and jurists had to rule on the basis of precedence only, with the *Quran* and *Hadith* as their sole sources. In such an environment no choice was open.

But to return to the philosophical problem left before. For many the notion embedded in Prof Nasr's statement that a plurality of sciences exists will sound a contradiction in terms. However, the common sense idea that one neutral science exists which progresses asymptotically toward Truth no longer goes unquestioned. Science is now thought by many to be as culture bound as other aspects of society.

For many years good historians have endeavoured not to write 'Whig' history which measures all against their own time and place, but instead to write history which evaluates epochs in their own terms. If science is ideological — and this book makes one of the best cases for this I have seen — then it too must be judged in its own terms. This at root is what Prof. Nasr has done for Islamic science, even if he didn't realise it.

This reclaiming of Islamic science has both a cause and a function. Western colonialism in both its overt and covert forms exercised its dominance not merely by the power relationships it established, nor by its economic subjection of its colonies, but by these joined to a cultural imperialism. Hence popular local knowledge and skills were eclipsed by the imperial state's own form of knowledge — Western science. Recently the struggles against colonialism and the realisation that Western science was in danger of leading mankind into an evolutionary cul-de-sac of environment pollution, resource depletion and human alienation — the distinction between Islamic science and Western science in these respects is too obvious to require illustration — have fused together. This is the cause.

The function such a rewriting fulfils is that it gives ideological backing in the tripartite struggle taking place in Prof. Nasr's own country — Iran — between the westernising technocrats, the left-wing guerrillas and the Muslim traditionalists, to this latter group. For it is firmly into this camp that our author falls.

Yet to end on a less contentious note. This book is illustrated by a wealth of splendid photographs. Roland Michand has amassed over a hundred and thirty colour plates and a hundred figures. These in themselves make for an outstanding book. The only pity is that these illustrations have not been integrated into the text by Prof. Nasr.

Gazelle Review No.4, 1978

6. Science in Society: Even the Truth is Relative

This article challenges one of the most deeply embedded myths in our culture — the idealist notion that science and technology are neutral. This has been so widely assimilated that even socialists leave it untouched. Such pious deference cannot continue.

Here the possible alternative views of science and technology will be set out and the reasons and functions the adoption of this myth served. Then in outline some illustrations of ideology in science will be discussed and, finally, the antidemocratic nature of nuclear technology will be explained.

The result of the belief in the neutrality, in essence, of science and technology is in epitome a model of use/abuse. Science and technology are value-free and as such rest below society as a firm substructure on which society can construct itself for good or ill. Thus science and technology can create no problems that cannot be narrowed down to problems of control. Under socialism riot-control technologies, heart transplant surgery and recombinant DNA research all have good things to offer society.

This view has not always been accepted. There are four ways in which science and technology can be viewed in relation to society. The correlation between the two can be taken as bad, good, neutral or mixed. All these various alternatives have at different times and in different cultures been accepted, sometimes by whole societies, at other times by classes or groups within societies.

The machine-breakers or Luddites in Yorkshire and Lancashire in the early decades of the nineteenth century shared with the world of medieval Islam a belief that *bid'a* (innovation) was detrimental to mankind. While in antithesis the rising bourgeoisie of late Victorian capitalism held that science and technology were God's beneficent gift to the English middle-class. In parallel to this their self-professed future expropriators directly equated socialism and science. In fact this belief was one of the few things which could bracket together such diverse socialists as Ramsey MacDonald and Lenin.

The last position took root in a virulent form in the 1930s of Stalinist Russia and Nazi Germany. In the former, with Stalin and 'Socialism in One Country', attempts were made by a number of scientists, most notably T.D. Lysenko, with their leader's support, to promote a socialist physics and a socialist biology. At the same time a similar manifestation was to be found with emergent Nazism in Germany with talk of 'Aryan' and 'non-Aryan' (i.e. Jewish) science.

The myth arose from a number of converging sets of circumstances after World War Two. Within the scientific community the explosions of Hiroshima and Nagasaki provoked a crisis of conscience about the fruits of their work. This was most easily salved by externalizing the problem they faced, which was one of responsibility. A belief in the neutrality of science enabled such an exclusion to occur. For then the physics and technology were split asunder from the uses to which they were put. Scientists could continue to do their physics while the rest of mankind grappled with the issues of conscience it threw up.

The related event within the wider community was the emergence after the war of large-scale state-funded science. The war itself had seen a massive mobilization of science and scientists behind the two protagonists. The very emergence of the atom bomb from this frenzy of activity and in particular the Manhattan Project ensured that Governments began to think science and technology might in peacetime be able to continue to be a handmaiden to the state.

But if the state was neutral in itself so must its handmaiden be. Thus a belief in the neutrality of science and technology served functions both internal and external to the scientific community. Both those giving and receiving funds had good reasons for wanting to believe themselves and wanting others to believe that science and technology were value-free.

The practice of science and technology is no more divorced from society than journalism. Philip Agee is deported for endangering the security of the state by his writing while Thomas Mancuso loses his job after suggesting that exposure to low-level radiation is much more dangerous than currently believed (*Nature* Vol.272, p.197).

Science and technology can never be neutral because their nature and directions are always framed — like other aspects of our culture — by the social and scientific context of the age. Today these two 'products' are generated within late capitalism and the style and packaging of these products reflect this environment. The major concern of the system as a unity is its own survival and extension. This aim inexorably shapes science and technology. Of course I am not suggesting that those in positions of power assemble in solemn secret conclave to decide what science and technology will be produced. It merely emerges from the logic of their shared way of viewing the world.

Science and technology are both heavily state-financed and there is always more of both of these waiting to be done than resources available. That which is undertaken can only be done at the expense of alternatives. Those who arbitrate between these possibilities do so on the basis of their own ideological presuppositions. To expect otherwise would be naive. Whereas few on the left will argue with the contention that the overwhelming majority of those in power are opposed to radical, let alone revolutionary change, they seem to baulk at the idea that such beliefs may impact upon science and technology. Yet they themselves loudly complain of this very bias with respect to all other aspects of our culture.

While the making of choices remains inevitable, these will be partisan and the output arising from such a system is unlikely to be neutral. This is not to say that the work of contemporary scientists and technologists always neatly meshes with the requirements of contemporary capitalism. Developments within science and technology emerge from an adversary process in which hypotheses compete for intellectual dominance.

New scientific laws are not brought to society like the tablets from mountains. They emerge from a field of competing alternatives all of which reflect to a greater or lesser extent aspects of the multidimensional world of nature. The determination of which is to be the victor is not a simple one. It is not determined purely on grounds of truth-content or to suit the implicit wishes of the ruling class, rather it comes from a continuous and multiple series of interactions between science, scientists and society. In these interactions which help to decide the outcome, factors like personal interests and prejudices, misunderstanding and incomplete knowledge all play their part.

A hypothetical situation may best illustrate the problem. A Chinese palaeontologist and member of the Communist Party would find it difficult to imagine — as a member of Chinese society with all its current beliefs — that some races are inherently inferior to others. Similarly, because of its implications, such a conditioning could well react on to his/her science when faced with interpreting a series of ambiguous humanoid remains suggestive of parallel evolution of similar but distinct races. For him such an alternative would be difficult to choose. Even if this palaeontologist did manage to think and publish such a theory, its successful reception in China would appear unlikely.

One does not have to resort to such hypothetical situations however to look for examples of ideology in science. One of the best examples to look at is the scientific theory which supported notions of feminine inferiority in the nineteenth century. Up to this time the belief in feminine inferiority was justified because of the moral defects associated with womankind. But in the years after 1865 this was supplemented and then replaced by an alternative justification based on the 'objective' criteria of science.

Women became — or at least middle- and upper-class women — weak and defective by nature. The medical theory on which this was based was the physiological law of the 'conservation of energy'. According to this law each human body contained a fixed quantity of energy which could be drawn upon by one organ or another, or used for one function or another. This meant that it was only possible to develop one organ or ability at the expense of others.

In particular the sexual organs competed with other organs for this limited energy. This theory, coupled with the belief that reproductivity was central to a women's biological life and that if sexual organs were starved of energy the resulting children were weak, sickly and unstable, was used to support current social policies, i.e. the exclusion of women from higher education was justified by the need to save the race from degeneration.

This theory did not create these inequalities, but it gave to their retention a scientific plausibility which helped to stem attempts at education emancipation for women. It may be tempting for some to argue that this was either 'bad science' and/or that this use of science no longer occurs. All that can be said in reply is look about you.

The ongoing Race-IQ debate has a similar element within it, while the associated work of Burt, recently cast into doubt by the *Sunday Times*, certainly influenced British educational policy and practices. The important point here being not so much that he 'massaged' his data but that his dubious work was so readily accepted and used as a theoretical basis for modelling our school system. But this is not totally surprising when one notices how closely his work was to thinking outside of science.

Nuclear power is one answer to the perceived problem of an imminent world energy shortage couched in a technology amenable to monopoly capitalism. Other alternative answers exist such as solar, wind and wave power, but little interest has been shown in them. Why? Despite the fact that nuclear power stations have high maintenance costs, short lifetimes and a high risk of causing major pollution, and that the fuel they use is limited, they do have the inestimable advantage of fitting readily into the institutional machinery developing within late Capitalism.

This is not true of the alternatives. Nuclear technology is a capital-intensive, large-scale, highly centralised technology and relates to an energy policy which attempts to maximise individual dependence on the system. This technology thrusts society inevitably further along the path towards late, or at best, State Capitalism. In this nuclear technology is not unique and the attitude adopted towards it would be unenthusiastic resignation.

However the new generations of nuclear power stations and their proposed exponential expansion in numbers lead towards the strong state. This arises from the peculiar threat nuclear technology brings to the whole of mankind. If a large scale release of radiation to the surrounding environment occurs either slowly or catastrophically, either accidentally or deliberately, then all are agreed mankind faces death and destruction on an unknown and long-term scale. The push towards the strong state comes from the political and social measures that the logic of capitalism dictates to cope with this contingency.

This threat is not one that is welcomed by those in positions of power and in our society, but it is one that the irrationality of capitalism is prepared to countenance rather than to promote the alternatives, for the emerging strong state holds no fears for them.

The United States Atomic Energy Commission has already proposed that a special federal police force be established to safeguard the security of plutonium plants and shipments. At the same time it has complained of court rulings protecting the individual privacy of citizens and urged the introduction of new legislation which would facilitate security checks on workers in nuclear industries.

In Britain, if the Birmingham pub bombings can get the Prevention of Terrorism Act through Parliament in twenty-four hours, what would be the result of a plutonium hijacking? Even if the strong state philosophy can initially be resisted by our liberal democratic traditions the pressure will rise with each year.

As new nuclear waste sites and abandoned nuclear power stations with their rusting barbed wire and bored security guards begin to dot the English countryside like an outbreak of measles on the face of the land, and as societal dependence on nuclear power grows the options facing the state will narrow mercilessly.

Finally, let it be stated that the point of view expressed here is not one of scientific or technological determinism. It is rather to present a real problem to socialists. Are we not to oppose a development that will make the achieving of socialism that much more difficult than it is today, and one which will leave any sort of society with an invisible but nonetheless terrifying hazard for tens of thousands of years into the future. The direction society is going in can be changed; the point I am making is that such a change is both necessary and possible.

Socialist Review No.4, July-August 1978

Natural Laws Rule, OK

I would like to make a short comment on Glyn Ford's 'Even the Truth is Relative' (*Socialist Review* July-August).

I have no quarrel with the author's conclusion about the dangers of nuclear power under capitalism. Indeed he could have strengthened his case by reference to the fact that since 6 August

1945, when the US Air Force obliterated Hiroshima, we have all lived under the shadow of the nuclear bomb and that 'peaceful' nuclear power production and nuclear weapon production are closely connected technologies.

But some of Glyn Ford's argumentation is, in my view, very dubious to say the least. And, since similar views seem to be fairly widespread on the left (including even sections of the Socialist Workers' Party), they need to be challenged.

What is at issue is whether there is or is not a real distinction between science (objective, operational) and ideology (more or less systematic mystification and false consciousness). Glyn Ford seems to cast doubt on the matter, if I have understood him correctly.

Marx and Engels took it for granted that there was such a distinction. In fact Marx's criticism of the post-Ricardo 'vulgar economists' is meaningless otherwise.

Putting it very crudely, there is bourgeois economics and there is marxian economics but there is no bourgeois physics and no marxian physics. There is only physics, which is operational and even 'value free' (although there are serious objections to this term) in the sense that, say, the laws of thermo-dynamics are the same for a marxist, a liberal, a conservative or whatever. They represent real (i.e. operative and objective) knowledge, or an approximation there to, not ideology.

That is to say science, scientific knowledge properly so-called, is part of our heritage and is an indispensable prerequisite for the construction of socialism. What is called social science in bourgeois institutions is, on the other hand, largely ideology. There can be no objective social science in a class society except insofar as it is revolutionary.

Naturally this does not mean that science and technology are somehow produced independently of society. That would be an absurd proposition, an idealist mystification. Very obviously technology develops in accordance with the requirements of the rulers of society. And not just technology. The same is true, at one or more removes, of the purest of 'pure' science.

Many years ago the Russian physicist Hessen wrote a paper for an international congress on the history of science entitled 'The Social and Economic Roots of Newton's *Principia*'. In it Hessen showed, as he put it, that 'the formation of ideas has to be explained by reference to material practice' and specifically demonstrated in detail that Newtonian mechanics was a synthesis made possible by the actual development of technology (socially conditioned) in the fields of transport, mining, gunnery and so on.

To put it very crudely again, even the austere mathematical logic of the *Principia* is not unconnected with the class struggle, though the connection is fairly remote. But, and it is a very big but, Newtonian mechanics is nevertheless objective, operative knowledge, and is science, whereas Hobbes's *Leviathan* or Locke's two *Treatises on Government*, both products of the same epoch, are ideology.

The fact that Newton's mechanics does not represent some 'absolute truth', that it was profoundly modified by the twentieth century 'revolution in physics' (relativity and the quantum theory) in no way alters its scientific character.

Does it matter? I think it matters a good deal. At a time when, as your editor points out in another connection, various 'left-wing' authors are mounting 'a thorough going attack on the theoretical foundations of classical marxism' (I do not mean, of course, to suggest that this is Glyn Ford's purpose) *Socialist Review* has the duty to defend them.

Not only because classical marxism is true (and I agree with Glyn Ford that even the truth is relative) but because truth, to a marxist, is operational, because there is an indissoluble connection between theory and practice, because marxism, unlike every trend in bourgeois social thought, is also *scientific*, as Engels rightly claimed.

Duncan Hallas
Socialist Review No.5, September 1978

Relatively Neutral

I would like the opportunity of clarifying a number of points arising from my article 'Even the Truth is Relative' (*Socialist Review* 4) in the light of Duncan Hallas' letter (*Socialist Review* 5). The reason I feel it necessary to do this is because I believe Duncan Hallas by insinuation at a number of points — unintentionally — misrepresents my position.

This may well be because my original article was not clear. In that case I would like to try to rectify the situation.

I did not suggest that science could be independent of nature, rather I suggested that its tenor is coloured to a greater or lesser extent by the social environment of its birth. For me science at any one time merely represents one face of a multifaceted reality.

Neither did I assert or imply that Newtonian mechanics was not science either prior to or post to its profound modification by the twentieth century 'revolution in physics'. The key question I tried to face was on a different level and was 'What are we saying when we call something Science?'.

For Duncan Hallas we are identifying objective knowledge. It is with this I disagree. 'Objective' for *Chambers Twentieth Century Dictionary* is 'setting forth what is external, actual, practical, uncoloured by one's own sensations or emotions' and I assume that it is with such a definition that Duncan Hallas is working.

Yet he himself at the same time seems to concede the argument. He admits that science and technology are produced in accordance with the requirements of the rulers of society. These requirements are multifold. They certainly include an operational control over nature which may lead to one kind of science or technology being pursued at the expense of another. This gives ideological support for their view of the world from what many falsely see as an independent network of authority, science. Such requirements are not conducive to the production of neutral science.

Duncan Hallas implies that despite being brought forth crippled by such requirements science grows up unblemished. What miracle is it that enables this cripple to discard its crutches? Unless Duncan Hallas can answer this his case is lost.

In concluding I must comment on the penultimate paragraphs of his letter. In these he pleads that his viewpoint warrants support as it is in concord with the views of Marx. If it is, and of this I'm not convinced, this is surely a singularly unmarxist argument for a Marxist!

Marx was a profound thinker, but surely few would agree with Hallas that he had a 'godlike' ability to write the last word on every subject. Socialism will hold few attractions for anyone who thinks if such religious dogmatism holds sway.

Glyn Ford
Socialist Review No.7, November 1978

7. Letter to *Socialist Challenge*

'Capital' and Darwin

Paul Tickell's letter (5 October) concerning science and Marxism asserted as support for its line of argumentation the 'fact' that Marx intended dedicating *Capital* to Darwin. Whilst I sympathise with the general tenor of the letter I would like to correct this false assertion.

It is true that the Soviet magazine *Under the Banner of Marxism* published in 1931 a letter which it claimed was from Darwin to

Marx in 1880 which graciously rejected the offer of a dedication. Recent work however has shown that this was a letter not from Darwin to Marx, but rather one from Darwin to Edward Aveling — that least attractive of Victorian socialists — in response to a request that he be allowed to dedicate his book *The Student's Darwin* to him.

Quite how this mistake was originally made is not known. Certainly Edward Aveling's character was such that little was beyond his fertile imagination, similarly the Russians might have had ulterior motives in 1931. The one thing that is clear is that Marx never offered to dedicate *Capital* to Darwin.

November 1978

8. Demolishing a Whale

The cowardly backsliding of the Panamanians under Japanese pressure at the thirtieth annual meeting of the International Whaling Commission (IWC), reported in the press, may well have been the final blow for the whale. The Panamanian withdrawal from the agenda of their proposal for a ten year moratorium on whaling may be seen as the last and final of a series of unheroic actions perpetuated by the IWC as it conserved the whale to extinction. Yet while aware of the widespread concern for the future of the whale it was not until last month that a combination of circumstances brought up to me the full futility and pathos of the whole whaling industry.

I had just arrived in the Faroe Islands when I learnt that a local whaling vessel had just harpooned a fin whale and was bringing it in under tow. The general excitement dragooned me into a party going out to the Whaling Station to see the arrival. The Whaling Station was a fifteen mile trip along the narrow cliff gripping roads of the main island *Streymoy* to a village *vid'Air*. This remaining station being the sole survivor of what had once been an island strong group of seven.

Here the events were doubly poignant, both from the point of view of the industry and its victims. The whalers themselves had not brought in a catch for twelve months until three days previously and now they had a second one. Yet from the condition and appearance of the factory the reported year's hiatus looked like a sad modesty. The place was seedy with crumbling wharves, rusting machinery and decaying buildings wrapped in the fishy sickly sweet smell of its last and present victim, all made unreal by the crowds morbidly drawn to the spot.

The poor beast who had met with the explosive harpoon was winched unceremoniously up the slipway and almost before the winch had stopped revolving the butchers fell upon it. This so recently living giant of the sea — sixty feet in length — was dismembered in one smooth practised operation. It's skin and subcutaneous blubber was stripped from the body by winches who peeled it back slowly as the scythe-like knives in the hands of the whalers hacked along the divide between the dark red flesh and the white blubber. As this proceeded the freshly exposed meat was cut from its body in steaming cubes. These coarse and fibrous lumps of flesh were then impaled on hooks and dragged across to pallets where they lay for later sale to the assembled throng. For the spectators were bipartisan in their interests. The Faroese had come because to the commercial whaling industry the meat is so much waste to be disposed of at knockdown prices. The local populace had congregated awaiting cheap meat, the tourists for cheap thrills.

As the cutting continued, at intervals a major blood vessel was severed and the blood gushed forth in a fierce arc whose trajectory slowly died to a gentle stream. Once on the slipway it meandered to and fro, at the whim of marooned flotsam, in a crimson ribbon to the sea. At length the lapping wavelets coloured red and began to spread this message around the bay. All the time the cutters moved deep into the cavities in the flesh created by their earlier efforts. With the sunset I left the half dismantled beast in its now despoiled glory to the mercies of those who were as much victims of the situation as the animal whose death had given them temporary consolation.

On returning the following day the evidence of the offence had all but gone. The meat had been sold, the remains of the carcase had been towed out to sea and abandoned, while the station deserted resumed uncompromisingly its air of industrial dereliction. All that remained at the top of the slip-way was that small portion of the whole meant to justify the exercise. Here the already yellowing blubber with its patena of black skin remained as the temporary and so small monument to the death of a whale.

The sordid aspects of the abattoir can never be glorified but they are an unavoidable accompaniment to an activity that has a rationale. Not until this morning did it really come home to me exactly how insane the whole thing is. An animal of outstanding beauty is over-exploited to such a degree that the industry exploiting it and the animals themselves are driven to the verge of extinction in order to produce from a fractional part of the beast products whose only uses are frivolous or ones for which substitutes are available. Such an insanity is rare amongst individuals but common amongst institutions.

Resurgence, March/April 1979

9. All at Sea with the Third World

In Geneva now the United Nations Law of the Sea Conference (UNLOSC) is meeting, yet again, in an attempt to resolve those complex issues of international jurisdiction over the oceans. For some of the remaining observers this Geneva meeting will see the 'big push' for agreement. Few observers remain however, as most of the media lost interest many 'final' meetings back in the decade long negotiations. It seems highly unlikely that this meeting will finalise anything new. It may well be that confrontation will replace compromise, for a new factor has entered into the negotiations.

In Washington last month Senate Bill S493 was introduced. This Bill proposes US domestic legislation to allow American Companies to proceed — in the absence of UN agreement — to mine the deep sea bed. The Group of Seventy Seven Underdeveloped Countries, at the UN, see this as a direct threat to their vision of a New International Economic Order based upon the Oceans as 'the common heritage of mankind'. Already members of this Group have threatened to boycott the American Companies, like Lockheed, Kennecott and US Steel, who might use the legislation as a basis on which to start mining. The whole American approach graphically reveals their continued lack of sensitivity in Government to Third World concerns.

The resources about which everyone is so concerned are manganese nodules. These are loose concretions, found resting on the seafloor in the deepest parts of the oceans, rich in manganese, nickel, cobalt, and copper. The Group of Seventy Seven are convinced that these nodules offer an enormous source of profit to whoever exploits them. Therefore within UNLOSC they have been bargaining very hard to ensure that they will not yet again find themselves standing on the sidelines as another portion of the world's limited resources find their way into the Industrialised World.

Despite this, Elliott Richardson — the American Ambassador to UNLOSC — is convinced that the imminence of US domestic legislation will help him force the negotiations through to a swift and satisfactory conclusion. This naivety is not shared elsewhere in America's elite circles. But some have a vested interest in maintaining Richardson in his misconceptions as he argues the Conference into impasse. The four international Consortia formed to mine these nodules are all dominated by US Companies, although companies from most of the western developed nations are involved. These Consortia all believe that any agreement achieved by the UN will be highly disadvantageous to their interests.

The present state of the negotiations are set out in the Informal Composite Negotiating Text (ICNT). The Consortia find in here the following; licensing of mine sites is to be undertaken by the International Sea Bed Authority (ISA) under UN control, an ISA mining company is to be established to mine some of the sites, the Consortia are to transfer their technology to this company, and in twenty-five years time the treaty is to be renegotiated, and during this twenty-five years production from deep sea mining is to be limited. These proposals in the ICNT plus the threat that the ISA company would eventually enter the marketing end of the operation, frighten the Consortia to death.

Within the next eighteen months these Consortia have to decide whether to go ahead or not. Before committing themselves fully they want to see a legal framework within which they can operate. This they see in the US Bill. This Bill, as it currently stands, is highly protectionist, due to the views of the Congressmen supporting it. Representative John Murphy (New York) and Senator Matsunaga (Hawaii) between them have ensured that the vessels used in the mining operation must be US flag ships, and that the plants for processing the three million tons a year of nodules from each mine site will be located in the US. The first makes work for the Eastcoast shipyards, while the second makes Hawaii or Southern California the prime sites for processing plants.

Unless the Bill is substantially amended, these and similar clauses will put the next British Government in a dilemma — which some are trying to deliberately engineer. If British companies involved, Rio-Tinto Zinc, Consolidated Goldfields, British Petroleum and Shell, are to be protected then similar legislation will have to be passed in Westminster and recognised by the American Government as being reciprocal. If this legislation is passed we will earn a share of the enmity of the Third World as we voluntarily take a share of America's censure. Britain's legislation is already written, say US commentators. The willingness of the last Labour Government to introduce it seemed revealed only a couple of weeks ago. In his reply to a question from Frank Hooley MP, (Labour, Sheffield Henley) asking if the UK Government would declare its opposition to British Companies mining in the deep sea prior to UNLOSC agreement, Gerald Kaufman from the Department of Industry said, 'No'.

Christine Marple (pseudonym)
New Statesman, 6 April 1979

10. Tameside: The Score Labour Has to Settle

The particularly reactionary nature of the Tory council in Tameside needs little introduction to those on the Left. The last-minute reversal of the entrained programme for comprehensive schools in the area following the Tories narrowly won control of the council became a *cause celebre* in 1976.

The series of legal actions initiated by the then Secretary of State for Education, Fred Mulley, and the final judgement of the Law Lords that the council had the right to be unreasonable are well known.

Less commonly known nationally is the series of bruising confrontations which the Tories have precipitated with local public sector unions, from the National Union of Teachers to the National and Local Government Officers' Association. In these disputes, Tory councillors have showered threats of dismissal upon their employees.

Again in character, they attempted to force through the Greater Manchester Bill in the district with its regressive clauses restricting the right to demonstrate, at the same time giving the freedom of Tameside to the National Front which, with implicit council approval, march, meet and even play football. This Tory council is now about to meets its end.

In one sense it was surprising that the Tories ever won control. Tameside — so charmingly misdescribed by one radio commentator in 1976 as a middle-class suburb of Manchester — consists of the old cotton towns of Ashton-under-Lyne, Stalybridge and Hyde. Here was the focus of so much of the Chartist agitation in the nineteenth century. Today this working-class character remains, with the area returning three Labour MPs in October 1976 with solid majorities.

But the local Tories were given notice to quit last year. Twelve months ago, when defending the council seats won in the exceptionally good year of 1973, Labour not only held its own but made gains against the gentle Conservative swing nationally, winning 15 out of 18 wards.

Donald Thorp, the Tory chairman of education directly responsible for the decision to retain the grammar schools, went and so, too, did Laurence Bell, their deputy leader.

This positive swing to Labour can be directly linked to the rejection by the electorate of the confrontational brand of politics directed by Colin Granthan, the leader of the Tory Group.

On May 3 the leader and deputy leader of the Labour Group, George Newton and Roy Oldham, along with the District Labour Party, are confident that Labour will be back in power, for this year Labour is defending only four seats inherited from the disastrous local elections of 1975 and needing to gain only two seats to take control.

The combination of the general election on the same day with the fact that two Tory-held seats (Ashton Number 1 and Longdendale) have majorities of four and 26 respectively, support the prediction that Tameside will return to its traditional allegiance.

Labour will then have the task of restoring the good industrial relations with council employees that existed before and implementing the too-long-delayed change to comprehensive schools in Tameside.

It is to be hoped that this sorry episode can be forgotten. The only good thing which may have come from it is that the Law Lords' judgement did seem to restore some degree of autonomy to local government. When a Tory government next comes to power, this precedent may well prove useful to Labour councils which attempt, like Clay Cross and others did before, to resist central government direction.

Tribune, 27 April 1979

Part 2

1980-1982

OTEC power generation system

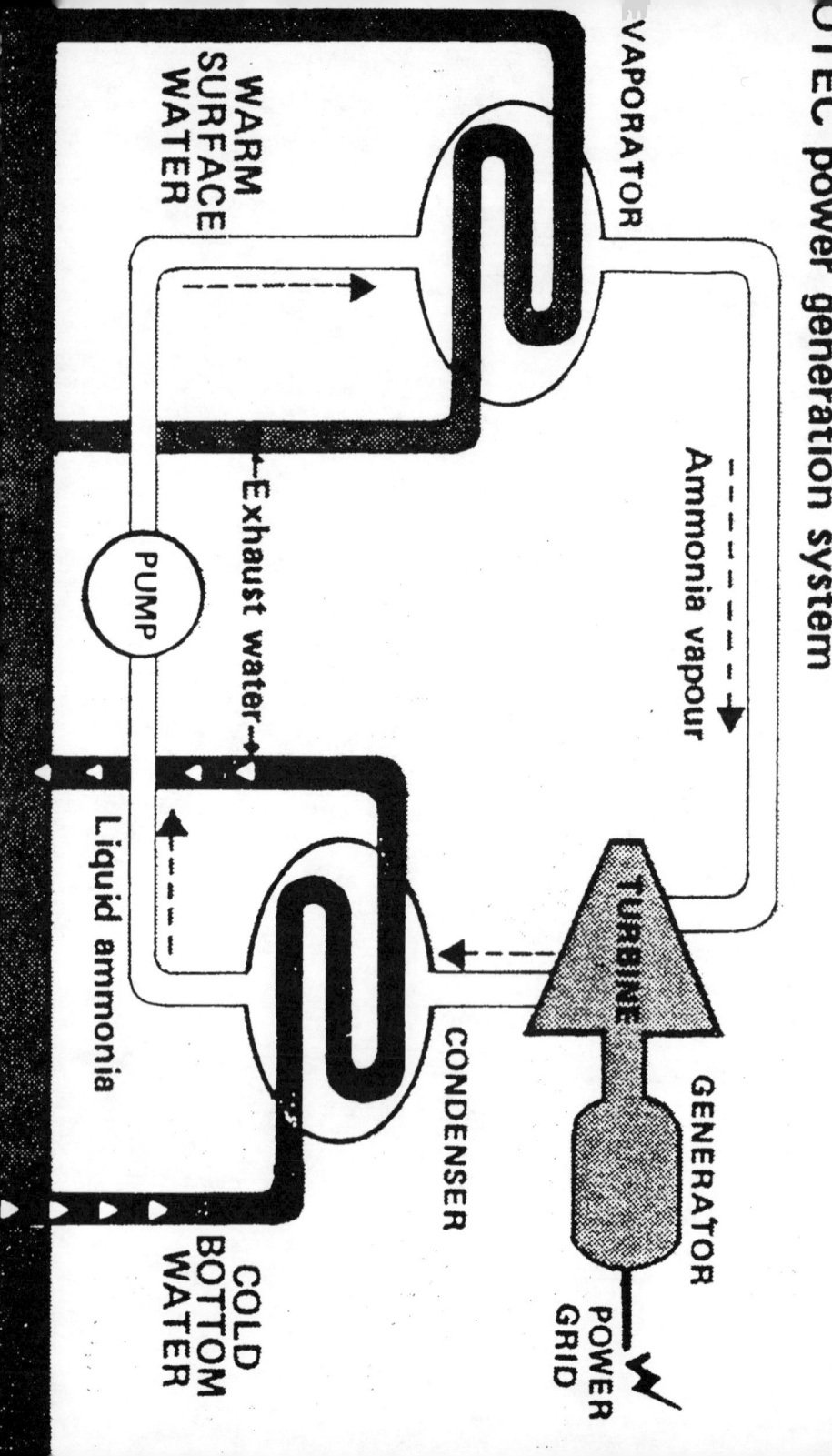

11. Letter to the *London Review of Books*

Orwell depoliticised

SIR: Samuel Hynes's review of Stansky and Abrahams' *Orwell: The Transformation* (*LRB*, Vol.2, No.1) was short on review and long on opinion. As a reader, I favour discursive reviewing, yet a writer who adopts this style has a duty to restrain his enthusiasm for his own political views and predilections. Hynes singularly fails to keep his under control. Admittedly, George Orwell — like most human beings — was a complex individual, difficult to categorise. Yet at least five assertions made by Hynes are bizarre enough to warrant comment. These are: Orwell was not a political thinker; had no philosophy of political action; was never able to relate himself comfortably to any political party; wrote nothing before 1936 that could be called political; his political idealism died in Barcelona in 1937.

Hynes turns Orwell into a minor literary figure of the Isaac Disraeli mould who flirted with politics. Orwell himself stated that he became a socialist in 1930, and the *Adelphi*, for which he wrote in the years following, was recognised as the vehicle of the intellectual Left within the Independent Labour Party. Similarly, if his idealistic socialism died in 1937, how come he joined the ILP in 1938 and later wrote so consistently for *Tribune*? As for Orwell's tendencies towards nationalism, Luddism and anti-intellectualism, and his limited philosophy of political action, he shared those with the British Left. They remain today — much to the disgust of the programmed Left — as part of that set of ideas held within, for example, the Labour Party. Finally, Orwell's political thinking in *Animal Farm* and *1984* has outlived the pronouncements of many of the political theorists of the succeeding decades. Ideagloy has yet to end, and as the US completes its switch in allies from Russia to China, *1984* keeps its point.

6 March 1980

12. Review

The Visible College by Gary Werskey

The Left Book Club's choices for May 1939 included a fairly straightforward text book, *Chemistry: A Survey*. There have been periods of course when the history and philosophy of science has

◀ *Ocean thermal energy conversion (OTEC): in the continuous cycle system, warm water vaporises ammonia to drive the turbine, and cold water re-condenses the ammonia (see item 21).*

been of some concern to socialists[1] and the choice of the book may have been quite consistent with the LBC's function, as expressed by key organiser John Lewis, "to supply relevant information and theoretical analysis of the problems of the day"; but the Club was unusual and possibly unique in taking its interest in science to the level of the laboratory bench and the test-tube rack.

Werskey's book provides insight into why this enthusiasm broke out when and where it did and, more importantly, into the theoretical basis of British Marxism. *The Visible College* is a collective biography of five prominent left-wing scientists who were politically active in the 1930s: J.D. Bernal, J.B.S. Haldane, Lancelot Hogben, Hyman Levy and Joseph Needham; but Bernal's presence is dominant.

The book attempts to integrate three themes. The first theme concerns what these left scientists were doing and saying during the period; the second is a reassessment of certain types of intellectuals who found their way into the pre-war left; and the third is an analysis of the impact of both the theory and practice of these scientists on socialists and socialism today.

The themes are treated with mixed success. The account of doings and sayings is superb and in magnificent detail, showing how the five men, and particularly Bernal, 'fashioned their own novel, coherent and contrasting interpretations of Marxism but closely linked their theoretical perspectives to a set of highly effective political practices as well'. This is undoubtedly an invaluable contribution to labour history, but the treatment of the other two themes is less satisfactory.

The treatment of the theme of intellectual recruitment is flawed because Werskey implicitly equates the left with the Communist Party, but there is much interesting material despite this limitation. In the 'social fascist' phase of Communist Party politics intellectuals were not encouraged to join the Party and natural scientists as the 'objective' lackeys of capital were particularly shunned. When the line changed in the early 1930s the minor literati continued to be allowed membership provided that they adapted themselves to the Party and were content to act as high-class commissionaires shepherding others into the organisation. They never had any central role or position however, unlike the new recruits from science, who became integral parts of the machine and entered into a symbiotic relationship which allowed some of them to help shape its future theory and practice. Bernal did much of this work while not officially a party member and his value was demonstrated in 1953 when he received the Stalin Peace Prize. Haldane actually became a member of the Party Executive Committee.

Why did this group of scientists become socialists? The scientific traditions of the early decades of the century were embodied in Cambridge 'High' science. The emphasis was on the virtues of hard, pure experimental research, conducted to the exclusion of all else and only by those with first-class brains, recruited from suitable aristocratic bourgeois or professional backgrounds. The cosseting which this implies would hardly seem to provide a fertile environment for the growth of left-wing commitment but the social isolation provided intellectual space and time for the development of a highly rationalistic ideology. The First World War intruded on this 'retreat' and the 'chemists' war brought them into society looking for political vehicles for their enthusiasm for efficiency and scientific planning. Many returned to seclusion after the war but some remained who felt, like the Fabians before them, that they had a duty to press for the modernisation of England and its way of life through science and rational administration. Sir Richard Gregory, the editor of Britain's leading scientific journal, *Nature*, welcomed the possibility of a Labour government as early as August 1919 because, "the causes of scientific education and scientific research stand to profit enormously". But the first Labour government was a profound disappointment and the cruel political and economic events of the subsequent years found many of the searchers drifting.

This was dramatically changed in 1931: the Second International Congress on the History of Science and Technology provided a programme and a party. This ordinary academic meeting was transformed by the unexpected arrival of a Russian delegation led by Bukharin which presented the Marxist view of the history of science. The Russians dominated the proceedings and our five scientists were particularly impressed by Boris Hessen's paper. 'The Social and Economic Roots of Newton's *Principia*',[2] which argued that it was capitalist entrepreneurs who were ultimately responsible for the scientific revolution of the seventeenth century; and 'Science develops out of production, and those social forms which become fetters upon production forces likewise become fetters upon science'. Bernal, in particular, found in Hessen's conclusion the starting point for the development of his own interpretation of Marxism.

This relates to Werskey's third theme, for what was Bernalism and what were its results? For Bernal, scientific theories are ideologically neutral to the extent that the 'practical value' can be demonstrated in production. Science is also inevitably progressive and, as it can only achieve its full potential in a socialist society, leads inexorably towards socialism. Thus, Bernalism echoes Lenin's response to American Scientific Management: 'a splendid example of technical progress under capitalism towards socialism'.[3] As Bernal saw it, the problem was merely to free science from its deprivation, for with adequate funds, management and co-ordination 'good scientists' could be left to produce good science. His utopia was a rationalistic world of oligarchy through democracy: in the rational world universal assent would be given to the running of the state in the interests of all by those most fit to govern. The first principle of being a good communist was to be a good scientist: here we see the influence of Cambridge 'High' science.

An expression of scientific meritocracy was to be found also in Haldane's *Why Professional Workers Should be Communists* (1945) and it is present in diluted form in Labour's post-war manifesto, *Let Us Face the Future*.[4] In this eleven-page document there are twenty-one occurrences of the word 'efficiency'. The enhanced prestige of science and scientists in the post-war period, under Labour, fell short of the hopes of both Bernal and Haldane, but for the majority of the scientific community it could be interpreted as a fulfilment of Bernalism. The claim had been made that the 'frustrations' of science could only be relieved through the achievement of socialism; and given a loose interpretation of 'socialism', and the fact that the removal of the frustrations was the primary consideration, social democracy was relatively comfortable. Christopher Caudwell had pointed out that Bernal's emphasis on science as the ultimate determinant — *the* revolutionary force — always risked collapsing Communism into science and the Lysenko affair bore this out. Bernal was the exception, but when science went against Lysenko most left scientists quickly shed their politics.

It is curious in this context that Werskey is content to explain the political stance of Bernal *et al* in terms of Labour reformism: there was no place to go to but the Communist Party. George Orwell was able to write as late as 1938 that 'the Independent Labour Party is the only British Party — at any rate the only one large enough to be worth considering — which aims at anything I should regard as Socialism'; and it was only in 1935 that the membership of the Communist Party exceeded that of the ILP. Hessen's message was obviously attractive and the politics of the Communist Party had a powerful resonance but why were the alternative vehicles of left politics rejected? The failure to consider this question may be related to a lack of awareness of events external to his group of scientists. The 1945-7 opposition to Bernalism is described as that of 'an ideologically heterogeneous grouping of literary intellectuals', including E.M. Forster, Arthur Koestler and George Orwell, 'anti-communist to a man'. But Orwell was anti-Communist (CP) and not anti-communist (left socialist). This is just one example of the need for a greater attention to matters which may come more readily within the purview of labour historians rather than social historians of science.

The importance of Bernalism is revealed perhaps in a single quote from Werskey. Bernal's 'single most important political act at home in the fifties was his continuing participation in a ginger group of scientists bent on changing the Labour Party's perspective on science and technology. Their meetings were regularly attended by Hugh Gaitskell, Jim Callaghan, Alf (later Lord) Robens and, eventually, Harold Wilson and Richard Crossman. Out of these discussions arose a new commitment on the part of Labour to modernise its own political image and fight the 1964 General Election on the basis of its ability to bring a "white hot" technological revolution to Britain'.[5] This history is also a useful starting point for present-day socialist consideration of the relation between science and socialism and it would be a pity if it did not gain a wide readership outside the relatively small groups associated with *Radical Science Journal* or the British Society for Social Responsibility in Science.

Bulletin of the Society for the Study of Labour History, Spring 1980

References
1. An interest in the history and philosophy of science has begun to emerge again on the more theoretical left. New Left Books have published Paul Feyerabend's *Against Method* (1975) and *Science in a Free Society* (1979).
2. All the Russian contributions were published in N. Bukharin *et al., Science at the Crossroads*, Kniga, London (1931). This was reprinted by Frank Cass in 1971.
3. A recent paper by Reginald Whitaker 'Scientific Management as Political Ideology', *Studies in Political Economy*, No.2 (1979) pp.75-108, deals with this and other issues.
4. This was nothing particularly new for the Labour Party. Haldane's pamphlet would have stood well next to Ramsay MacDonald's, *Socialism for Businessmen* (1925).
5. This exaggerates the Labour Party's distance from Bernalism since it has had its own 'Bernals' from its formation, but the point is well made for all that.

13. Review

The Heyday of Natural History by Lynn Barber and *Science and Colonial Expansion; The Role of British Royal Botanic Gardens* by Lucile H. Brockway

The two growth areas of the last few years are video games and studies of the social history of science. The latter should be unequivocally welcomed. No more is science seen as a value-free form of knowledge that inevitably imposes its logic and results upon society. No more is the history of science seen as the arrow in Zeno's paradox ever approaching but never closing with absolute truth.

In their separate ways both of these books illustrate this new perspective; where science is seen as both a product *and* a moulder of society. The first is a beautifully illustrated apolitical history of the Victorian mania for natural history, while the latter is a 'marxist' analysis of botany's contribution to imperialism.

The Heyday of Natural History traces in some detail the wave of fashion that brought the subject in from the cold and as far as the boudoir. Natural history helped to fill in the 'interminable leisure hours' opening up in front of the emerging middle class. It was entertaining, provided useful instruction and, most importantly, provided evidence of God's beneficence in creating the natural world for the use of mankind and in particular the English. Natural history was a celebration of religion. It was nothing more nor less than the enumeration and classification of the product of God's handiwork.

This enthusiasm embraced all classes from Lancashire weavers through to the aristocracy; even women. A hearty welcome was extended to working-class devotees of the study, especially when, like Hugh Miller, they urged their fellow workers to avoid the snares of Chartism by taking up natural history. The ladies were a problem. The sexual classification of plants by Linnaeus was thought to be more than female modesty could endure. As a result texts were prepared omitting these indelicacies.

The majority of enthusiasts were never more than mere specimen collectors. Yet some made solid contributions to natural history. H.W. Bates, one collector who turned his hobby into a profession, discovered in the Amazon 8,000 new species. Yet over-all this popular enthusiasm, and its associated science, was flawed. It took place in a vacuum. The magazines and journals for the devotees of this static, desiccated science were silent on the debates about the 'Age of the Earth' and 'Evolution'. Its leaders, Richard Owen, Roderick Murchison and Louis Agassiz, were swept into the footnotes of history when the power of Darwin's evolutionism struck home. The piety of nature as the product of the artisan watchmaker was destroyed as Darwin showed its production was the result not of skilled craftsmanship but of blind variation meeting savage destruction. In many senses Hugh Miller, the working-class naturalist and theologian made good, summed up the impact of

Darwin on the popular enthusiasm for natural history. Miller committed suicide.

Barber shows us an aspect of mid-Victorian science separate from the inchoate preamble to Darwin more commonly seen as the totality of science of the period. *This* science had different problems, different purposes and was a positive barrier to Evolution. It was a regression from much that had come before and as such it is important to know about it.

As the second book points out, British society is littered with relics of our history. Gin and tonic is one of them. The managers of our Indian Empire in the late 19th century found that the most pleasant way to take their 'medicine' was to combine it with their before-dinner drinks. The function has died, but like the House of Lords, the institution remains. *Science and Colonial Expansion* puts this minor historical excursion into a wider perspective.

Britain and the other countries of Western Europe dragged themselves across the barrier between feudalism and industrialisation by mobilising world capital in its broadest sense. They used precious metals, plants, animals and technology as tools to speed up the exploitation of colonies. This is a study of how Kew Gardens contributed with enthusiasm its 'mite' to the support and furtherance of colonialism; and how this both maintained and changed the nature of imperialism.

Kew, established in 1841, became the central institution of a global network of scientists specialising in economic botany, drawing together in the process the work of collectors who ranged the world searching for plants whose properties or appearance offered a profit. Even the private collectors, like Bates, looked at their victims with the eye of imperialism. As far as the work centred around Kew went, it was impossible to draw the line between science, commerce and imperialism. This did not trouble Kew's directors, whose rationale was 'aiding the Mother Country in everything that is useful in the vegetable Kingdom'. This role meant Kew acted as a kind of scientific clearing house; new plants were sought out, obtained by fair means or foul, brought to England for evaluation and improvement, finally transhipped to the colonies for exploitation. Kew's role is best demonstrated in the three case studies of plant transfers — Cinchona, Rubber and Sisal — included in the book. These were all plants native to South and Central America which were transferred, more or less successfully, from there via Kew to Asia.

The reason, Brockway suggests, for these transfers was that in South America Britain lacked full control and labour was both in short supply and unreliable. In Asia both control and labour were available. For example, in India Britain had a pliant, formal colony whose displaced peasants made ideal disciplined plantation labour. In some cases both plant and labour were transported, with British pockets benefiting from South American rubber grown on Malayan plantations and harvested by Indian labour. The transfers themselves were not simple. Numerous attempts were made to transfer rubber to Kew. It was only finally achieved when forebears of the rubber trees in Malaysia today were smuggled out under the noses of Brazilian customs officials.

The broad picture Lucile Brockway paints of botany as *one* of the servants of imperialism is well-drawn. Yet when she attempts to apply this same marxist approach at a more detailed level one's credulity is stretched to the limit, as the picture dissolves into a multitude of individual events. For example, in the Nilgiri Hills of India the plantation system was not pushed to its logical extreme, she says, because the British wanted to protect the environment for their own enjoyment.

With regard to sisal, the fact that the *Kew Bulletin* published information enabling Germany to establish a profitable sisal industry in its African colonies is explained by saying 'Botanical imperialism had shifted by the end of the 19th century from organised plant raids to the diffusion of information among the scientific and technological elite of the world'. At this level Brockway's marxism explains so much that it explains nothing.

Yet it is worth reading for the chapter on Cinchona alone, which offers a couple of interesting insights. First, the introduction of quinine, particularly into India, promoted racism.

For following its introduction there was a flood of English women joining their husbands on colonial service. With the coming of family ties the British began to congregate separately. No longer was the white man a temporary bachelor who sought company and often a wife among the natives. He was now a family man who had a tradition to uphold and a taboo to enforce by distance. This apartheid was legitimised through racism.

Second, quinine enabled a prolonging of Empire. As a senior British Army officer wrote, 'if portions of Britannia's tropical empire are upheld on the bayonet, the arm that wields the weapon would be nerveless but for the Cinchona bark and its active principles'. Thus, in 1890, when Britain faced an economic crisis as severe as today's, we were able to opt for further colonisation rather than the modernisation we are still awaiting.

New Statesman, 30 January 1981

14. Science for All

Britain's Education system is under severe strain at all levels. Within primary and secondary education as local government finance is cut back, education expenditure shrinks. This is unavoidable when education spending outweighs *all* other expenditure on local services for those authorities with education responsibilities. Mark Carlisle, the Secretary of State for Education, has admitted (almost in as many words) that education standards will fall over the next few years. The real level of resources per pupil is falling, however, and this will be compounded by the problem of falling school rolls. In the next decade or so the number of pupils in secondary education will shrink by a quarter. If present pupil to teacher ratios are held, then the breadth of the curriculum available within secondary schools will narrow markedly, and for some time there will be almost no recruitment nationwide into the teaching profession.

At present, local authorities have much autonomy on the curriculum taught within schools, and almost all this freedom is passed down to individual headteachers. Despite this, in the face of common problems the responses will be similar, and science education will come under threat. Economic and demographic restrictions on recruitment will hit hardest at science, and the concomitant 'progressive' set of subjects that require constant updating. It will be exacerbated by the fact that we are already short of qualified teachers for the 'harder' sciences like physics and chemistry. Gaps could soon appear in the *curriculum* especially among the 'harder' sciences.

The prospects are not made any the more cheerful by the current national picture of science education. The most recent readily available summary is to be found in *Aspects of Secondary Education in England: A Survey by HM Inspectors of Schools* (HMSO, 1979). The HMIs 'intended to assess science education across the curriculum', however, they found that 'little science appeared anywhere in the curriculum outside science subjects themselves'. They found things even more disturbing when a survey was taken of science provision in the fourth- and fifth-year curricula of over 200 schools. It revealed that 9 per cent of boys and 17 per cent of girls did no science in their fourth and fifth years, and 50 and 60 per cent respectively were studying only one science subject. With the absence of science elsewhere in the curriculum, that means that 1 in 11 boys and 1 in 6 girls have started and finished their science education in three short years.

These figures are confirmed by a survey from Tameside Education Authority showing that 11 per cent of boys and 18 per cent of girls do no science in their fifth year. In as much as Tameside is typical, some other interesting findings emerge. Schools show a wide variation in the uptake of science. The proportion of pupils who take no science varies from 0 up to 48 per cent. Similarly the range of 'sciences' on offer varies between three and eight subjects. At worst, two schools do not offer chemistry (this is an area where one in eight jobs are chemically related!) and offer only physics, biology and general science. At best, these four are offered together with geology, human biology, rural studies and applied science. The time allocated to science shows a similar variation. In the first three years this ranged from 1 hour per week to 3 hours 25 minutes, while in the fourth and fifth years each separate science could receive anything between 2 and 4 hours per week on the timetable.

The only science subject that is taken by 50 per cent of all pupils in the fourth and fifth years is biology, while physics and chemistry are taken by less than 30 and 25 per cent of pupils respectively. Other sciences outside of the 'Big Three' barely exist in schools. Any one of geology, applied science, rural studies is taken by no more than 1 pupil in 20. Yet one of the major problems of our age is natural resources and their availability. Much lip-service is paid to this need but it has failed to have much impact at school level.

The recent Finniston Report, *Engineering Our Future* (HMSO, 1980), complained about the low status of engineers in Britain — and rightly so. Yet applied science in schools is considered by some sectors of society to be a second-class activity. If a modern industrial system is to be established in Britain and if new enterprises are to emerge to replace traditional industries then we require a distinct cultural change. One component of this would be an increased commitment to education in applied science.

The cocktail of science taught in our schools nowadays is outmoded in many other ways. However the coming of the new technology in the form of micro-electronics is beginning to lead towards a proliferation of computer study courses in schools. Now with the support of the Department of Education and Science the possibility of every school having its own microcomputer is in sight. Computer programming may be taught to a few but what is not being taught is how the coming of microelectronics (and, for that matter, biotechnology) is going to affect the kind of society we live in and the sort of lives we shall be leading in the future.

Science teaching has rarely included within its remit the social implications of its subjects. Much of science is taught as subjects independent and autonomous from society — as the latest message from outside as to how the machine works. The past two decades have seen this myth badly damaged within the universities. It is now widely conceded that scientific theories are not neutral, value-free statements about the world; rather they are partial, and less than fully certain generalisations.

Science teaching should include some appreciation of the limits of its subjects — physics, chemistry etc — and the illegitimate uses to which they can be put. Such an appreciation is one that cannot be limited to only those pupils who decide to specialise in science. It is as important — if not more so — for a critical appreciation of science to be understood by those who have no intention of ever becoming scientists. The encouragement of syllabus changes by examining boards to include aspects of science within history, geography and other syllabuses would help.

One fact leaps out from both the HMI report and the Tameside survey: apart from biology, science is for males. In 1976 fewer than one-fifth of the entrants for CSE and O-level physics were girls, while for chemistry less than a third were. Even those girls who opt for science persistently underachieve. The most significant causes of all this are the reluctance of girls to enter and to compete within what they (and many of their peers) consider to be a male preserve; their anxiety about the apparent difficulty of physical science; and pressure from staff, parents and peers to conform to stereotype. Teaching methods and the content of physical sciences need to be modified, and must make allowance for the different experience of boys and girls when they enter school. Boys tend to be acquainted with cars, chemistry sets and mechanical toys; girls are rarely so.

Science education in both its nature and extent is failing future generations. It is vital for all pupils to have a good acquaintance with science. Ideally, science should be a compulsory part of school curricula; at least a programme of encouraging more science is required. But along with *more*, must come *different*. The present concentration virtually to the exclusion of all else on science's 'Big Three', physics, chemistry and biology, needs justification. Certainly if the British economy is to be re-industrialised there must be greater emphasis on applied science. This will require a cultural change, but a start in schools can be made.

New Scientist, 2 July 1981

15. Review

Science and Sexual Oppression by Brian Easlea

This is Brian Easlea's third book exploring the complex of links between scientific activity and the 'external' social environment. The first, *Liberation and the Aims of Science* (1973, and reprinted last year) examined the interpenetration of scientific and social issues from Copernicus to Keynes and beyond. The second, *Witch Hunting, Magic and the New Philosophy* (1980), looked more specifically at these issues in the context of the scientific revolution in early modern Europe. This third book surveys sexism in Western society and shows how science has acted through its practice to affirm 'masculinity' and, through its theories, to legitimate sexual oppression.

Easlea has welded together a monumental number of sources ranging from Orwell to Kelvin and Newton to Reich. He demonstrates how — as in Nazi Germany where physicians, scientists and technologists collaborated first in the articulation of theories to 'prove' the 'inferiority' of Jews and then in their mass murder through the developments of scientifically sophisticated gassing techniques — science has been used against women. For example, women's exclusion from higher education was justified on the basis of a need to conserve their limited energy, given their physical weakness and intellectual inferiority, for child bearing; their threat to male superiority through their sexuality was controlled by the assiduous propagation of the image of women as passive receivers of male sexual activity. This notion was generally accepted by women. But where it failed, science justified genital mutilation. Between 1870 and 1900 in America some 150,000 women had either their ovaries or clitoris removed because they were diagnosed as 'suffering from excessive' sexual activity. But practical examples of sexism in science are only one aspect of Easlea's book. For him the key message is that the 'masculine philosophy' that has been modern science, and whose aims have been to dominate and mechanise the external world, must be feminised. This 'masculine philosophy' has infected not only the fascist image of the world, but also that of socialists and most particularly communists. Easlea wants a struggle for gentleness based on a socialist feminism. The imagery that we must conjure with is not that of J.D. Bernal's *The World, the Flesh and the Devil* — Bernal was Britain's most prominent Marxist scientist of the Thirties and Forties — where the future is a non-stop mechanical thrusting forward of mankind, but rather that of making slow love in a meadow with the gentle flow of Morris's *News from Nowhere*.

New Statesman, 27 November 1981

16. Review

The Baroque Arsenal by Mary Kaldor

Only three of the eight RH-53D helicopters used by the US on the abortive mission to Iran to rescue the American hostages broke down. This was an above average performance. The mean time between failures of the RH-53D is less than the flying time from the Nimitz aircraft carrier in the Persian Gulf to the landing site in Iran. Mary Kaldor attempts to explain this bizarre state of affairs and much else.

The arms race is out of control. It is no longer directed by the politicians who are now merely dragged along in its wake. She uses as her explanatory key the symbiotic relationship that exists between the military and the prime industrial contractors in the US, for it is in America that the pace is set. The military is technologically conservative, unable to break away from the style of 'hardware' that won the last war. The prime contractors hobbled by the weight of experience, plant, equipment and people are capable only of supplying successive generations of the same basic technology. This continues because of the political clout of the military industrial complex.

In consequence there is now a crisis of diminishing returns. Increased weapons performance is at the expense of increased complexity with reliability declining and costs rising exponentially. The results are planes with inventories of nearly one hundred thousand separate spare parts which in flight have component failures every 12 minutes, and 'skirmishes' like Vietnam and Afghanistan where the most advanced military technology in the world impotently tries to crush peasant armies with primitive weapons.

But the effects are not limited either to the developed world or to the military sector. Major distortions of national economies are to be found both when this technology is 'parachuted' into the Third World and when it continues to dominate R&D in the industrialised nations. In the Third World it leads to a form of industrialisation that is capital intensive, decadent and incapable of providing an appropriate basis — or any basis at all — for self-sustained development. When the prime contractors attempt to diversify into non-military applications the result is over-engineered *quasi* weapons systems like Concorde and the Glomar Explorer.

Yet despite the above, Mary Kaldor believes that the current situation offers an opportunity. Because modern weapons systems are so expensive and ineffective it is possible to opt out of the arms race without sacrificing defence capability. This may be true, but it seems more probable that the edifice will not atrophy away. Rather it will collapse when some future 'skirmish' acts, like the Battle of Sedan in 1870, to show an alternative military technology has come of age; be it chemical weapons, biological weapons or precision guided munitions. Then round the survivors go again.

New Scientist, 8 April 1982

17. Japan Stakes its Industrial Future in the Sea

The Japanese skill in pursuing, and surpassing, others' technology is about to take to the water in an effort to support the nation's land-based industry. Because they are short of land and resources the Japanese have always seen ocean development as a priority — hence, the nation's strong support for its fishing, shipbuilding and, offshore oil and gas industries. More recent are the Japanese programmes to develop three technologies that are hardly new — ocean thermal energy conversion (OTEC), the extraction of uranium from seawater and deep sea-bed mining. But in each case the Japanese are pushing development work carried out elsewhere toward a commercial scale.

The main thrust for developing OTEC is coming from private industry. The principle — using the temperature difference between the warm surface waters of the tropical oceans and the cold deep water at around 1000m — has been understood for over a century but interest was revived only in the mid-1970s. The Carter administration in the US set aside $1000 million for the development of huge 400 MW floating plants. This has all but disappeared in President Reagan's budget cuts, and the contractors for earlier work — TRW, Lockheed and Global Marine — are turning toward lucrative defence contracts. Reagan's argument is that OTEC is now commercial.

In Japan, private and public efforts seem to live comfortably together. The Japanese National Sunshine Project for solar energy has within it a limited programme to develop a large, floating OTEC plant, while industry has concentrated on shorter-term technical and commercial developments. Industry's immediate target is the construction of land-based plants with capacities of up to 10 MW. The Tokyo Electrical Power Services Company, Shimizu Construction and Toshiba have successfully operated a pilot plant on the Pacific Island of Nauru since last autumn. Although there is only a limited number of suitable sites for OTEC in the tropics there is scope for commercial development to help Japanese engineers gain valuable experience of operating conditions, and the detail — heat exchangers and turbines — of the technology. The government contributed 40 per cent of the cost of the Nauru plant.

At the same time, power companies such as the Cache Electric Power Company are considering using OTEC to increase the efficiency of conventional power stations by raising the temperature of the warm water intake with waste heat. A plant for Tokunoshima island is already under construction.

The government is far more the senior partner in attempts to extract uranium from seawater, but industry is closely involved, mainly through the medium of 'entrusted' research. The technology — like OTEC — is far from new. Fritz Haber — inventor of the process for making ammonia — attempted to pay off Germany's First World War reparations by extracting gold from seawater. While massive quantities of metals are present in the oceans the concentrations are so low that processes for their extraction are usually uneconomic. For instance, a British project to extract uranium from seawater showed promise in the 1960s, but promptly died.

With a heavy commitment to nuclear power and no indigenous supplies of uranium to fuel plants the Japanese government is supporting a programme to extract uranium from seawater on an unprecedented scale. A pilot plant, which will cost £10 million, is under construction. This will pump about 40 million litres of seawater each day through a bed of titanium oxide — to yield 10 kg of uranium a year. The eventual plan is to build a plant producing 1000 tonnes of uranium a year. Uranium from seawater will hardly compete with land-based production, but the Japanese are willing to pay a premium on the fuel to secure energy independence.

The government adopts similar arguments in mining for manganese nodules on the sea-bed. The various American and European consortia involved in sea-bed mining have over the past few years drifted into a state of limbo, awaiting both the outcome of the Third United Nations Conference on the Law of the Sea (UNCLOS III) and a rise in metal prices. There is little sign of a dramatic rise in prices, and the indecisive end to UNCLOS — where all the mining countries, with the exception of France and Japan, voted against or abstained from an agreement — has done nothing to reduce the uncertainty. Japan's aim is not so much to make big profits as to assure supplies of nickel, cobalt and manganese to feed its giant steel industry. The involvement of Japanese companies with American-led consortia did not seem an adequate guarantee, so the Ministry of International Trade and Industry (MITI) became involved in deep sea mining a few years ago. Recently, the ministry's programme has gained a budget of £50 million to pursue over the next seven years, a pilot-scale test for nodule-mining. The project seems to be starting almost from first principles.

There is no simple explanation for Japan's policy on ocean technology. While it is true that the Japanese are acutely aware of their vulnerability to interruptions of supply of raw materials, or price rises, such arguments apply also to the US and Europe. One factor seems to be the commitment of both industry and government to longer term development work; companies in Japan seem not to be pursuing quick profits and Japanese government policy is more stable than other governments. This is partly because the Liberal Democratic Party has been in power almost continuously since the end of the Second World War, and because Japanese policy is based on a consensus of opinion from government and industry. For marine technology there is a Council for Ocean Development, which includes roughly equal numbers of industrialists, academics and civil servants, who recommend to the Prime Minister the long-term strategy for marine technology. These reports do not lead the way; rather they act as a summary of common consensus.

Glyn Ford and Luke Georghiou
New Scientist, 3 June 1982

18. The Costs of Good Intentions

Many Labour councils — and some Tory ones — are, in their attempts to maintain services, creating a situation that could lead to severe financial problems in the years ahead. In some cases this has happened unwittingly, whilst in others it is supposedly a short-term expedient to hold out until the election of a new Labour Government in 1984. The limits of such a strategy need to be made clear.

Since the last General Election local government expenditure has been under constant attack. Each year the Rate Support Grant settlement has been lower and the figures built in for wage rises and inflation unrealistic. At the same time more responsibilities have been offloaded onto local government, and a marked politically motivated shift of resources has occurred from the generally Labour controlled urban areas to the Conservative shires. To compound this National Government has sought to limit overall expenditure by controlling rate increases through legal and financial constraints, with 'hold-back' and 'claw-back' negating any benefits possible from rate increases outside of increasing proscribed limits. At the same time it has become clear that Labour's own supporters are not prepared to shoulder the repeated annual burden of thirty per cent increases and above. The response to supplementary rates in Greater London and elsewhere, plus the results of the Coventry referendum have made this clear. The realisation of this has led to sections of Labour's left attempting to abolish the laws of mathematics through slogans like, 'No rate rises, No cuts in services'.

In a situation where local government has lost in real terms something between a fifth and a sixth of its purchasing power, Labour Councillors are in the invidious position of being subject to two countervailing pressures. Firstly from Heseltine to restrict rate rises and secondly, from the Party's own activists, to maintain services. This latter pressure is more potent than it once was because of the constitutional changes in the Party. Only two ways out are available, Fight or Hide. A small number of Labour Councils have bravely chosen the former and lost; Lambeth to the voters, Lothian to the law and the GLC to Lord Denning. Most have chosen the latter. The result has been that the cuts imposed have been much less severe than might have been anticipated. Redundancies have been the exception rather than the rule and services have been maintained at surprisingly high levels.

Exactly how this has been achieved is not clear. Press reports in general report only the consequences of Council decisions and leave the detailed smallprint of how this is to be achieved well alone. Nevertheless indications from various Councils suggest that a number of techniques are in use. Firstly local government has transferred some portion of its slimming down costs back to National Government by the use of generous early retirement and voluntary redundancy schemes that have proved extremely attractive to middle and senior management. Secondly it has been successful in finding ways of circumventing the laws of mathematics in the short-term, i.e. maintaining levels of expenditure well in excess of income.

This has been done in a number of ways, and working down the list from the least contentious to the most the following can be seen. The majority of councils have drawn on their balances quite heavily, and while most Labour Councils have rightly resisted the sale of Council Houses, the same has not been true for the disposal of other capital assets. Civic buildings, land in Council ownership and leases have all been sold off. In some cases sale and lease back agreements have been suggested. Capital built up over the decades has been disposed of in as many months. While those councils who got in on the act early didn't do too badly, over the past twelve months it has increasingly become a buyer's market and prices are now rock-bottom. Similarly repair and maintenance is being capitalised, and goods and equipment leased rather than bought outright. In the short term massive savings are available. For example a medium sized Council can easily save a million pounds by doing this *in the first year* on vehicles alone. But, of course, as time passes the savings disappear and the ultimate result is more expensive than before.

The two final examples are debt rescheduling and internal manipulation of finances. Many of the new councils established by the 1973 local government reorganisation felt it necessary to construct new civic complexes as symbols of their status. Some of these were to be paid for under deferred purchase agreements. These repayments are now being negotiated to extend the payback period. Internally various funds are being switched around to allow certain statutory requirements to be met.

Certainly part of this overall exercise is to enable various loopholes in the Government's expenditure restrictions to be exploited, nevertheless the overall result is to build up longer term expenditure and debt in the interests of maintaining jobs and services in the short-term. It is argued that the consequences of this build up will be mitigated by a sharp decline in interest rates of the next few years which will sharply reduce interest charges. The belief is an act of faith. This also fails to take into account the increasing burden that will inevitably fall on local councils from: population changes, where the number of people over seventy-five is beginning to increase dramatically with the necessary burden falling on Social Services Departments; Youth Unemployment, where stay-on rates in the 16-18 age group are leaping up; and the many other stress areas.

Financial controls on local government in England and Wales are stringent, and it would be difficult for Councils to allow this to get wildly out of hand. But there are lessons available as to the consequences of taking this strategy too far. Charles Morris' recent book *The Cost of Good Intentions: New York City and the Liberal Experiment* (McGraw-Hill, 1981) details the financial gimmicks and evasions that allowed New York to slide to the very edge of bankruptcy in 1975. In kind, but not extent, the same pattern is now being repeated in Britain. In his epilogue, Morris claims that the budget directors in New York City did not understand where the City's financial policies were leading. They were unable to grasp the totality of all the various evasions and gimmicks that allowed the imbalance between income and expenditure to take them on the lemming-like rush to the financial cliffs.

In Britain it seems equally as easy. Councillors are only too delighted to be told that there is a way out, that they can avoid the Rates or Services dilemma. In this coming year the pressure will be even more severe as many councils pare their rate demands to increases of only twelve per cent or so. Councillors can fail to understand or even question the financial implications behind the monthly or annual miracles that are presented for their approval. This cannot continue.

This is not to argue that there is anything wrong with pursuing this strategy *in the short term*. But it must be pursued openly and clearly, as otherwise there are twin dangers. Firstly electors when they see services maintained following government cutbacks will begin to believe that the Tories were right in claiming local government was beset with gross inefficiencies that are now being weeded out. Secondly Councillors will get addicted to an option of continually deferring the evil days until a time when it can be deferred no longer.

The policy of this government is inhumane. Their current policies will massively increase levels of misery amongst the poor, the aged and the infirm. Labour Councils must say that they are maintaining at great cost a standard of service above the levels implicit in Government policies, because they believe that these levels are the *bare minimum* required for a caring society. But it will be impossible to stop a sharp reduction in services and employment if extra funds are not made available within the next couple of years. The watershed will clearly be the next General Election. If the Tories are elected, or the SDP-Liberal Alliance, then services will have to be severely curtailed. At the same time the Labour Party and the PLP must come clean. The gaps between promise and reality in the post-war years have been widening when Labour Governments have been in office. 1984 will see any incoming Government facing a series of grave crises. Councils must know whether local government will figure amongst the highest financial priorities for a newly elected Labour Government. If not, extremely painful political decisions will have to be made now and not deferred.

Ashton Labour Voice, June 1982

19. Review

Kew: Gardens for Science and Pleasure, edited by F. Nigel Hepper

Kew is a highly decorative collection of essays on various aspects of the world famous Royal Botanic Gardens. These describe the history, development and scientific research of Kew and its Sussex annex, Wakenhurst Place. The result is less than satisfactory, for the political economy of Kew is submerged beneath its more minor function as spectacle. The elements of what would constitute a good book on Kew are present.

We learn, for example, that the emergence of the conservatory in the middle nineteenth century, as the new appendage to the Victorian mansion, was a conjunction of technology and politics; a combination of the availability of good quality sheet glass plus new construction techniques in iron, and the removal of the glass tax in 1845. Similarly we learn, almost in passing, that current forestry practices predicated on maximising returns by planting conifers rather than deciduous woods are threatening wildlife, and that the International Union for the Conservation of Nature has produced a *Red Data Book* estimating that worldwide, at least 20,000 plant species are in danger of extinction. These and similar comments remain isolated and unconnected.

Instead the ornamental side of Kew dominates. The balance is such that it is as if a book on the British Army devoted the majority of its length to the ceremony of 'trooping the colour'. Those who are satisfied with the appearance will be well served by the beautiful pictures and illustrations making up the 'coffee table' aspect of this book. However, those who wish to delve deeper into Kew's function as another arm of the British state should turn instead to Lucile Brockway's *Science and Colonial Expansion: The Role of the British Royal Botanic Gardens*.

New Statesman, 20 August 1982

20. Independence for Gib

This is my second visit to Gibraltar. The first was fifteen years ago just prior to the Referendum. In the interim, the political situation here has evolved with changing circumstances. In many ways they seem to have mirrored developments of a decade and more ago in Britain's other fortress colony in the Mediterranean, Malta. There, a wish for integration changed to a demand for independence. I believe the same forces are acting here.

Of course, Gibraltar's situation is not identical with that of Malta. The two key differences are size and geographical setting. I believe that neither of these precludes the Independence option from being taken. The size argument is simplest to deal with; the world already has a number of Independent states smaller than Gibraltar which are successful in maintaining and improving the quality of life of their peoples.

Dealing with the second problem is slightly more complex. British imperialism, once it got into its stride in the Victorian era, painted as much of the world red as was possible. Rich prizes like India, Southern Africa and Australia were grabbed. Other crumbs like the Falklands, Malta and Gibraltar were just swept up together with the rest. Such colonization leaves behind it many legacies. In the case of Gibraltar this last two hundred and seventy eight years of occupation has created a new people, as waves of migrations have successively been incorporated into a common stock. Geographical logic is confounded by the legacy of colonialism. This separate people have a right to self-determination. Certainly recent history would suggest that integration with Spain holds few attractions.

Equally I would suggest integration with Britain is both politically and economically unviable. Britain would not favour integration, nor should the people of Gibraltar. This country had a function with a particular technology as the staging post and outwork of imperialism and world power status. With the passage of the ship, the Empire and Britain's position in the world have now gone. The result of integration would be for Gibraltar to become a forgotten appendage of the UK. Those who want to foresee the future with integration could do well to look at some of Britain's own islands off Scotland and their current state.

Britain does owe Gibraltar much. This capital should be used up in demanding financial and political support for the establishment of an independent Gibraltar from Britain. Gibraltarians should go forward with the vision of an independent Gibraltar making its own way in the world — with all the problems and promises that it implies — hopefully in mutual collaboration with its cultural and geographical neighbours — in Spain and Britain.

The People, 25 August 1982
(Weekly paper of the Gibraltan Socialist Labour Party)

21. Energy: The Hot and Cold Solution

New hope for future power from the ocean is being raised by the successful operation of a small pilot plant on the tiny island of Nauru in the South Pacific, using a renewable energy technology that was practically written off by the world energy conference four years ago.

Ocean thermal energy conversion (Otec), first conceived over a century ago, has yet to solve the problems of high plant cost and low efficiency — at present about 3 per cent — but is seen as an energy source of the future for tropical Third World countries.

The technique was first outlined in 1881, when French scientist Jacques D'Ansorval suggested electricity could be generated by exploiting temperature differences between the ocean's warm surface waters and the cold, deep waters flowing from the poles.

A D'Ansorval disciple put the idea into practice 50 years later — but his 22kW plant at Matanzas, Cuba, was wrecked by a hurricane two weeks after it was built.

The 1973 oil price rises, which sparked off a host of renewable energy schemes, gave Otec its first solid boost.

Although Otec is only workable in the tropics, where temperature differences between the surface and deeps reach at least the required 20 degrees centigrade, it has several key advantages: unlike other renewable energy sources, it provides 'base load' power — meaning a continuous electricity flow; and its byproducts — fresh water and easier shellfish harvesting — may prove more profitable than electricity supply.

In one system, warm surface water vaporises ammonia, which drives a turbine and is then condensed by the cold water, in a continuous cycle. Although it would be cheaper and easier to build plants onshore, most future Otec set-ups will have to be fixed on the continental shelf or — more likely — built on floating platforms, with power transmitted to shore by submarine cable. This is because the cold ocean floor water is at a depth of around 1000m. Few sites plunge to that depth a short distance from the shore.

The major challenge in the operating procedure is to improve the efficiency of heat exchange where the ammonia vapour is condensed by cold water. The present 3 per cent efficiency is 10 times lower than that achieved in thermal power stations — though this is offset by the fact that the seawater 'fuel' is not a cost factor.

Like other renewable sources — and nuclear power — Otec plants require high capital investment and offer low operating costs. Estimates of power costs range widely — from US$1500kW for projected 500MW floating stations to over US$7,000/kW for a 2.5MW plant, and from US3.1c to US27c per kilowatt/hour.

It is clear that the largescale plants favoured by US planners will not be viable in the near future. The next 10 years is likely to see the introduction of the smaller 40MW plants that deliver energy at high unit cost. These will still be cheaper than small oil-fired power stations operated in many Third World areas. The technology will at first be provided by the industrialised countries.

Federal funding for a major US long-term project in the Gulf of Mexico has been drastically cut by the Reagan Administration and is scheduled to be halted next year, with further Otec research left in the hands of the private sector. Remaining US Department of Energy funds for Otec are earmarked for two plant design schemes for 40MW land-based and shelf-mounted plants for Kahe Point, Hawaii. A commercial consortium has plans to build a 48MW land-based plant for the island of Guam.

Japanese interest has centred on the Pacific. While there is a government research and development programme for a large-scale floating plant, the main impetus comes from private industry with some government backing. The Tokyo Electric Power Services Company and partners built the onshore demonstration plant for the Republic of Naura last year, and it produces 100KW of electricity. Plans are now in an advanced stage for a large plant that would meet all the island's energy demands.

The French government agency CNEXO is planning to construct a pilot plant by 1985, possibly in Tahiti. Holland, Sweden and India have had small programmes, and the latest entrant into the field is Britain. A consortium based around a company called Otecs Limited has government support for the first stages of a small floating pilot plant, likely to be located in the Caribbean.

If future supply of Otec plants is looking healthy, so is demand. The success of Japan's Nauru plant has prompted inquiries from China, Indonesia, North Yemen and a clutch of Pacific island states. US companies have had feelers from India and Guam. Jamaica has links with the Swedish programme.

One advantage of the technology, particularly the land-based version, is that it is suited to joint ventures. Plant construction and the production of some components will provide local employment.

Among technologies for tapping the power of the oceans Otec is best suited for Third World countries. But among a host of others are two with a lot of promise.

Tidal energy harnesses daily tides and operates on the same basic principle as a hydroelectric station. The coastal basin is dammed and the flow that activates the turbines is regulated through gates. The energy potential of this source is large, but there are under 40 spots where tides are high enough to make it viable. The two best-known plants are La Rance in France and Kislaya Guba in the Soviet Union, which generate 340MW and 400MW respectively. Canada and Britain have suitable sites for large tidal power projects. Tidal energy is the only ocean power resource being commercially exploited.

Wave energy offers potentially 10 times more power than tides, and waves can be harnessed more cheaply. But the ideal waves are over 30 degrees North of the Equator and out of the reach of most developing countries, except parts of the West African coast, Indonesia, Papua New Guinea and Mauritius. Mauritius may become the first developing country to operate a wave energy system, which will provide electricity cheaper than diesel power.

Otec is an obvious candidate for development funding, but this will only be forthcoming once the technology is proven on a commercial scale. The potential is enormous. A survey for the United Nations Nairobi conference last year on 'new and renewable sources of energy' showed that 98 nations and territories — almost all developing — were suitable for Otec.

Glyn Ford and Luke Georghiou
South, November 1982

Part 3

1983-1985

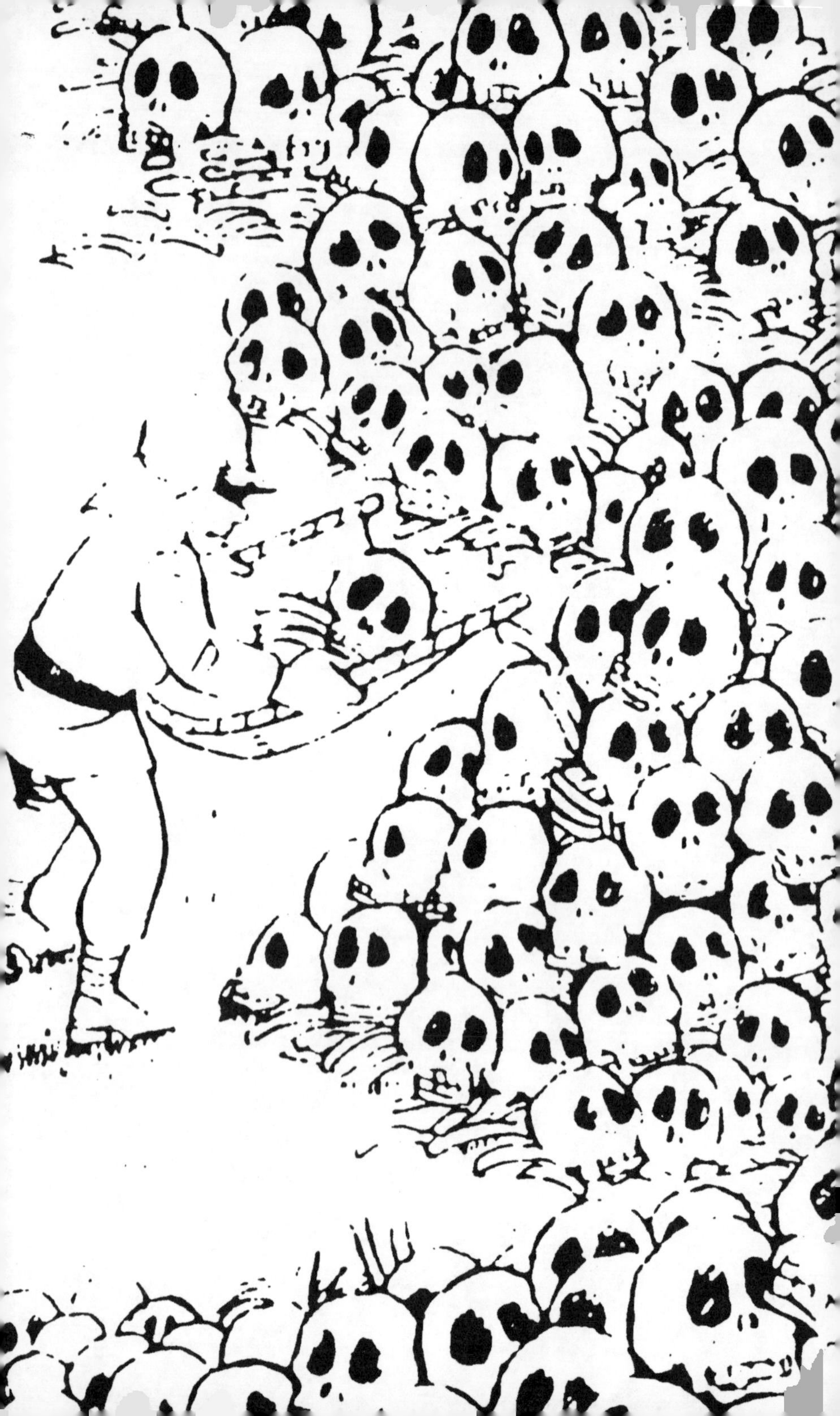

22. Letter from Port Blair

As Marshall McLuhan once wrote 'the medium is the message'. To visit the Andaman and Nicobar Islands to see the emerging tensions between Cultural Preservation, Tourism, Resource Exploitation and Defence requires a close acquaintance with facets of Indian life that would not be missed. This chain of over two hundred separate islands is a Union Territory of India administered from Delhi, and which is categorised by the Administration as falling into an 'Inner-line Zone'. Thus requiring non-Indian nationals to obtain travel permits in advance which are for tourism only. In fact some of the islands require permits for Indian nationals to visit them. Obtaining permission is not so much difficult as haphazard. At the Indian Consulate in Berlin it is deceptively easy, yet elsewhere it can be all but impossible. This is the first, not the final hurdle.

Port Blair, the capital, is three days or almost a thousand kilometres of rough sailing from the Indian mainland on a route that is irregular at best. The result is that pressure on India Air's twice weekly flights from Calcutta to the capital is extreme. The 'OK list', 'priority lists', 'waiting list' and 'chance list' seem to be in a constant state of flux that becomes increasingly frantic as departure approaches. Confidence that you are going to fly only comes as you board the plane. On board the dissipated apprehension is replaced by a dawning puzzlement. The plane whose seats were so precious is more than a third empty on take-off.

In flight, the plane sweeps along the length of the forest covered Andamans. The first sighting, in the far distance, is of the handful of Burmese islands at the north of the chain, where, it is said, Ne Win's friends spend their lives in close custody. Two hours after departure touchdown crashes the pieces of the nagging puzzle into place. Landing is short, fierce and nasty. Off the plane waiting to be shuttled to immigration the reason is obvious. The broad black sweep of the runway is abruptly swallowed beneath a threatening cliff. A full load on a hot day might not make it.

At immigration control the limits of freedom prove to be short. As passports are stamped, it is revealed that permits are necessary for travel outside of the tightly constricted municipality of Port Blair. These have to be applied for, take time, and are unlikely to be granted outside of a narrow list of selected destinations. The newly opened road to North Andaman, the first land route, is not on the list.

The town itself turns out to be a small dusty one, sprawled across the south western arc of the low hills embracing the natural harbour to which it owes its origins. In a quaint, almost 'colonial' manner

◄ *Manga mania in Japan: a frame from one of the few political comics (see item 23).*

Port Blair manages a cosmopolitan air. Evidence of Muslim, Hindu, Christian and Buddhist influence co-exist within a few hundred metres, with a temple, mosque and wat within sight of each other; while the bland rural flavour is spiced by a small naval base whose personnel require the services common to sailors everywhere.

Port Blair has had its footnotes in history. Locally there is a fierce pride in the presence of the Cellular Jail, built by the British to hold those Indian nationalists and revolutionaries who figured so little in Attenborough's *Gandhi*. Here hundreds were incarcerated under a brutal regime and scores put to death. Today the jail serves both as a national monument and a lodging for Thai smugglers caught in Indian waters around the Islands. Nor was the role of the Islands in the struggle limited to the surrogate activities of those held in its Jail. It was in Port Blair that Bose raised the flag of Indian Independence for the first time in 1942 as his Indian National Liberation Army established its presence in the Japanese occupied fringes of India.

Yet in 1947 the Islands were almost an embarrassment to an India burdened with so many riches and troubles. Just after Independence land on the Islands was offered to Anglo-Indians to entice them out of the limelight. Few took up the offer. More recently other settlers have been more successfully impressed. Bangladeshi refugees and retired Indian Army personnel have both helped to swell the Islands' population towards the two hundred thousand mark. Equally communications have moved on with the replacement of a weekly flight to the Islands from Calcutta to Rangoon, with an overnight stop before flying on the next day, by the much faster and more thrilling direct flight.

The town now boasts two hotels that you are allowed to stop at. The first is a tourist hotel five miles out of town set back from a crescent of palm fringed beach, where local fishermen haul in meagre catches and where docile rocks nose their way above the gentle swell. The idyllic picture is only spoilt by a lame Japanese pillbox blindly looking to repel the invasion that never came. The guests are either Italians besotted with the colourful fauna of the as yet unspoilt coral reefs around the Island, or Russians helping to balance India's imports from the Soviet Union. The Russians seem to consist of lower ranking Party Officials and lonely Stakhanovites who remain inspired by the ideals of the thirties half a century on.

Despite the strict prohibition in force in the town, the Russians do an attractive trade in Russian Champagne, Vodka and Caviar in exchange for Indian rupees. Away from the hotel they are less forward, looking and acting lost as their burly minders shepherd them round the rather limited circle of sights culminating in the iniquities of British Imperialism as illustrated by the Cellular Jail. The second hotel is a world apart. An 'International' hotel whose backers caught wind that the opening up of the Islands might be slower than they hoped during construction, it remains half built without significant clientele, perched in splendid isolation on the other side of the town looking across the entrance to the harbour. Here all possible facilities are available tomorrow or next month. Appropriate local flavour sees the completed blocks named after the indigenous aboriginal tribes, the Onge, the Nicobarese, the Sentinelese and the notorious Jawaras. The only clients are Texas oilmen supervising the probing for offshore oil, who drink endless 'omelettes' every night — prohibition requires gentle massage of receipts — and Indian Officials and Businessmen overnighting before flying back to the mainland.

These Islands have a future, the question is, which one? Both local and mainland entrepreneurs have been lobbying for the Islands to be opened up for large-scale tourism. But the Indian bureaucracy responsible for the Islands has been dominated until recently by a faction that wanted to protect the unique anthropological environment, leaving for posterity the still unbefriended Jawaras, mitigated by a little gentle development. The tourist lobby could not compete with the reality of the Islands' isolation in the age of jet holidays rather than expeditions.

More recently two other new and linked factors have upset this balance. There has always been an awareness of the timber resources available here, but distance and a lack of infrastructure has meant that useful exploitation has been limited. However, the recent discovery of a small offshore gas field forty kilometres from Port Blair means that a new wave of oilmen is arriving. Improved dockyard facilities are likely to follow. The Islands geological provenance suggests that offshore hydrocarbons might be matched by onshore metal ores. Resource exploitation would threaten the delicate social structure of both the settlers and the natives. Yet the resource argument is a powerful one, as is defence.

The other factor is the military one. Recent events in the South Atlantic have made many countries look to their more remote appendages. National pride or resources or both have spurred India to build up its naval strength in these once almost forgotten islands. Port Blair's naval base is to be improved and a new and larger naval base is scheduled for Great Nicobar so close to Sumatra. It has already been claimed that the ex-Army settlers on this island have been allowed to clear much of the natural vegetation to maximise agricultural production on the island to help feed the new base.

The evolving struggle within Delhi's bureaucracy over the Islands' future is likely to be conducted in private. The outcome may best be determined possibly by where the Islands are next publicised. The choices appear to be the *Petroleum Times*, upmarket travel brochures or the foreign pages of the quality press.

Christine Marple (pseudonym)
Far Eastern Economic Review, 25 August 1983

23. Manga Mania in Japan

Colourful pastel comics, or *manga*, of telephone directory proportions are read by all post-war generations in Japan and their presence whispers itself in turning pages everywhere — at coffee shops, in restaurants, on public transport. The most popular boys' comic, *Shonen Jump*, sells almost three million copies each week. In all, over eleven hundred million comics are sold every year, or ten for each man, woman and child in Japan.

Their origins go back almost a thousand years, as Fredrick Schodt describes in *The World of Japanese Comics*. The satirical *Chojugiga* (animal scrolls) drawn by a Buddhist monk in the 12th century show all the elements later to form the core of Japanese narrative art: simplicity and mockery in a cartoon form that at times becomes almost surreal. By the Edo period (1600-1867) the development of popular secular print-making was advanced, though its subject-matter was limited to life's sensual pleasures, for the *Ukiyo* or 'floating world' offered almost the only safe pictures under Japan's feudal dictatorships. The Edo order crumbled with the forceful arrival of the Americans in 1853 and after that the limits of cartooning were thrown open.

By the end of the First World War political cartooning was making its presence felt. Leftist groups like the Japan Proletarian Arts League were formed to mobilise narrative art in support of the class struggle, but the militarisation of Japan saw these groups compulsorily disbanded. Some of their members fled abroad and Yashimo Taro*, for one, continued his opposition from America where he produced, during the Second World War, a comic strip *Unganaizo* (You're Out of Luck!) for Allied propaganda leaflets. It was between the end of the War and the end of the Occupation (1952) that need to escape from life's harsh realities started the metamorphosis of this minor art form into a whole popular culture.

The first post-war comics were for primary-school children, but their initial readers have never given them up. Now there are comics for all age groups. Adult comics are also sexually differentiated, even if with a remarkably large cross-over readership. Each issue of a more popular weekly may have over 500 pages and individual stories can go on almost indefinitely. For example, *Tsurikichi Sampei*, a fishing story, has run since 1973 in *Shonen Magazine* and has been compiled into over 50 paperback volumes.

Manga have the most improbable heroes and plots, with whole comics devoted to stores about *mah jongg* while heroes include trainee *Sushi* (raw fish) chefs, *rakugo* (story teller) and *kugishi*. (The *kugishi*, or nailman, has the bizarre profession of adjusting the nails in the machines in a *Pachinko* parlour so that they do not run true, *Pachinko* being an adult version of bagatelle.) More ordinary stories — school life, space travel, historical romances, sport — all illustrate Japan's idiosyncrasies. But mass-market comics are overtly apolitical, the major exception being Nakazawa Keiji's long-running *Hadashi no Gen* (Barefoot Gen), the semi-autobiographical account of a child victim of Hiroshima. In reprinted form this runs at present to eight volumes. Attempts are being made to get it published in other languages and two volumes are already available in English,** and it is to be published shortly in French.

The content of some stories would shock many who are far from being candidate members of the Festival of Light. In children's comics innocent stories of school life are interleaved with others that go far beyond western limits. There is a current fashion in young girls' comics for tales of male homosexual love, for example *Kaze-to-ki-no-Uta* (The Song of the Wind and Trees), and of incest. In *The Great Railway Bazaar*, Paul Theroux expressed disgust for the content of a Japanese comic he picked up, but he had not met the children's series, *Toiretto Hakase* (Professor Toilet), about a scientist who specialises in scatology and works in a toilet-shaped laboratory. Violence is also prevalent: heads roll, eyes are gouged out and the pages are showered with blood.

The 'adult' comic market respects few constraints outside the, now almost ritual avoidance of genitals and of actual sexual intercourse. Story titles include 'Flesh Slave Dolls' and 'Enema Rock Climbing'. The comics are sexist and degrade women. In the worst, sado-masochism is common and a trend towards paedophilia is emerging. Many of the stories suggest, as has already been noted elsewhere, that no Japanese lover is properly equipped for a date unless bedecked with a selection of ropes and chains.

Yet Japan is a very conservative society and the crime rate is low. It was while comic sales soared, in the Fifties and Sixties, that the crime rate began its long decline. The Japanese experience seems to stand on its head the logic of those who suggest that the one causes the other. In America, in the Fifties, a coalition of educators, religious leaders and politicians demanded the censorship of comics in order to save children from depravity and juvenile delinquency. The comic industry was so intimidated it established a self-censoring body, the Comics Code Authority, rather like the British Board of Film Censors. The Authority's tunnel vision about what was permissible emasculated the American comic and the industry has declined to less than a seventh the size it was in its heyday. Yet in America the crime rate climbed.

Popular culture can provide windows that allow visions deep inside a society. Today Japan is less the land of the tea ceremony than of *Manga*. It is tempting to see the comic industry there as a paper parallel to *Coronation Street*, but a better analogy would be *The Archers*, for the stories contain the same wealth of useful information so paternalistically presented by the 'everyday story of countryfolk'. And, like both of these, Japan's comics include hidden cultural and political messages.

Manga are both part of contemporary Japanese culture and at the same time subversive of it. Comic culture is another face of the 'Walkman' generation. This has a passive, autistic element that does not disturb Japanese vertical society where the group is more important than the individual and consensus outweighs conflict. Here duty, obedience and high technology are held in high esteem, while woman are subordinate. Nevertheless the subversive side is more important. The very success of the cartoonists has created among some of them attitudes and life-styles that are reflected in stories that exemplify the Smilesian vision of self-help through hard work. These undermine group society in the interests of Western-style individualism. The portrayal of women in 'adult' comics at times shows a fear; almost a wish to school obedience into the other sex, rather than merely to reconfirm their second-class status.

Tom Nairn has written about the unique problems facing Britain because of its vanguard role in industrialising. Today Japan, with the most advanced consumer technology, has the advantage of an almost feudal social structure and set of attitudes. It may well be that *manga* will make a greater contribution to breaking these down, and creating more equal competition, than any of the more profound social theorists. If the businessmen don't like it, at least the women will be pleased.

*In accordance with East Asian practice, the surname is placed first in all Japanese names.
**Further details available from Alan Gleason, Project Gen, 1280 Fourth Avenue #3, San Francisco CA 94122, USA.

Glyn Ford and Nakajima Keiko
New Statesman, 7 October 1983

24. Review

Geophysics in the Affairs of Man by C. Bates, T. Gaskell, and R. Rice

This tome, for it is too long and over-detailed to be properly called a book, sets out to describe 'the geophysical enterprise as an interplay of technical, social and economic factors'. It is not therefore an historian's history of a neglected branch of science, but rather one produced by practitioners. The book's subtitle summarises it best, 'A personalised history of exploration geophysics and its allied sciences of seismology and oceanography'. *Geophysics in the affairs of man* is a fusion of history, reminiscence and collective autobiography.

As an analysis it is best early on when the historical dimension dominates. Here are described the origins of geophysics and its developments, academic and technical, up to and through the Second World War and into the 1960s. From this high level, the latter half declines to little more than horoscope writing — too general, too optimistic and irrelevant — as to the future prospects for the private major geophysical companies. Nevertheless, the first half of the book is a useful quarry from which much of value can be recovered, and which will serve as a guide to original sources.

For geophysics is a young science that really only emerged this century. Yet it is one whose history contains lessons that scientists should *remember*. Harold Jeffries' brilliance was tempered with a myopic arrogance that could damn Alfred Wegener's theory of continental drift with 'quantitatively insufficient and qualitatively inapplicable. It is an explanation that explains nothing which we wish to explain.'

Charles Bates, Thomas Gaskell and Robert Rice do show how the increasing demand for oil to keep industry's wheels turning in the developed world forced the pace of progress in geophysical prospecting over the past half century. Yet they do more than establish this link between science and the economics of social demand. They implicitly show that social attitudes and demands upon and within science play a crucial role in shaping and directing its continuing transformations.

The progress of geophysics has been constantly spurred by wars, hot and cold, in all its subdisciplines from oceanography to seismology. As the authors point out, earthquakes can cause more death and destruction than did the atomic bombs on Hiroshima and Nagasaki. The Tokyo earthquake of 1923 killed 130,000, while the

Tangshan earthquake in China in 1976 killed between 240,000 and 650,000 people outright.

But seismology has not been funded down the path of better earthquake prediction by governments. Instead they have sent it chasing forensic seismological criteria capable of distinguishing underground nuclear tests in territories belonging to the 'other side' from earthquakes on the basis of either seismic signature and bizarre ways of disguising the former to look like the latter for themselves. A message that seismologists and others in Tokyo and San Francisco may ponder. The authors have an explanation. "Things worth doing are worth doing for money..."

New Scientist, 13 October 1983

25. Revealing Illness: Radical Science in Japan

The Japanese Radical Science Movement today, distinguishing it from those groups that have always had purely environmental concerns, exists as elements within a number of functionally distinct organisations. These various groups aim to provide information and co-ordination for national and international campaigns over pollution issues. There is little interest outside of environmental issues, and even here interest is increasingly focused on the nuclear issue alone. Like their counterparts elsewhere in the world they face increasing apathy, at best, or positive hostility, at worst, from the Conservative tide that is flowing in Japan. In Japan the nuclear issue is the high ground to which a strategic withdrawal can be made. For here anti-nuclear campaigns of all descriptions, for obvious reasons, generate support across the political spectrum. Japan is after all a 'nuclear-free zone'. Under a Prime Minister who is as conservative as any that have held the office during the right-wing Liberal Democratic Party's (LDP) twenty-eight year rule. Thus the current stance of the Radical Science Movement in Japan is very different from that envisaged by its founders fifteen years ago, although it has maintained many facets of its original style of operation.

The late sixties in Japan, as in Europe and the United States, saw prolonged upheaval in the Universities. The University of Tokyo — Japan's most prestigious — barely functioned during 1968/69. The student struggles in *Todai* (Tokyo University) culminated in a three day pitched battle with the police around the Yasuda auditorium. But outside the Universities the struggles produced bewilderment and hostility. The crucial importance of this failure to communicate outside of the narrow confines of the student movement was clear to a number of sympathetic observers of both the student movement and its defeat. They urged the student leaders in *Todai* and, more widely, with *Zengakuren* (the National Student Federation), to break their isolation by going to the people 'narodnik' fashion through issues and campaigns with which they could identify.

An ideal issue was at hand, plus leaders with a message. The issue was that of *kogai*. This can be translated as 'public hazard' or 'public nuisance', but it is wider than this. It includes problems of factory noise, excessive vibration, obstruction of sunlight, traffic congestion and water shortage.

The increasing pace of postwar industrialisation in Japan had multiplied incidents of *kogai*. It was in the late fifties that the first indications of what later came to be called 'Minamata disease' were detected. The disease was named after the town of Minamata in south western Kyushu, Japan's most southerly 'home' island. The disease causing blindness and paralysis eventually proved to be mercury poisoning caused by waste from the Chisso Corporation's chemical plant that was allowed to be dumped into the local bay. The mercury was ingested by the fish in the area and eventually poisoned the local townspeople through their fishing industry. In 1964 a second 'Minamata disease' was detected along the Agano River near Niigata. This time the culprit proved to be the Showa Denko chemical plant.

Similarly Mitsui Mining and Smelting Company dumped cadmium in the Jinzu River near Tokyo. This caused outbreaks of *itai-itai byo* (ouch-ouch disease) named because as the cadmium weakened its victims bones they were subject to terrible pain. These examples were only the earliest and most prominent of a catalogue of other occurrences. Initially all the Companies concerned denied any responsibility. This position was generally supported by their Trade Unions and the Local Authorities. The victims often became the criminals, as Ibsen's Enemy of the People was played for real in Towns throughout Japan.

Initially the only groups that fought these cases were the *jumin undo* (local citizens groups), made up more often than not from the victims themselves. These groups were very different from the politicised, urbanised citizens groups *(shimin undo* who led the demonstrations over the Security Treaty and similar issues also in the Sixties. The *jumin undo* were often uneducated farmers, factory workers or fishermen from Japan's multitude of small towns and villages.

The catalyst for 'fusing together the concerns of the *jumin undo* with those of the students' was the existence of a small number of radical scientists. Many of these had been radicalised during campaigns against America's Vietnam War, and the use of biological and chemical weapons in that war (this parallels, in many ways, the path followed by the founders of the British Society for Social Responsibility in Science). The reaction was started by Jun Ui, a member of the Engineering Department at *Todai*. It was his thinking that in many ways set the frame within which the movement operated over the next decade and more. By the end of the Sixties he had come to believe that the University system was so tied in to the Government and Industry Complex that it could never be other than on the side of those causing *kogai*. Therefore, using the slogan 'Don't trust our present Science! Don't trust our present Education!', he established the *Jishu Koza* (Free University) in October 1970 to discuss *kogai* issues.

This 'Free University' came to take two forms. First, there were large open forums every Monday evening in front of the Yasuda auditorium — where the student struggle two years before had culminated. These meetings heard lectures from academics, but more importantly they also heard from the crippled *higaisha* (victims) of Minamata and other towns, as well as from old labour movement activists who had been involved in struggles over work-place conditions in mines and factories before the war.

These meetings had to be held outside because there were often more than a thousand people present and this was too many to be accommodated in any of the lecture theatres. Of these, as many as a third were ordinary citizens. Jun Ui tried to use these open forums to illustrate the social and economic roots of pollution. The 'curriculum' explained that the creation of *kogai* was not an unthinking by-product of breakneck industrialisation, but rather, along with low wages and trade protection, it played an essential part in allowing Japan's economic success.

Second, to parallel the plenary meetings, a variety of study groups were established to consider individual issues in depth. Subjects chosen, amongst others, included synthetic detergents, pesticides, and energy problems. This was an attempt to arm the *Jishu Koza* movement technically by producing knowledgeable groups and individuals outside of the Establishment. In some cases this was emphasised by their practice. The energy group, for example, required participating members to attend twenty hours of lectures on resource physics that considered the energy problem from a scientific and technical point of view. This was also reflected in the movement's magazine, initially also called *Jishu Koza*, which reported the main research findings indicating the possible causes of the various outbreaks of *kogai* related diseases. Of course, this 'cult of the expert' had its opponents. Some scientists in the movement rejected the political implications of 'expertise' and imposed self-denying ordinances to not involve themselves in struggles where their own expertise was concerned. This approach has softened with time.

Both of *Jushu Koza's* two initial activities still continue. The open forums outside the Yasuda auditorium still take place on Monday nights, but now it's tradition and not numbers that keep the meetings outside. Meetings are no longer held every week and the audiences rarely exceed two hundred. This decline reflects the shifting political attitudes in Japan and the fact that the LDP Government was forced to respond to the early campaigns of the *jumin undo* because they piled up evidence to indict the negligence of Japanese industrialists. As early as 1971 an Environmental Agency was established. Nevertheless it was kept firmly in a subordinate position. For example in 1978 it was forced to relax NO_x tolerance levels after industry lobbied Japan's powerful Ministry of International Trade and Industry (MITI), saying that the new standards were adversely affecting their competitiveness in the world market. Despite this undeniable improvements in the environment in Japan have partly defused the *kogai* issue. Thus now in terms of mass support the nuclear issues are uniquely appealing.

The specialist groups still continue to operate. Some use descriptive titles, while others have more cryptic names indicating merely where they originally met. As the major issues have been reduced to the nuclear one, so the groups have moved from a technical to a political role. Some have moved so far in this direction that they almost fall outside the definition of radical science groups apart from their origins.

When Ui established the 'Free University' he argued that the only way to beat *kogai* was through absolute opposition. Every case must be fought right through to the end. The Japanese legal system makes this a long road to follow. Ui himself appeared on behalf of the victims of the 'Second Minamata disease' in a court case against the Company in Niigata, cross-examining the parade of expert witnesses appearing on behalf of Showa Denko. In 1973, more than eight years after the first victims were identified, the Company finally admitted liability.

In the case of Minamata itself the issues have been even more protracted. Although the main issue of compensation is now settled, subsidiary issues are still in dispute. The Japanese Supreme Court finally upheld a ruling by a lower Court that invalidated the Chisso

Corporation's 1970 Shareholders' Meeting, because it was not allowed to consider a resolution that had been tabled that would have accepted responsibility for the disease. The meeting had to be reconvened.

The task of continuing to assist the *higaisha* and the associated citizens' groups is undertaken by the *Kasugo Group*. Recently they have helped with citizens' group injunctions against nuclear power plants, both in operation and proposed. Although, until recently when a dissident anti-nuclear group took part for the first time, no anti-nuclear groups participated in the formal safety hearings organised by MITI. The feeling is that these are pre-determined and to participate only gives them a legitimacy that they otherwise lack.

In his initial case against *kogai*, Jun Ui warned that one consequence of Japanese Corporations being forced to alleviate pollution would be that they would export it instead to the rest of East Asia and the Pacific. Thus the *Han-kogai Yushutsu Tsuho Center* (Committee Against the Export of Pollution) campaigns to alert the unknowing recipients that this is taking place. Again the last few years has seen them increasingly concentrate on the export of nuclear power technology.

Another campaign on an international basis is co-ordinated through the group around *Han-Genpatsu* (Anti-Nuclear) *News*. They publish material from around the World on the anti-nuclear campaign although it is in fact mainly from the Eastern Hemisphere. Recently they have devoted most of their efforts to publicising the Pacific states campaign for a 'nuclear free' Pacific, and hence to the practical issues of ocean dumping and French nuclear tests. The newsletter has a circulation of just about a thousand, but as reflects the group's international orientation few are circulated in Japan. About half are sent to contacts within the Pacific and South East Asian Countries, while the remainder are divided almost evenly between North America and Europe.

The domestic side is oriented around the magazine *Tsuchino-koe Tamino-koe* (Voice of the Earth, Voice of the People) and its production group. This was the original *Jushu Koza* magazine mentioned above, but was transformed into an overtly political magazine in the middle seventies, and now provides arguments showing the social and economic causes of *kogai*. Other groups include the *Mizu Group* concerned with water supply and pollution, and *Daigaku-ron* that campaigns for the reform of Japan's ponderous and stultifying higher education system.

All the above groups are direct descendents of *Jishu Koza's* founders in their practice. They are 'outsider' groups that step aside from Japan's consensual style of politics, avoiding the 'unofficial' and the 'off the record' meetings between business and other organisations. These groups co-ordinate their activities through regular monthly meetings. The central core of activists is small; no more than thirty or forty. But the domestic, like the international network, has over a thousand contacts.

One other significant group exists that derives from the original *Jishu Koza* network, although it is now outside of the present organisation. This is the *People's Research Institute for Energy and Environment* (PRIEE), whose roots lay with the small group organised within the 'Free University' in 1974 to argue the case for soft energy paths in the wake of the 'oil shock'. This was the group that insisted upon the training mentioned above before admission into full membership. The Institute itself was established in May 1978 and analyses the influence of nuclear power, while promoting technical and social alternatives. Since the formal establishment of PRIEE they have published a number of handbooks, including a handbook of alternative energy schemes in Japan.

The Institute works closely with the broad citizens movements and the Japan Consumers' Union. Its philosophy is to provide expertise and it is more accommodating than the other groups in response to outside organisations. Some of its activists have been involved in advising the Japan Socialist Party and the *Komeito* (Clean Government) Party. The latter is the political wing of *Soka Gakkai*, a new Buddhist revivalist movement whose membership is concentrated amongst those marginal groups who have been left economically and socially isolated by the pace of change in Japan since the War. While the Japan Communist Party has campaigned consistently on environmental issues over the years its organisation and its attitude towards science means that it has little time for the theoretical stance of the radical science movement although it has co-operated on particular campaigns.

Thus the radical science movement in Japan is dissolving itself into a group of organisations whose main target is the nuclear issue in all of its many dimensions. Like anti-nuclear groups all over the world, because of the political economy of the nuclear enterprise, there are few trained nuclear scientists in their ranks — although there are some. Nevertheless, focused on one issue they do have considerable strength especially when the issue is one that has such deep resonances within the people of Japan. The past decade has seen the movement go from *kogai* to nuclear power. What will be the result of the next decade?

Science for People, Winter 1983

26. Review

Betrayers of the Truth: Fraud and Deceit in the Halls of Science, William Broad and Nicholas Wade

Scientists lie, cheat and steal. In this they are no different from the rest of mankind. Yet a myth exists that while they exhibit these normal human failings outside of the laboratory, once inside this *sanctum sanctorum* they exhibit a purity of thought and deed worthy of any priest. Admittedly, this is only partly attributed to the natural goodness of the scientists, and lays much of the responsibility at the door of science's informal, but nonetheless rigorous and formidable, system of self-control. This system only allocates recognition to the scientist in exchange for original work capable of replication.

Betrayers of the Truth catalogues the numerous cases of fraud and deceit by scientists, showing that many of our 'heroes of science' were flawed: Galileo cheated, Newton lied, Darwin stole. More importantly the authors claim that these blemishes in the production process of science are not isolated and exceptional events, but rather the needle peaks of a widespread phenomenon. Some of these deceits can go undetected for decades, and can distort political and technical choices. One example of this is Cyril Burt's work on 'Levedity' that was so vital in shaping Britain's postwar education system in to the rigid and hierarchical trinity of Grammar, Technical and Secondary Modern schools. This was based on spurious studies of identical twins that it was claimed demonstrated that intelligence was more than seventy-five per cent inherited. Yet it was not until 1976 that the *Sunday Times* — not the scientific press — exposed Burt's half century of scientific work as a fabrication based on a tissue of lies.

The implications of this and similar events is that the healthy scepticism that politicians so often suspend in the face of science's claims to be able to arbitrate between political choices must be maintained. Broad and Wade have shown science's other side. To mirror the 'heroes of science' of the past perhaps we should have the trio of Margaret Howard, Elias A.K. Alsabti and Jocelyn Bell. The first was one of Burt's ghostly collaborators, the second published scores, if not hundreds, of forged scientific papers, while the third was the graduate student who discovered in the sixties the novel pulsating radio stars known as 'pulsars' and whose reward was to see her discovery earn not her but her supervisor, Dr. Antony Hamish, the Nobel Prize for Physics in 1974. We should remember them.

New Statesman, 24 February 1984

27. Review

The Japanese Mind, Robert C. Christopher

Robert Christopher is an ageing American who has worked for both *Time* and *Newsweek*. This book is therefore moulded by the thought patterns and concerns of 'greying' executive America. It reads strangely to English eyes with a language that is epitomised by chapter headings like, 'Mom, Pop and the Robots'. Yet it is worth reading for two reasons. First, while it gives a partial portrait of Japan it is one that is far more real than many of the current 'off the peg' images of Japan available. Secondly, *The Japanese Mind* is revealing of the American mind.

The Japan of Robert Christopher is a land of harmony, efficiency and beauty through utility. Yet these are at least seen as only one face of Japan. The harmony of 'Japan Inc.' is broken by the struggles of the *Sanrizuka* farmers against Narita Airport and the bombings and killings of groups like *Chukaku-ha* whose internecine warfare with other left groups still continues. The efficiency matches Nissan's Zama plant where robots, neatly labelled and bedecked with feminine names and portraits, spew out cars at rates unmatched in Europe or the US or FANUC where robots build robots, with a creaking victorian distribution system where numerous intermediaries edge products towards the ultimate consumers. The beauty contrasts the naturalness of the lesser arts in the Imperial Villa at Katsura with the brashness of Japan's sex-tourism industry and Tokyo Disneyland. The land of contrast does at least feature here.

What is missing, however, is the analysis of why this is the case, and how Japan's corporate capitalism is evolving. Here we have the disjointed elements of what should serve as illustrations to a coherent whole. But to produce such an analysis would require a way of thought that sees these elements as visual manifestations of deeper social forces rather than the product of chance. It would require the scientific approach of a professional rather than that of the amateur anthropologist. Here we must be satisfied with a vision that moves from the chrysanthemum and the sword to the micro and MITI.

New Statesman, May 1984

28. The Tide of Racism Sweeps over Europe

It would be hard to exaggerate the importance of the rise of racism in Europe, says the report of an all-party European Parliament committee of inquiry published this week in Brussels.

The report compares the situation in each of the community's ten member states, plus its neighbours, and demonstrates that recent events are not evidence of a peculiarly British problem. They are a national expression of a deep-seated malaise which has been spreading throughout Europe alongside mass unemployment, the crisis in the inner cities and the crisis of the education system.

Racial tensions find their expression in racial attacks and in the revival of so-called scientific racist ideas. Every day racism within the state apparatus, particularly the police, can make a dangerous situation explosive.

Incidents such as the shooting of Mrs Groce (in Brixton) or the death of Mrs Jarrett (in Tottenham) are just the short fuse. The report points out that xenophobia, which is perhaps almost endemic, is not quite the same as racism. It lists the political parties in Europe which openly appeal to xenophobia and challenge the democratic structure of their countries. The European Parliament now has a political group many of whose members make no secret of their fascist sympathies.

The committee, which looked into the rise of fascism and racism in Europe, was a product of the European elections of June 1984. While in Britain there was a swing to Labour, doubling its representation to 32, the major tremor was in France where the extreme right Front National under the leadership of the former Poujadist deputy and long time extreme-right activist Jean-Marie Le Pen, polled 10.95 per cent of the votes all but overtaking the French Communist Party and returning 10 members to Europe. In Italy the self-confessed neo-fascist Movimento Sociale Italiano (MSI) increased its representation compared with 1979 from four to five and in Greece Ethniki Politiki Enossis (EPEN), apologists for the colonel's regime, returned its first member. With a total of 16 members, the extreme right was able to establish the Group of the European Right in the Parliament and consequently gain substantial financial support and political legitimacy.

The report provides a wealth of detail concerning right-wing extremist parties. For example, Romain Marie — real name Bernard Antony — one of the Front Nationale's representatives in the European Parliament was the founder of the daily *Present* which described M. Robert Badinter, France's Jewish Minister of Justice in

June 1983 as 'a Bohemian with blood-stained lips.' Marie had earlier also written in *Present*: 'The modern world is once again facing the Jewish problem. Jews are at the centre of contemporary debate. Marx and Rothschild can be said to represent two sides of the same medal ... another aspect of the Jewish problem is the propensity of Jews to occupy all the key posts in Western societies.'

The report sees the use of such language as a clear symptom of a problem that should not be allowed to grow as a result of complacency by democratic parties throughout Europe.

The Socialist Group saw these election results as a re-emerging political problem that needed highlighting and at their initiative the inquiry was established. The report provides details of the links between extreme-right groups in Europe, their common ideology and vision of Europe's future. It refers to the horrifying level of rightwing terrorism in Italy, making clear that this is not an isolated marginal factor. MSI members have been goaled for terrorist activities. In this light, Britain's continuing refusal to hand over Italian terrorists to the courts in Italy is all the more unacceptable.

The report proposed not only to strengthen anti-terrorist co-operation but argues that Europe should also strengthen its civic education to meet the needs of a multi-racial society. Immigrant organisations should have a consultative body based in Brussels and combating xenophobia should become one of the objectives of the EEC policy. The committee held a series of public hearings in Brussels and heard evidence from 39 witnesses including Prof Bhiku Parekh, Jean-Francois Revel, Andre Glucksman, Prof Ernest Mandel, Prof Stephen Rose and Simon Wiesental and received thousands of pages of written submissions.

Early on the European right withdrew from the committee threatening to frustrate its work and begin judicial proceedings in the European Court. This last matter is still sub-judice. As the French daily *Liberation* said recently of this last action — why is it that Le Pen, who claims neither to be a racist or a fascist, is spending so much effort trying to prevent an inquiry into fascism and racism?

Now the committee's work is almost complete. The report has been prepared by Dimitrious Evrigenis, a Greek Christian Democrat, a judge at the European Court of Human Rights, a member of the United Nations Committee on Racial Discrimination, and someone who was goaled under the colonels' regime in Greece. It will be approved along with a list of recommendations at the end of the month before finally being presented to the European Parliament.

The report deals with the elements of racial discrimination which can be found in the legislatory case law and above all perhaps to the administrative practices of European countries. This means that minority groups face discrimination in both their working and private lives. Recent figures from Birmingham and Manchester show the bias within the Youth Training Scheme against young blacks. All the indications are that the pressures on ethnic minority groups will continue to increase. Xenophobia throughout Europe has reached alarming levels with racist attacks and even murder common events. The victims vary. In France it is the immigrants from the Mahgreb, in Germany the Turkish guestworkers, in Britain Asians and West Indians, in Denmark the Iranians and in Ireland the travellers.

At the moment we are against the stream. Many of the ideas from the extremist groups in the European right and their British equivalent, the National Front, have a currency and a resonance far outside their limited membership and following. They may use subtle ideographic formulations that substitute 'difference' for 'inferior' but we all know what the new right is saying. Their influence goes far wider, touching democratic parties in Europe.

Immigration is a major issue in the run-up to the National Assembly elections in France. However the answer is not to make out the victims to be the criminals. Lord Denning said recently in the *Mail on Sunday* that "what is happening on the streets of Britain today is a war." He like so many was blaming the victims rather than the criminals, but in one sense he was right: it is a war, but the battle is against ignorance, bigotry and prejudice and the neglect that together is creating the social problems that will disrupt the fabric of our society.

Politicians from all democratic parties in Europe have to be forced to take action. Anti-discriminatory legislation must be strengthened; the European Parliament has done Europe a service in drawing attention to this situation. Now the Council of Ministers and the Commission is taking up the issue. What is needed are public campaigns that start to shift the terms of the debate. In France SOS Racisme the youth group campaigning for a multiracial society has started to mobilise millions of young people. In Britain the anti-fascist alliance may do the same. Unless something is done we will all lose. Maybe standing back at a European level made the problem clearer. Certainly now, in the light of recent events, it is only the blind who cannot see.

The Guardian, 8 November 1985

Part 4

1986

論壇

日本のSDI参加に反対

核の恐怖知る大国の責任果たせ

グリン・フォード

すでに参加に踏み切った英国、西独では、政府の秘密主義のゆえに、微妙な問題点を抱えているのに、両国の議会は論議を尽くすことができなかった。そして今度は日本が人類の未来にとって重大な意味をもつ選択を迫

る。これらの議論はいずれも厳密な検証に堪えぬものだ。日本はSDIに決して参加すべきでない、と考える。

日本はSDIに参加するに先立って、何ら公開討議がなされなかった。SDIはきわめて複雑、微妙な問題点を抱えているのに、政府の秘密主義のゆえに、両国の議会は論議を尽くすことができなかった。そして今度は日本が人類の未来にとって重大な意味をもつ選択を迫

な軍事技術を開発し、相手方計画、と認識されている。これらの兵器はミサイル・サイロや堅固化された他の標的の核ミサイルが突破し得ぬ「かさ」を創出する、という防衛に用いられよう。

これはごまかしの核ミサイルが突破し得ぬもしくは錯誤によってキューバ危機のような事態が生ずる不安定な時期に、偶然、故意と警戒しているからだ。

日本は二つの原爆の犠牲者である。核戦争をだれより知っているが国際関係で威信を高めつつある今こそ、米ソる危険な道を食い止べく、その道義的責任を果たすときである。ロ

なら、それは即「ボタン戦争」につながるだろう。

レーガン大統領が日本の参加を望む理由は、その政治的支援を誇示して、米国内のSDI反対派を抑えるためだ。人は核軍拡競争に歯止めをかけることに貢献するで

ある。そうすることは、政府がSDI参加サインしないよう要

航ミサイルの侵入を阻むことはできぬからである。

近ごろでは、技術のとうしだ。それは早い時期に欧州と極東に配備されるだろう。

その結果として軍拡競争は激化する。スターウォーズ技術の研究はソ連でも進行してできぬ既成事実を今のうちにつくっておきたいのである。

英国政府との覚書によって実現の可能性が高いのは、ソ連の中距離・短距離核兵器を防ぐ戦術ミサイル防衛技術

である。なぜなら、完ぺきな「かさ」できず、爆撃機や巡

た現実がSDI宣伝を無力化しつつある。私は最近、十日間米国に滞在したが、米国は熱狂的なSDI推進派や先端技術企業ロビーを除き、飛んでくる大陸間弾道ミサイルすれば、軍事支出は急上昇

将来、民主党政権が生まれたとしても、くつがえすことができぬ既成事実を今のうちにつくっておきたいのである。双方がこの技術を配備いる。

対米合意の覚書にサインす

（欧州議会議員・ギー研究技術委DI問題担当者在住）

29. Star Wars Secret Could Cost Us Dear

The memorandum of understanding signed in December between the British and United States governments for the UK participation in the Star Wars research programme has a series of political, military and financial consequences that need the fullest possible debate, but which have been kept secret from the British public and Parliament, and maybe even from members of the current Cabinet. First, the memorandum makes a commitment on behalf of the UK Government to provide up to a third of the costs of research agreed on the basis of government to government contracts, which could total hundreds of millions of pounds. Secondly, it contains penalty clauses for non-performance that would match these figures in cancellation payments should the programme be abandoned. Thirdly, should technologies be deployed, in consequence of tearing up the 1972 Anti-Ballistic Missile Treaty and building up the arms race, they would be deployed first in Europe. Finally, if mutual deployment by both East and West was to occur, there would in all probability be a period of time during the build-up when a major military advantage would lie with whoever struck first. During this period, a crisis could spark off a race for the button.

In March, 1983, Ronald Reagan, seemingly almost as an afterthought at the end of a speech, announced the Strategic Defence Initiative (SDI). This research programme, known as Star Wars, was to produce a variety of military technologies, including laser-beam weapons, that would act in series to form an 'umbrella' impenetrable to incoming nuclear missiles, effectively precluding nuclear war. The claim that Star Wars would abolish nuclear war was a spurious one, since even a perfect umbrella could be underflown with bombers.

How much Reagan believed his own rhetoric is uncertain, but his enthusiasm for the programme was clear, and it quickly became another potent virility symbol held up before the American people. Appearing to offer protection to civilians instead of silos, SDI became popular with the public, certainly compared with the MX programme. SDI also provided massive new sustenance to the military-industrial complex.

Shortly after the initial speech, participation in the programme was offered on a sixty-day option to America's allies in Europe and elsewhere. The USSR saw this as another racking up of the arms race, as a clear breach of the 1972 ABM treaty, and in consequence, as a clear indication of the insincerity of America and her allies in engaging in meaningful arms reduction negotiations. While research

◀ *April 1986: an appeal to the people of Japan about Star Wars (see item 30).*

is not banned by the ABM treaty, testing and deployment are, and these are envisaged for the later stages of the programme. When coupled with other American weapons developments, SDI could enable hardened point targets to be taken out. Consequently, the USSR sees SDI as part of a strategy to achieve an American first strike capability.

European worries about the political implications and the technological feasibility of SDI stretched the sixty-day option very elastically. In spite of early coolness from Sir Geoffrey Howe, the UK remained America's staunchest ally. The size of the SDI research programme is enormous. Funding in the current fiscal year is $2.75 billion with a planned rise next year to $4.2 billion, a figure three times that of Government funded research and development in Britain. At first Britain tried to trade political support for cash, in terms of up to $1.5 billion of guaranteed contracts for UK firms during the programme. This offer was firmly rejected. Because of Prime Ministerial insistence that a deal had to be made to maintain the Ron-Margaret axis, and because of the clear indication that no memorandum of understanding meant no contracts of any significance, Michael Heseltine, then Minister of Defence, was forced to settle for what he could get. Perhaps it was the experience of these negotiations that helped turn Heseltine's opinion on Westland from indifference to pro-European. When the memo was signed in December it was announced that its terms were to remain secret *in perpetuity*. Now that Britain has gone boldly forward, negotiations are in an advanced stage for other agreements with West Germany, Italy, Japan, and Israel. The German government, unlike Britain, has announced that no public money will be available for the programme.

Under the terms of the US-UK memo, money is available to British firms in two ways. First, it can be obtained through direct contract between individual companies and the US government, with the UK government acting as security overlord channelling secret information to the companies and vetting their employees. It has been estimated that $300-$1,000 million is available for *all* states signing an agreement during the next five years, and this will have to be bid for against American competition and pork-barrel politics. The second route is through government-to-government contracts where, in exchange for a substantial financial contribution, the US will allocate responsibility for a whole section of research to another government to sub-contract. It is only through this mechanism that UK firms like British Aerospace, Plessey, and GEC may obtain the orders they so desperately want.

The sector most likely to be sub-contracted is that of anti-tactical missile defence. Within Nato the Americans have long been pressing the case for improving European Air Defences. The message has been getting home recently, and now the US is arguing that Nato members should work on the development of anti-tactical missiles technology that would serve to defend against a whole range of intermediate offensive weapons. These technologies, which are reasonably advanced, could be pursued jointly by Nato countries in Europe that have signed agreements, and would be available for deployment, with obvious political consequences, fairly quickly.

In order to protect US interests, and as a useful political lever for the present government in Britain, the memo contains penalty clauses for non-performance that would make it expensive for an incoming government to abandon any research already sub-contracted, much as this might be their wish. Of course, it is readily acknowledged that governments frequently make commitments that extend beyond their term of office, and must continue to do so if they are to govern effectively. However, it is not acceptable that the public or politicians, apart from a very limited number of individuals within the highest reaches of government, are unaware of what the UK has committed itself to.

On the left in Britain and in Europe there is a great, but unfounded, belief that the problem of Star Wars will dissolve itself because it will not work. Certainly the technologies required for an impenetrable umbrella are far beyond the current state of the art. Space-based missile defence systems make the Shuttle engineering look like child's play. The software required for battle management will far exceed that available today, and it will be impossible to test such a system before Armageddon. But, this is tilting at windmills.

No-one in the US — outside the lunatic fringe — expects the creation of a Star Wars shield to spell the end of nuclear weapons. Instead, SDI is being conceived as a research programme that will lead to the successful deployment of defensive weapons technologies, enhancing US military superiority. These technologies will be used for point defence of missile silos and other hardened targets, with only the most limited attempt to extend their deployment to protect cities, because the Pentagon strategists know that the limit of their effectiveness is likely to remain substantially below 100 per cent. On this basis it is clear that SDI could work.

The public must realise the truth that lies behind the successful public relations exercise still being conducted in the US. Inevitable increase in the arms race lies behind the reality of SDI as opposed to the nuclear weapon-free world of the rhetoric. Recognition must also be given to the destabilising situation that can arise during deployment of the systems. As deployment takes place, defensive capability will increase gradually so that successively 20 per cent, 40 per cent, 60 per cent, and 80 per cent of incoming missiles can be destroyed. If ever such a deployment occurs simultaneously in the US and USSR, there will be a significant period of time during the deployment phase when both sides will gain an advantage. Translated into military terms this means that whoever strikes first *wins* a nuclear war. A situation like the Cuban missile crisis arising through accident, design, or miscalculation would lead to a race to shoot.

In Britain little detailed discussion has occurred about the implications of SDI as a tactical defence system or its implications for destabilisation. The financial commitment of the UK and the leading political and military role Europe will play have received small attention. No full scale debate has yet taken place in Westminster. These issues need to be raised, and the links explored between the various existing high technology programmes like Alvey in Britain, Esprit in Europe, and SDI research. It is only when some of these questions have been answered that we will know exactly what kind of bastardised runt Michael Heseltine purchased for Britain in December's 'pig in a poke.'

The Guardian, 17 February 1986

30. An Appeal to the People of Japan — Don't Play Star Wars

Over the next weeks and months you will be subject to a barrage of subtle propaganda justifying the signature by Japan of a memorandum of understanding (MOU) with the United States to participate in President Reagan's Star Wars programme. These arguments will be couched in military, political and economic terms. None of them stand up to close scrutiny. In both Britain and Germany, who signed agreements in December and March respectively, there was virtually no public discussion on the implications of Star Wars. In neither country was there a debate in the national parliament before signature. America has made it clear that Japan is the next target for signature. You are now centre stage in what may be a crucial decision for the future of mankind. *I urge you to demand that your Government does not sign such an agreement.* In doing so you will be making a major contribution to braking the nuclear arms race.

The military-political arguments are as follows. In March 1983, when President Reagan announced the Strategic Defence Initiative (SDI), commonly known as Star Wars, he marketed it as a research programme that would effectively make nuclear weapons redundant, by developing a variety of military technologies, including laser weapons, which would act in series to create an 'umbrella' impenetrable to incoming nuclear missiles. Even this initial claim was spurious, since the most perfect umbrella could be underflown by bombers and cruise missiles.

More recently the technological realities have begun to prevail over the rhetoric. No-one in America, outside of the lunatic fringe and the High Frontier lobby, now even pretends that it will be possible to create a defence system totally impenetrable to incoming Intercontinental Ballistic Missiles. Rather, SDI is now being conceived of as a programme that will allow defensive weapons to be deployed, enhancing American military superiority and enabling them to win a nuclear war. These weapons will be used for point defence of missile silos and other hardened targets, and will be first deployed in Europe and the Far East.

The consequences will be a further acceleration of the arms race. Russian research on Star Wars technologies is also underway. Should both sides deploy these technologies, and it is difficult to conceive of a situation when this would not occur, the overall level of defence spending would climb steeply again creating a new level of terror. More dangerously during deployment there would be a period of time when a major military advantage would lie with which ever of the superpowers struck first in a nuclear exchange. In this unstable period, a situation like the Cuban missile crisis — whether it arose through accident, design or miscalculation — would lead to a 'race for the button'.

The reason President Reagan wants an agreement with Japan is to demonstrate domestic and international political support for this military initiative. He wants to create a bandwagon that will be unstoppable by a new incoming Democratic administration. The supposed trade-off for countries who sign agreements will be contracts for SDI work. Yet this will be a one-way trade. Contracts will be available through three routes. First, money could be obtained through direct contract between companies and the American government with the Japanese government acting as security overlord channelling information and vetting employees. Secondly, money would be available through American companies subcontracting work to Japanese firms. The third route is direct government to government contracts where, *in exchange for a substantial financial contribution,* and with the acceptance of penalty clauses for 'non-performance', America will allocate the responsibility of managing a whole area of research to another government. The first two of these mechanisms will be available without any MOU. American industry has made it clear that it is determined to minimise foreign involvement to those areas of research where the technologies are unavailable in the United States. This is because they fear that Japanese and European companies could gain a competitive edge from the spin-offs of SDI work. Thus Japan's industry will gain *nothing* from signing an MOU.

Japanese industry and individuals in the Ministries are well aware of this situation, and many are opposed, or are at least unenthusiastic about Japan's involvement in SDI, which is why the alternative of a Human Frontier programme has been proposed. The pressure for such a political gesture — for that is all it is — comes only from Prime Minister Nakasone's think tank, the *Niu-Isseiki Vijin-Ni Kai* (21st Century Vision Study Association), headed by Professor Fukada the former President of Tsukuba University. Japan knows well the horrors of nuclear war being the unfortunate victim of the world's only two nuclear explosions. Japan and the Japanese people have a duty to stand out against the folly of SDI. It is you, now Japan is regaining its political authority in world affairs, that have the moral responsibility of starting the process that stops both Russia and America from imposing this new high and very dangerous frontier on the rest of the world.

Ashahi Shimbunan (Japanese Newspaper), 8 April 1986

31. Review

Aborted Discovery by Susantha Goonatilake

This is how Europe under-developed south Asia. In *Aborted Discovery*, Susantha Goonatilake details the way in which Western imperialism manifested itself in the 18th century by intellectually devaluing and delegitimising south Asia's own science and technology and de-industrialising the region. Prior to this, in a strange irony, Europe's industrial revolution — like Japan's after the Second World War — had been fuelled by 'borrowings' from non-Western science and technology.

The process of undermining was aided and abetted by scientists in India and elsewhere who collaborated just as they do today. But Goonatilake has not written just another revisionist history of science which attempts to transfer scientific recognition from occident to orient. It does more than demonstrate the cultural bias of the historiography of science by looking at the contemporary implications for science and technology policy for development. This, in Goonatilake's view, requires a radical transformation from peripheral Western-led science, so doggedly and uselessly followed by Asia's present technocrats, to a science rooted in the needs and culture of south Asia.

Goonatilake shows the existence of south Asia's own distinct science and technology prior to colonisation and how it anticipated the West at both the mundane and theoretical level. There was an interpenetration of science and culture at a number of levels. Indian plastic surgery was initially developed to rebuild noses chopped off as a punishment, while acoustics and phonetics were developed because of the need for the 'correct' recitation of religious texts. An effective smallpox vaccination existed, and it was from India that, Goonatilake claims, the stirrup came.

Science and technology in south Asia had a sound theoretical foundation derived from a search for systems of reality that was serious, rich and sophisticated. The major Ayurvedic texts, the *Charaka*, *Susruta* and *Astanga* contained large stores of codified knowledge based on a thoroughgoing scientific discipline with a realistic approach to nature. For example the *Charaka Sanhitha* is based on four concepts: disease; the cause of disease; the treatment of disease; and the introduction of health. Equally, an atomic theory was developed by Pakudha Katayayana that anticipated Democritus, and Aryablata proposed that the Earth rotated and explained planetary motion by means of epicycles.

What are the lessons the author offers for today? The possibility of detaching science from links with its centre is dismissed. Cutting off the external links scientists have with the West, where the current scientific communities depend for their intellectual sustenance, would create an intellectual orphanage in which knowledge would become fossilised at its present level and where scientific endeavour, even compared to its current level, would atrophy and eventually die. Instead, what Goonatilake demands is reformism rather than revolution. Attempts should be made to legitimise Western knowledge in terms of past south Asian knowledge, and to build a new south Asian science by searching for new additions to the structure from the West. In effect, this would reverse the intellectual traffic between East and West today.

This eclectic book is only marginally spoilt by a thin rash of textual errors that, for example, misdate the publication of Hessen's key Marxist revisionist text *The Social and Economic Roots of Newton's Principia*. Goonatilake has also misread Feyerabend's anarchistic philosophy of science. The imponderable is whether it is possible for "a thousand flowers to bloom" without the ground being cleared of the choking ivy of Western science.

New Scientist, 14 August 1986

32. Kamikaze Politics or the Collective Madness that Grips Labour in Europe

There is an urgent need to mobilise the substantial resources available to the British Labour Members of the European Parliament in assisting a general election victory, in sustaining a radical Labour government and in maximising support for our policies in Europe. We are not convinced that the party or the British Labour Group have so far acted in a manner that recognises and grasps that reality or that opportunity.

Immediately after the 1983 general election, Robin Cook offered a very pessimistic analysis of Labour's foreign policy, as outlined in the election manifesto: on defence we were going to upset the Americans; on trade we were going to offend the newly industrialised countries and, most especially, the Japanese; on the EEC we were going to fall out with most of Western Europe. This was a case of the whole being less than the sum of the parts, for while individually each position made sense, collectively they would leave Britain dangerously alone in the world.

Now we face another general election, probably within the next twelve months, and if Labour wins, the party will face massive *overt* and *covert* economic and political pressure from both Republicans and Democrats in the United States to renege on our defence policy. Equally if the Party's commitment to set manufacturing industry moving again is to have any real basis, hard decisions concerning trade policy, transnational financial institutions and manufacturing investment will have to be made.

Nothing is more important than winning the next general election. At the same time Labour will also need friends abroad to support a Labour government trying to implement its policies. In both these areas a significant contribution could be made by the Labour members of the European Parliament. Yet nothing is being done because, as Nietzsche said, if 'madness is rare in individuals', it is 'common in parties, groups and organisations'. This collective madness is compounded by a clear lack of direction from the Labour leadership in Walworth Road.

One of the barriers to changing these attitudes is the mouldering corpse of a long-dead debate on the Common Market whose decaying stench suffocates any attempt at fresh thinking.

If we allow reality to intrude for a moment, it is becoming clear that the Labour movement no longer wants to put a lot of energy into resurrecting the debate on membership of the Common Market, and the lack of party conference and TUC resolutions on the subject, reflects this. At the same time, the Labour leadership is not falling over itself to make a check-list of reasons for withdrawal. So the probability is that Britain will still be a member of the European Community at the beginning of the twenty-first century, whether we like it or not.

Yet where is the strategy for building European support for Labour's programme? Where are the coherent arguments for the fundamental reforms that would make continued membership of the EEC more bearable?

After nearly twelve months of deliberation, the British Labour Group of MEP's recently produced a discussion document on the EEC. This document, at best, made a reasonable case for not joining the Community in 1973, and at worst served as a collective comforter to be nursed against the threatened intrusion of the real world. What that document should have discussed was how socialists, working and co-operating together, could make use of the EEC to tackle the major international issues of our times, despite the Treaty of Rome.

The Common Agricultural Policy is a disaster, but we cannot content ourselves by fiddling with farm prices while South Africa burns; sixteen million Europeans are on the dole; women are losing out in the restructuring of the labour market; and our forests and lakes are dying. If we are to remain within the EEC, the party must develop a political vision of the Europe it wants to create. What we must avoid is becoming tenants in a building where the owner lives in Washington and the first floor is occupied by the multinationals. Yet our day-to-day activities in Europe are governed by a form of revolutionary nihilism whose legitimation is our 'imminent departure', whose practice is intimidatory, and whose forward vision is lemming-like.

The current epithet for the British Labour Members, which originated amongst the Spanish Socialists, is *Los Japoneses* (The Japanese) deriving from the occasional discovery in remote island jungles of Japanese soldiers who didn't know the war was over. This is a rather over generous comparison. At least Yokoi Shoichai, who emerged from the jungle in Guam in 1970, had the excuse that he had been isolated for almost a quarter of a century. The same is not true either of the British Labour Group or the Labour leadership.

Members of the British Labour Group have raced toy woodpeckers down sticks while the Parliament has been voting on the food aid sections of the budget. At committee meetings some have attended three-quarters of the meetings, but only participated in five per cent of the votes. On at least three occasions, on defence issues such as Star Wars and European security, British Labour members have voted against the Socialist Group and Labour Group whip because, in the classic style of what Lenin called Parliamentary cretinism, they have mistaken the trees for the wood and have aided the Right in its enthusiasm for Reagan's Strategic Defence Initiatives because of 'theological' objections to some obscure paragraph. At one stage a decision was taken to postpone agreeing that we will vote for our own Socialist Group candidate against the Tory Sir Henry Plumb in January's elections for the presidency of the Parliament.

The British Labour Group has at least one million pounds to spend between now and 1988 on political campaigning. In the last Parliament this money was given directly to the party, but now is totally controlled by the Group, although there are restrictions on its usage. It has not been suggested that it be used over the next twelve months fitting within the tenor, style and subject of national Labour Party campaigns; instead it is being suggested that it be used spread evenly over the next three years to fund such campaigns as 'Why we should leave the Common Market', this action being aided and abetted by the leadership in Walworth Road, who refuse to involve themselves seriously in the discussion of how the money might be spent. While many members of the Labour Party could never be accused of being overgenerous in their praise of the British Labour Group, few, however, would want to see such a valuable resource dribbled into the sand.

Members of the Labour Party must start to make clear to *all* those involved that nothing is more important than the next general election, and ensuring that our policies have the maximum support and understanding everywhere. At the moment far from rushing to our aid, Socialists in Europe will cynically shrug as they watch British Socialism sharply stopped by the self-imposed limits of the autonomous nation state. If this is allowed to continue, Labour are indulging in nothing less than self-immolation.

Never has there been a more important time for the Labour Party to reassert its internationalism and to dismiss the chauvinism that leads us to claim that we have nothing to learn from Socialists in other countries.

Glyn Ford, Christine Crawley, David Morris, David Martin
Tribune, 12 December 1986

33. Rebirth of Islamic Science*

And now, what will become of us without barbarians?
They were a kind of solution.
C.P. Cavafy [1]

Science and technology in their current manifestation pose a profound threat to the future of mankind. While this threat has its clearest form in the shadow of the nuclear bomb, there are the no less dangerous problems of environmental destruction, and community disintegration. A break with the present dominant trends requires new ways of perceiving and handling the natural world and *dar al islam* has much to contribute. Historically it has done this, although few seem aware of it, and an opportunity exists to do it again.

Yet the idea that Western science and technology are the unavoidable truth about the world, has mesmerised mankind for a hundred years and more, and helped to create this crisis. This view of science as 'objective truth' is a *myth* that serves a political purpose. *Science and technology are not neutral, but value-laden.* They carry the values of the West into everywhere and everything they penetrate; as the Trojan horse brought the Greeks into Troy. Until this is recognised the vicious circle of technology creating problems that more technology is imported to solve will continue. For the Third World has found to its cost that imported technologies bring with them an inexorable logic that forces the pace of change along a narrow Western path.

Yet modern historiography of science is beginning to show that alternative science did exist. However, Western historians of science had rewritten this past to sanitise it for their own purpose. For while these historians had not met in solemn conclave to conspire together, their shared values and social situations produced an essential unity of thought. In attempting to reclaim this past, Islamic scientists can gain confidence to change their future.

Islamic culture has shared the fate of all non-Western cultures in the hands of the few who arbitrate upon these issues and set the fashion from their havens within the major cities of the industrialised world. This intellectual imperialism is especially potent in relation to 'science' for a number of reasons, which will be discussed below. The history of Islamic science had been re-read in the language of Western values and as a consequence it has been damned with faint praise. Its aims have been axiomatically assumed to parallel those of Western science and its major achievements have been written down as mere footnotes to the Greek classics. Islamic science's prime function has been presented as that of a preserving medium in which the science of antiquity was stored during these unfortunate centuries when Europe forgot its destiny. Thus, when Europe's temporary amnesia ended with the Renaissance, Islamic science had fulfilled its preordained mission of short-term custodianship and passed the torch of civilisation — the texts and techniques of Greek science — back to its rightful owners. This view is pervasive outside the West itself. The inaugural issue of *The Journal for the History of Arabic Science*[2] had a statement explaining the new journal's aims that merely qualified this view as neglectful of the contribution of Islamic culture, rather than fundamentally dissenting from it. At its worst this 'formaldehyde' analysis of Islamic science then attempts to cleanse this science of its Islamic content completely.

Yet there was an Islamic science worthy of an independent existence that dealt with the questions raised within its own framework of ideas. To reclaim the possibility of an Islamic science that is more than what Muslims discover *qua* Western scientists operating within the framework of values and concerns of the West, it is important to explain how this myth arose and how it became universally accepted. For unless this can be done, and the lessons of recent philosophical advances accepted, the same intellectual straitjacket will prevent any rebirth within the era of late capitalism.

This myth and its acceptance had behind it a combination of economic, political and even technical causes. A key one was the legacy of imperialism with its subjection of the 'less developed' world by the industrialising nations. For the subjection was not only a political and economic phenomenon but also a cultural one. Western prestige and power led to a self-abnegation, within the Third World, of all aspects of indigenous culture. This was especially true of science and technology. For it was here that the cultural clash was most direct, and most weighted in favour of the West. Western military technology decisively proved its superiority again and again as the European nations painted the globe in their various national hues. The result was that Western technical advisers began to litter the court circles of the Middle East and elsewhere. In many cases, the courts wanted their influence strictly contained within the military sphere. But this was a barrier that was impossible to hold. The technology itself required a skilled 'workforce', and it was therefore necessary to send suitable candidates abroad to receive appropriate technical training. When these neophytes returned from the imperial homeland and took their place as junior officers they began to want to generalise the application of what they had learnt outside the military sphere. The power of Western exemplars meant that the demand for 'modernisation' swept all before it.³

Most important, this was at a time when Western culture was becoming increasingly secularised as the progress of the war between science and religion entailed the steady surrender of intellectual spheres of influence by the sacred into the hands of the profane. Science was the pursuit of objective truth. This belief meant that Western science — and who was to deny its claims? — took precedence over all other realms of knowledge. Inevitably, therefore, the only value of scientific achievements outside its limits was either as caretaker or precursor, where it had anticipated the future findings of occidental science. This myth can be destroyed creating an opportunity for an appropriate science for the Muslim world. There is now a conjunction of circumstances that allows this to be done. Western colonialism, both formally and informally, is weaker than it has been this century. The demands for national liberation after the Second World War has led to the break-up of empire, and the post-1973 economic independence of much of *dar al islam* has weakened, or even in some cases reversed, the hierarchy of informal subordination. Intellectually a similar process has occurred with longheld truths of the West's *Weltanschauung* being sceptically reappraised. Here is not the appropriate place to discuss the causes, but the aid of righteous self-confidence among the Western intelligentsia has given way to scepticism and doubt. This is not unconnected with the darker results of Western industrialisation, the direct product of its science and technology.

The material conditions for 'opening' the West's intellectual hegemony are a necessary aspect of developments, but they are by no means sufficient. For at the same time alternative frameworks for thought must be available. In re-evaluating science with hindsight, two key events in the history of ideas offer to legitimate the existence of culturally dependent sciences as facets of the complex world of nature.

The earlier of these was the transformation of the methodology of history, which took place between the two World Wars. The second was the much more recent changed perception of the nature of science itself among both some of its practitioners and philosophers. Unfortunately, these two developments — although both consequent upon the same change of tenor within the world — came into the wrong order for them to be smoothly integrated by historians of science into their discipline. Until recently the former was ruled by the historians to be uniquely inapplicable to the history of science because of the belief they held about the nature of science. For them science, unlike other disciplines, was the pursuit of an objective truth. Thus, the history of science was unique as a form of history, being little, if anything, more than a chronicle of the mapping of this objective reality. This view of the special nature of scientific enquiry, as was mentioned above, is no longer taken for granted. It is these changes which create an opportunity for the re-evaluation and rebirth of Islamic and other non-Western sciences.

This first event was, in epitome, the restructuring of the 'Whig, scissors and paste' history of the nineteenth century into the analytical history of today. The former was characterised by both its subject matter and its construction. It studied the past with reference to the present. As Butterfield wrote, 'though there may be a sense in which this is unobjectionable if its implications are carefully considered, and there may be a sense in which it is inescapable, it has often been an obstruction to historical understanding because it has been taken to mean the study of the past with direct and perpetual reference to the present. Through this system of immediate reference to the present day, historical personages can easily and irresistibly be classed into the men who furthered progress and the men who tried to hinder it.'[4] Thus Whig history stood at the summit of time organising the past from the point of view of the present. It was built up from raw materials quarried from original sources and rearranged to form a diachronous picture of development whose lacunae were covered by the interpolations of linking narrative.

Thus history was atomised into its constituent 'facts' and these were winnowed by the winds of progress. What remained were the components of a well rounded and polished portrayal of the origins of the present. This subsidiary element was a fetish, a cult, of facts. The empiricist derivation supposed a complete separation between subject and object. Thus history was a corpus of ascertained facts. As E.H. Carr wrote, 'The historian collects them, takes them home, and cooks and serves them in whatever style appeals to him.'[5] The style of serving was as a demonstration of apparently infinite progress towards higher things, and despite claims to the contrary, implied a rigid set of selection criteria as to what constituted a fact and what did not. Clearly if mundane history became a glorification, and self-justification of the *status quo*, how much truer was this of science history where the facts themselves are up-dated and where the achievements of one's predecessors are mere steps on which to stand.

This kind of history has been replaced by one which is less egocentric, more analytical and less cavalier. Many historians contributed towards this change to studying the past in its own terms, including Croce, the Italian historian, and many others. While social, economic and political historians found that the belief that the present was the key to the past was relatively easy to put aside, how was this undertaken in methodological terms?

This may be illustrated by looking at the ideas of R.G. Collingwood (1889-1943), the only British thinker in the present century who has made a serious contribution to the philosophy of history, and who was one of the earliest and clearest exponents of these ideas. The choice of Collingwood as a model is made because of the clarity with which he expressed his ideas, even though he did not live to write the systematic treatise he planned, and because he was one of only a small number of philosopher historians who showed any interest in the history of science. His methodology, as expounded in his posthumous collection of writings, *The Idea of History*,[6] rested upon three concepts: (1) the logic of question and answer, (2) the notion of historical evidence and (3) the leitmotif of development.

1. Francis Bacon wrote that it was the duty of scientists to 'put nature to the question'. Collingwood in parallel demanded that historians subject history to interrogation. The trial was for the purpose of determining the questions to which the events of history were the answers and to establish the problems motivating its actors, rather than to merely superimpose those of today. The interrogation was conducted within the mind of the historian as an iterative process, the historian asking him/herself a series of consequential questions.

For like a detective investigation (a particularly apt analogy, for the success of the investigation depends upon getting into someone else's mind), every step of the argument depends on asking a question. The question is the charge of gas, exploded in the cylinder head, which is the motive force of every piston-stroke. But the metaphor is not fully adequate because each new piston-stroke is produced not by exploding another charge of the same old mixture but by exploding a charge of a new kind. No one with any grasp of method will go on asking the same questions all the time, 'Who killed John Doe?' One asks a new question, every time. And it is not enough to cover the ground by having a catalogue of all the questions that have to be asked and asking every one of them sooner or later: they must be asked in the right order.

2. History is an activity whose business is to study events no longer open to our direct observation. These events must therefore be studied inferentially, arguing from the 'evidence' available. This is how questions like, 'Did Hitler commit suicide?', 'Why did the Romans withdraw from Britain?' and 'What problems were Jabir ibn

Hayyan, Muhammad ibn Musa al-Khuwarizimi and Al-Farabi trying to solve when they were doing science?', for which we have no direct evidence, must be handled. Any relic from the past has a potential for providing evidence hidden within it. It is the job of the historian to trigger such a release by his questioning addressed to the evidence. The culture within which events occur determine the frame of values within which the questions are formulated.

3. The concept of development is one of 'arising'. Any step forward involves a simultaneous step backwards. Human history is a seamless web containing no sharp breaks. It is unbroken, but it is not the continuity of the straight line scoring its way across the page, but rather that of an irregular spiral. All changes involve dual opposing movements. A new development arises by a return to an old position which is transposed to a higher level. It is thus simultaneously old and new. Old in its nature, new in its transformation.

These three concepts form in themselves a unity and a justification. The third gives history a role in intellectual life which wishes to interact with the world, the second allows evidence, apart from the purely mundane kind, to be available to the historian, while the first gives a method which can generate such evidence. Perhaps some trivial examples of Collingwood's methodology at work will help. One rather simple example is the problem of why did Julius Caesar invade Britain twice, a question rarely asked by historians. No evidence exists apart from Caesar's own narrative in the *Commentaries* which nowhere says what his intention was. This concealment itself suggests that Caesar failed in his objective. Thus his intention must have been more than a mere punitive expedition or demonstration of force. A comparison of the strength of his expeditionary force with that sent over by Claudius nearly a century later shows that it was consistent with an attempt to conquer the country completely. Thus an event for which no direct evidence exists can be explained in a manner which is entirely consistent with the information available and which goes beyond the 'scissors and paste' history that implies nothing can be said about a subject with *direct* evidence. Collingwood and other historians in related schools would claim that by such an approach they can distance themselves sufficiently, although obviously not entirely, from the present so as to begin to explain the past in its own terms.

If science, like other intellectual disciplines, is culturally determined, then such an approach can be applied to its history. Thus an evaluation can be made of Islamic science that uses as its framework the particular problems and concerns of the period and environment and its successes and failures can be measured in its own terms, rather than by criteria alien, in many senses, to the concerns of its practitioners. This would be a radical departure for the historiography of science within Islam. To date, the controversy in this area has been limited to a purely quantitative dispute. At one extreme many historians of science have all but ignored the contribution of Muslim scientists to the development of the discipline; Dampier and Bernal on two political extremes both fall to greater or lesser extents in this camp. To be fair, Bernal's *Social Function of Science* and his rather overgeneralised *Science in History* did recognise the class structure of science, but it went no further.[7] This was partly redressed by George Sarton's *An Introduction to the History of Science*[8] which set out in great detail the achievements of the Muslim scientists in foreseeing and anticipating elements and theories of Western science, and forms the other end of the spectrum. Here it is being suggested that Islamic science can be viewed from an entirely different perspective. Obviously a close corollary of this is that once the existence of such a science can be shown, then the lessons can be applied to the re-creation of sciences today in *dar al islam* that embody the concerns and values of Islam itself, instead of apeing those of the West, which have so lamentably failed to deal with the issues facing mankind. However, all this presupposes the results of recent scholarship in the philosophy of science.

The twentieth-century doubts and worries about the inevitability of progress, which helped to give birth to the new history, have recently touched science. The rather sterile work of those logicians and mechanics that comprised the philosophy of science community until this time received two intellectual blows. These originally emanated from two individuals, Karl Popper and Thomas Kuhn.

The first of these, Popper, was concerned that the methodology of science, with its aim of 'proving' theories, rested upon a logical fallacy.[9] For no number, however large, of confirming instances supporting a proposition can *prove* that the next will not confound all those that went before. This threatened to undermine the notion of science as a rational enterprise, and was already being exploited by unfalsifiable pseudo-sciences such as Marxism and psychoanalysis that were claiming the legitimacy of sciences for themselves and were capable of assimilating any and all events as yet further confirmations of their veracity. Popper's response was to propose a 'technical fix' that would get around the inherent illogicality. For him the driving force behind science was no longer to be confirmation, but rather *refutation*. Scientists should proceed by advancing, along with their hypotheses, a series of tests that could prove these to be false; and should then rigorously apply them until the theory fell, giving rise to a new theory of greater explanatory power that would be tested in a similar way.

Certainly Popper's ideas, and here there is only the briefest summary, are of some value to the working scientists in avoiding some of the pitfalls of theory development. Nevertheless, at a strategic level of long-term scientific development, they are at best prescriptive of what should occur but in fact does not, and at worst dangerous in that their rigid application could prevent rather than promote scientific changes that were radical rather than merely incremental additions to what had gone before.

For many it has been the second of these philosophers, Thomas Kuhn, who has proved crucial. Kuhn, in a survey of the history of science, claimed that two very different and alternating types of scientific practice were to be found. These he termed 'normal' and 'revolutionary' science respectively.[10] The first of these is what the vast majority of scientists undertake all of the time and all scientists do most of the time. It is the refined articulation of scientific ideas within a rigid framework of accepted practices and beliefs about nature that remain unquestioned. Thus for example Ptolemaic astronomy had, as aspects of its framework, a geocentric universe where the celestial bodies moved in perfect circles. This kind of matrix determines the kinds of problems investigated; the style in which solutions to these puzzles are offered; and the criteria of acceptability that these solutions have to meet. This framework of fundamental beliefs and accepted practices Kuhn termed a paradigm. By definition during periods of normal science the ruling paradigm in a particular field remains inviolate.

However, eventually progress within any template falters. The paradigm itself ceases to pose interesting questions, and anomalies are discovered that resist persistent attempts to incorporate them within the accepted framework. A crisis begins to develop within normal science, which if not speedily brought under control by the successful spiriting away of anomalies, forces some individual scientists to call into question the paradigm itself in an attempt to make explicable those elements of nature they consider important but outside the pale of the current paradigm's explanatory powers. This is revolutionary science. The crisis acts like rain in the Sahara. A desert blooming of alternative paradigms takes place, all of which threatens to cast into oblivion much of the work undertaken as normal science under the previous paradigm. This is obviously resisted by those whose life's work is threatened with extinction.

They persist in attempting *ad hoc* modifications of what went before.

The period of revolutionary science is short-lived. It is not long before scientists begin to group themselves behind one or other of the new alternatives, and very rapidly these options mercilessly start to narrow as they compete with each other for survival; until to remain a scientist one must subscribe to *the* new paradigm within whose limits normal science recommences. This period of revolutionary science is one in which 'survival of the fittest' operates to its limits: only one survives. The test of fitness here is that the new paradigm must make explicable those facets of nature whose understanding is important to the scientists of the period.

The most important point is that Kuhn contends that the selection of the new paradigm, when in a period of revolutionary science the process of resolving the options down to one new underpinning schema is occurring, is not free from the influence of personal and partisan considerations on the part of scientists. For Kuhn believes that, in the last analysis, there is no unambiguous scientific test that enables individual scientists to choose between competing paradigms. These, to use his own terminology, are incommensurable. It is at this point that the belief of science as objective, neutral and value-free collapses. For with personal and partisan considerations influencing paradigm choice, science clearly loses its claimed unique character. Scientists are part of society. Their personal beliefs reflect those of the society in which they live and the important issues they wish science to handle are thus not independent of social values. Thus science is society.

In 1931 Boris Hessen wrote a paper, 'The Social and Economic Roots of Newton's Principia', in which he argued from a Marxist standpoint that the *Principia* was not an isolated product of scientific genius generated by the internal logic of science alone, but rather had emerged as a consequence of the needs of the developing British bourgeoisie.[11] This materialist analysis indicates the style of arguments science is opened to by Kuhn, although of course man's motives are not only a product of economics, but also religion, morality and ideology that fall outside the naive purview of Marxism.

Since 1962, when the first edition of Kuhn's *The Structure of Scientific Revolutions* was published, a furious dispute has taken place among philosophers of science.[12] And interestingly enough this quarrel itself exhibits many of the irrational characteristics Kuhn — to his opponents' great chagrin — suggests are exhibited in paradigm choice. Claims that his work is a vindication of irrational behaviour and that it threatens, almost, the foundations of Western civilisation has forced Kuhn to recant to a degree. He has taken the step of denying the logic of his own arguments in the face of scientific indignation, and abandoned some of his erstwhile disciples. In effect following the famous precedent of Marx, he has declared himself a non-Kuhnian. This has not stopped others going further. Some have proclaimed anarchy in science[13] while others have declared that there is an ideology *of* and *in* science.[14] But one does not have to go so far to recognise that the position of science in the world has changed. Now that Kuhn has removed the blinkers, the fact that science is not neutral and value-free emerges clearly from the fog of accepted dogma. As Huxley said of Darwin's *Origin of Species*, 'How stupid not to have thought of it before.' The Lysenko affair in Russia in the 1930s is just one example,[15] while others are available from the history of non-Western sciences.[16]

Islamic Science

To put it at its simplest: if science is not the unique intellectual construct which until so recently it was portrayed, if the history of science is not the history of iterative movements towards the truth about the natural world, but rather the history of various social constructions of reality mediated through science, scientists and society, then there exists the possibility of an Islamic science that will be one facet, or more likely a series of facets, of a multi-dimensional world of nature, all of which are imbued with the very essence of Islamic society. In this it only parallels those commonly accepted links between culture and society exclusive of science. For example, the development and evolution of Islamic calligraphy can be shown to be mediated through societal changes. Early Kufic in its simplicity and austerity reflects the puritanism of the century following the death of Prophet Muhammad, while the coming of a more settled urban existence is shown as this gives way to the dynamic and workmanlike Nashki. As Muslim society began to stagnate so did the ponderous and sombre Thuluth Script arrive.[17] Just as with the development of calligraphy, it is not possible to divorce Islamic science and society from one another.

Thus, Islamic science could be evaluated in its own terms rather than as just an aberrant sub-species of Western science. This evaluation will have much to contribute to the style in which a rebirth of Islamic science could be promoted in the future. This evaluation will require an analysis of the history of Islamic science before it succumbs to Western cultural imperialism as the answers to questions posed within its own framework, rather than cripple its rich promise by forcing it into the mould of Western thought patterns and concerns. For it is here that Islamic science will have already shown its distinct concerns and will illustrate, albeit not fully, the elements which may constitute a new Islamic science.

What would such a re-evaluation look like? We can obtain some idea by looking at the work of Seyyed Hossein Nasr. Nasr is not an ideal example, because of the strong elements of Sufi theology within his beliefs. However, if this can be borne in mind, Nasr's *Islamic Science: an Illustrated Study*[18] shows one picture. He maintains that historically there was a distinct Islamic science that was separate from, but related to, its origins. For him all ideas entering the citadel of Islamic thought from outside, including the Greek scientific heritage, were transposed into a new spiritual and intellectual form capable of meshing into the Islamic world picture.

The structure of this world picture was pre-determined by its theory of knowledge and it was this theory of knowledge which shaped the science of *dar al-islam*. Nasr believes that for Muslims there was a number of kinds of knowledge. There was 'acquired' knowledge in its twin forms of the transmitted and the intellectual sciences, and the 'presential' knowledge of vision and experience. In the West it would be maintained today that the form of knowledge termed intellectual science is, if not the only form of knowledge, that against which all others must be compared. Yet, for the Muslim, these different forms of knowledge were all of equal standing, locked within a metaphysical hierarchy whose source was the Qur'an and whose totality was a unity. Hence the quest for all knowledge was impregnated with a religious aura. This was the frame that determined both the problems the Muslim scientists tried to solve and the types of solution offered and accepted.

This symbiotic relationship between science and culture operated at a number of levels. At its most direct, religious rites, through their concern with the direction of the *quiblah* and the timing of the rising of the sun and moon, created a pragmatic interest in geodesy and astronomy. At another level the belief that science — as we would use the term now — reveals only one aspect of a multidimensional reality tempered the science itself. Scientists gave answers which were not posed in the unilateral manner of analytical and quantitative science, but were rather an art form of qualities and symbols.

To imagine such a 'science' is not easy for those steeped in contemporary ways of seeing science. Yet Nasr is able to give some feel for its distinctiveness through its technology. The science emerging from an Islamic cosmology emphasising harmony, equilibrium and balance, led Muslims to create technologies that utilised natural forces through the maximum use of human skills and with the minimum disturbance of the natural environment. Technical change in and for itself was frowned upon. Like the Chinese who had gunpowder but never made guns, Muslim technology harmonised with the environment. The technical artefacts that were manufactured, especially those for liturgical use, had the beauty that came from utility.

Yet this and future evaluations from other Muslim perspectives by historians will only show that a distinct Islamic science did have a fitful existence in the past. While this certainly demonstrates the possibility of a rebirth, this will not be a return to the past, but rather a step into the future. A new Islamic science will have to be a science for the late twentieth century, and will bear the marks of its period. But this will require an appreciation of principles that should guide the foundations of an Islamic science. Ziauddin Sardar[19] has put forward a set of values that could do this. Sardar believes that there are ten values at the core of Islamic thought: four standing alone, namely *tawheed* (unity), *khilafah* (trusteeship), *ibadah* (workship) and *ilm* (knowledge), plus three opposing pairs. These pairs are *halal* (praiseworthy) v. *haram* (blameworthy), *adl* (social justice) v. *zulm* (tyranny), and *istislah* (public interest) v. *dhiya* (waste).

In attempting to reconstruct such a science these values could be put against technical and research programmes to establish whether such programmes fall within the ambit of Islamic science. Questions can be asked as to whether the results of a particular programme will lead to a higher measure of social justice or reinforce tyranny; will respect or not the position of trusteeship of man with respect to the world of nature; will promote public interest rather than waste. Such questions would clearly have put certain high technology projects outside of the pale. For example, the Kufra oasis development project in Libya would have never started. The idea was to turn the desert green by the importation of skilled techniques and large quantities of fertiliser plus the use of water from an immense underground natural reservoir. Hundreds of acres of alfalfa was to be grown and this was to be the basis of lamb-breeding for meat. This project breaks the values of both *istislah* and *khilafah* as it increases reliance on Western 'experts' at the expense of the subsistence farmers, and depends upon a water supply — connate water — which has been retained in the rocks since their formation and is not being replenished.

Similarly, many of the town planning schemes implemented in the Middle East pay no attention to Islamic *mores*. The extended family is inevitably destroyed as Western-style urbanisation takes its toll with its ubiquitous and alienating tower blocks and expressways. The sense of community is atomised as improved communications lead to an insistence on mobility and the production of flat-dwelling, capital-hopping 'gypsies' of the twentieth century. In industry the embrace of Taylorite scientific management with its destruction of the skills of craft through the ceaseless fission of the work process goes against *tawheed* and *ilm*. The whole architecture, where man becomes dwarfed by his own creations, replaces the worship of nature's wonders with a concrete and steel materialism.

All of these and many others subvert Islamic values. But these examples are all negative ones in that they show where Western science has failed the Muslim world. Obviously the positive side of a new Islamic science is less easy to illustrate, for it requires foreknowledge of something that does not as yet exist. Certainly it is not possible even to imagine the new paradigms that would emerge to frame this science. Nevertheless some pointers to its concerns can be given. These would all show a closer match to Sardar's Islamic values than current scientific concerns which sadly neglect fundamental areas of interest to Muslims through the dictates of the big high technology science fashion in the West.

These areas would include, among others, the following. In agriculture, the enhancement of subsistence farming in all its aspects from farm machinery to crop development, in desert environments techniques that used this environment rather than attempted to change it. In pharmacology, a balanced concern that dealt with the effect of all drugs on human physiology rather than the one-sided over-concern with those traditional ones coming from outside Western culture. In animal husbandry, work on the domesticated animals of the Muslim world, along with serious work on the origins of dietary taboos. In energy technology, an emphasis on small-scale renewable energy sources such as solar energy, ocean thermal energy conversion (OTEC), etc., rather than fossil fuels and nuclear power. The physics of wind-blown sand and desert dunes rather than the n plus 1 elementary particle. In chemistry, work on the causes of soil infertility in low precipitation environments rather than on synthetic chocolate or artificial colouring agents.

Among the softer sciences, architecture and town planning could attempt to use natural materials to create an urban environment that did not produce the alienation and atomisation of the inner city 'no go' areas of the West, but instead maintained and strengthened it by the feeling of community and the value of the individual rather than the anomie of mass culture.

The mix of science undertaken within any given society is a reflection of that society's concerns and indicates the path it is taking. Science in the Muslim world today reflects the values and concerns of Western society; and it is turning Muslim societies into poor replicas of Western ones. A re-orientated research programme that reflected the concerns of Muslim society would eventually lead, if Kuhn is right, to the inevitable production of an Islamic scientific paradigm. Only by counterposing an alternative science and technology will it be possible to halt and reverse the impact Western science's hidden values are having upon *dar al islam*. The way is now open.[20]

Islamic Cultural Identity and Scientific Technological Development, edited by Klaus Gottstein, published by Nomos Verlagsgesellschaft, Baden-Baden, 1986

*Reprinted from the book *The Touch of Midas* (Manchester University Press, 1984. Editor: Z. Sardar) with the kind permission of the author and of the publishers.

References
1. C.P. Cavafy, *Collected Poems*, Chatto and Windus, London 1975.
2. S. Hamarneh 'An Editorial: Arabic Science and Technology', *Journal for the History of Arabic Science*', Vol.1, pp.3-7, 1977.
3. See for example: B. Lewis, *The Emergence of Modern Turkey*, 2nd edition, Oxford University Press, London, 1968.
4. H. Butterfield, *The Whig Interpretation of History*, Penguin, Harmondsworth, 1973, pp.17-18.
5. E.H. Carr, *What is History?* Penguin, Harmondsworth, 1964, p.9.
6. R.G. Collingwood, *The Idea of History*, Oxford University Press, London, 1961. See also his *An Autobiography*, Oxford University Press, London, 1939, and *The Idea of Nature*, Oxford University Press, London, 1945. Despite Collingwood's interest in science, it should be noted that his analysis contains only inchoate traces of what is outlined here.
7. J.D. Bernal, *The Social Function of Science*, Routledge and Kegan Paul, London, 1939, and *Science in History*, Watts, London, 1954.
8. G. Sarton, *An Introduction to the History of Science*, 5 vols., Williams and Wilkins, Baltimore, 1927, p.48.
9. K.R. Popper, *Conjectures and Refutations*, Routledge and Kegan Paul, London, 1963. See also his *Objective Knowledge*, Oxford University Press, London, 1972.
10. T.S. Kuhn, *The Structure of Scientific Revolutions*, 2nd edition, University of Chicago Press, Chicago, 1970.
11. B. Hessen, 'The Social and Economic Roots of Newton's "Principia"' in *Science at the Crossroads*, Kniga, London, 1931.
12. See for example: I. Lakatos and A. Musgrave (eds), *Criticism and the Growth of Knowledge*, Cambridge University Press, London, 1970.
13. A. Feyerabend, *Against Method*, New Left Books, London, 1975, and his *Science in a Free Society*, New Left Books, London, 1978.
14. H. Rose and S. Rose (eds.), *Ideology of/in the Natural Sciences*, 2 vols; Vol.1, *The Radicalisation of Science;*, Vol.2, *The Political Economy of Science*, Macmillan, London, 1976.
15. Z.A. Medvedev, *The Rise and Fall of T.D. Lysenko*, Doubleday, Anchor, New York, 1971.
16. J. Needham, *Science and Civilisation in China*, numerous ongoing vols, Cambridge University Press, London, 1954-.
17. The ideas behind this analogy owe much to A. Lycett, 'The Ageless Magnificence

of Islamic Calligraphy', *Azure* 2, pp.30-33, 1978.
18. S.H. Nasr, *Islamic Science: An Illustrated Study*, World of Islam Festival Publishing Company, London, 1976.
19. Z. Sardar, 'Why Islam Needs Islamic Science', *New Scientist*, Vol.94, pp.25-28, 1982.
20. The origins of this chapter are to be found in G. Ford, 'A Framework for a New View of Islamic Science', *Adiyat Halab*, Vols.4/5, pp.68-74, 1978/9.

Part 5

1987

34. Letter from Urumqi

Urumqi is the centre of the Earth, or rather it's the most inland city in the World. It feels that way, three and a half hours flying time from Beijing across the Gobi desert with the western edge of Mongolia to the north, central Tibet to the south, and the Soviet Union to the immediate east. Descending out of the haze towards the airport there is a glimpse of snow-capped mountains to the distance south and a brown alluvial fan smothering acres of desert. Then there appears a patch of green thrown carelessly across the fan's fringes. The airport is less than busy. The flow of pedestrians and cyclists across the runway only momentarily ceases for the unaccustomed landing of a plane, resuming even before it has taxied to a halt.

Outside, the immediate impression is not of China proper. The terminal building, despite it's 1950's utilitarian concrete architecture, illustrates this through it's labelling in both an Arabic script and Chinese. This epigraphic dichotomy shows itself at the personal level. The majority of officials, not in the olive-green uniform of the PLA, wear colourful embroidered skullcaps. Travelling into the city only reinforces this impression. The *Central Business District* is more reminiscent of the cities of Anatolia or Afghanistan than Anhwei, with adobe walled buildings engulfing scattered mosques in those areas that have not as yet surrendered to the ubiquitous concrete.

The roads are beset with 'Soviet realist' lorries ploughing through thronging bicycles that miraculously clear from their immediate path. It is the outskirts of the city where the cause of all this industry is located. Just beyond the neat geometrically laid out apartment blocks, there is in the process of creation the equivalent of Birmingham in the early nineteenth century; a region blasted with mine, factory and furnace, coloured by leaping flames and columns of black smoke. Acres are covered with men and women batch producing the concrete slabs to provide the skins for the next phase of concrete boxes, while alongside them others are quarrying the detritus from a recent river valley and sieving it by hand to provide sand for their neighbours, creating cairns of cobbles for some mysterious future function. Criss-crossing this lunar wasteland are rows of tipsy telegraph poles at jaunty angles. The rough roads are cornered by small one-storey teahouses, outside of which the local lads play a version of bar billiards.

Travelling from the suburbs into the countryside shows a further step back into the past. Here the old Silk Road might still run its course, as barrack style housing first shrinks to a single storey before giving way to yurts, and as sheep, horses and even camels start to outnumber people. Here are the remnants of nomadic life. The people look different; no longer the Han Chinese these are the Kazaks. In appearance many could pass as Balkans. They almost wistfully perform for visitors their feats of horsemanship, including a team sport with unfathomable rules that seems to be a version of tug-of-war with a dead sheep substituting for a rope. It is only a few clues that locate them in the twentieth century global village, such as the presence of baseball caps advertising the virtues of damaging one's health through the consumption of the world's most popular cigarette. Further still out of Urumqi there is Tianchi Lake, high in the mountains, the whole area of which could be relocated in Switzerland without anyone being any the wiser.

Western Xinjiang is a strange *mélange*. It is a frontier province where the Han Chinese and the indigenous inhabitants have an essentially immiscible existence. China is a country with many faces, yet of them all this is one of the most untypical. In Urumqi industry has the usual ubiquitous Japanese presence. For example the Tian Shah Woollen Spinning and Knitting Company is a joint venture set up in 1980 with Toyo Boshi Kogyo and two Hong Kong companies producing cashmere and lambswool products. The Chinese provide the labour — 1300 workers and staff members *including minorities* as their brochure states — the Japanese provide the technical equipment and the management style, while Hong Kong provides the quotas with some of the yarn being made up there to avoid export restrictions.

The minority group most obvious in Urumqi is the Uighur. They are also the group that is currently most at odds with Beijing. *The Guardian* reported (24 December 1985) that Uighur students at Beijing's Institute of Cultural Minorities marched around Tiananmen Square protesting about the fact that Xinjiang is used for nuclear testing. They then presented written demands at the Communist Party headquarters at Zhongnanhai that included an end to the policy of sending criminals to labour camps in Xinjiang, democratic elections to allow minority peoples to become officials in the region, more support for the education of minority peoples, an end to forced birth control, and greater political and economic autonomy. It was also reported that in Urumqi itself thousands had demonstrated for greater political freedom. Certainly there were demonstrations in Urumqi in the beginning of May concerning the dangers of drifting clouds of radioactive fallout from the Chernobyl disaster. It may well be these that have helped to contribute to

Beijing's slow, but perceptible shift, to review China's nuclear programme.

Xinjiang is China's frontier province in more than one sense of the term. It is virgin territory that offers the promise of rich mineral wealth as well as being a buffer against the Soviet Union. But China faces a problem, the future is seen to lie with the 'Special Economic Zones' and these are lightyears away, geographically and industrially, from Urumqi. And the inhabitants know this. Beijing cannot afford to be seen to neglect these areas or their peoples, who retain a deep suspicion of remote bureaucracy. Yet here what is necessary is the development of a kind of heavy industry that is now distinctly unfashionable in ruling circles, where *homo economicus* has replaced Stakhanov. At the same time the process cannot alienate the minorities in the region by too dramatically disrupting their present way of life. The border clash in the province last month with the Russians can only reinforce the delicate tightrope the centre has to walk in relation to the periphery on what was the ring where the colonial powers played out their 'Great Game' at the end of the last century.

To give more autonomy is to lose control; to emphasise the SEZ's in the South East is to create resentment in the North West. China's central power will have to learn to balance its approach. As they say, if you can't ride two horses at the same time you shouldn't be in the bloody circus. The only question is whether Beijing realises it must indulge in acrobatics and is sufficiently supple to be able to do so.

Far Eastern Economic Review, 19 March 1987

35. Top Gun — Designer Death

Video commercials are now an everyday part of our lives and their messages and style often pass unnoticed. It is only when we see them in a new context that we begin to notice the incorporation and interpenetration of the signs and symbols of what would, initially at least, be thought of as different or even alien cultural forms legitimising the illegitimate. Last week the Energy, Research and Technology Committee of the European Parliament met in Madrid for three days, and during that time the Spanish Government arranged a number of Industrial visits for Committee members. The last of these was to *Construcciones Aeronauticas, S.A.* (CASA), Spain's dominant aerospace company, where the Directors arranged the usual PR presentation, with a difference. The stars of the show were the two commercials for selling the C-212 and the C-101 military aircraft to Third World arms purchasers.

It was only fifteen months ago that *Live Aid* demonstrated that *rock* really cares, much to the satisfaction of the artists and everyone else; apart from the churlish few who either thought that the whole thing was a media hype or who saw no necessary connection between organising even global rock concerts, and efficiently and swiftly distributing development aid to the Sahel. At CASA the talents of Jean Michel Jarre were being put to rather different uses. *Concerts in China* provided the throbbing background beat to the voice over describing the use of the C-101 as a ground attack aircraft with fitted 12.7mm machine guns and 4,000lb of mixed weapons load, all demonstrated by pirouetting aircraft in a more purposive aerial version of synchronised swimming, and reaching a crescendo with the seemingly clinching statement that the C-101 had *napalm capability.*

The whole style was a kind of sub-*Top Gun* combined with elements from *The Wild Geese* — a film from a few years ago glorying a bunch of bloodthirsty mercenaries — apart from the fact that the acting was not quite as wooden as in the films. Files of fully equipped men merged on the trot to fill the hold of the C-212 and promptly streamed out again as showers of parachutists. Fully laden Jeeps bumped aboard to be deposited back on the ground by parachute release from planes flying at head height. Racks folded down to handle the wounded and it was even possible to imagine where the body bags would go. The ideal counter-insurgency support aircraft.

Spain has a socialist Government with a solid majority that was confirmed in power earlier this year, shortly after Felipe Gonzalez's victory in the referendum to stay in NATO. This Government has an astigmatic vision that sees CASA as a high technology company to be emulated by the rest of Spanish industry. Not for them any notions of 'socially useful production' as a route to dismantling the military-industrial complex — in Spain something that is vitally necessary — nor even the easy morality of vetting the purchasers for their political acceptability. The people who gave the World the atrocities of East Timor and the stadiums of Santiago have both recently purchased military or *dual use* planes from CASA.

This brief event has levels of questions embedded within it. First, will the next Labour Government, with its commitment to a greater production and, one assumes, consumption of conventional arms, be willing or able to exercise effective control over the defence export market. Secondly, how do socialists start to break peoples' perceptions of what it means to fire guns, and napalm, in anger from the *Tom and Jerry* world of *Top Gun*, where only the bad guys get hurt and even they die cleanly, to the realities of death, pain, disfigurement and despair. Finally, if rock music is ultimately anti-establishment how do we stop its prostitution in this way. Otherwise, if Victor Jara had played to the right beat his posthumous fingers might have provided the pace for the commercials selling death to those who mutilated and killed him.

Tribune, 3 April 1987

36. Japan Bids for a Corner in the World Power Triad

Ohmae Kenichi, Japan's most fashionable economist, has characterised the current world economic order as one dominated by the 'triad powers' of Japan, Europe, and the United States. Industrially it is the mix of collaboration and competition between these three that sets the world economic stage. High technology threatens to unbalance this relationship to the detriment of Europe. Technology is the foundation of wealth creation.

America is attempting to underpin its technological future with the Strategic Defence Initiative (SDI), the ultimate in Victorian technology. Europe is currently trying to find the political will to fund the European Communities Framework Programme, the £5 billion necessary being almost the 'small change' of any serious programme.

Meanwhile, in Japan — partly in response to SDI — they are in the final stages of preparing the Human Frontier Science Programme for launch at the Economic Summit in Venice in May. This programme is to try to set a new technological trajectory that is organic, rather than electronic. How does Europe respond?

The Japanese programme is to be an attempt to redirect contemporary science and technology towards solving the problems that will confront people in the 21st century. The key themes will be research on the ageing process, photosynthesis, renewable energy, minimal pollution technologies, and the person-machine relationship. The programme will have a budget of $10 billion over ten years.

It is claimed that all the work will be 'basic' research.

It is almost certain that this will translate into strategic research. In May, Prime Minister Nakasone will invite the member states of the World Economic Summit plus the European Commission to participate.

The important secondary motives of SDI research, to 'pump prime' American science and technology in the belief that the spin-off from military research will provide the US with a technological lead in the commercial environment are neglected.

The claim that civilian spin off follows automatically from military R and D is not proven. Nevertheless one cannot doubt that £33 billion available over five years for Star Wars will produce some significant technological developments. SDI funds will also be used to unlock the scientific work carried out in Europe.

The availability of funds from the SDI programme means Europe will lose some of its best brains and ideas to the United States, mentally if not geographically. The intellectual property rights to SDI work carried out in Europe will not remain here. European governments, rather than being partners in SDI, are in reality mainly sub-contractors. The technology developed is likely to end up on the Military Critical Technologies list compiled by the American defence department, meaning it will be unavailable for commercial exploitation.

Most European governments, in particular the French, are aware of these various threats that SDI poses to our technological future, but have found it difficult to know how to respond. The first reaction from President Mitterrand was to propose a European version of Star Wars. But, apart from the difficulty of finding the resources to match SDI, it would have allowed American military imperatives to establish the scientific framework for European technologies.

The early recognition of the need for a purely civil programme was fortuitous. Mitterrand's initiative, which came to be known as Eureka, (European Research Coordinating Agency) rapidly shifted into a programme for stimulating high technology in the civilian sector with the aim of improving the competitiveness of European industry *vis à vis* Japan and the United States.

Eureka, despite its failings, cannot be rejected. Some good will come from the 109 projects agreed with aggregated funds of £2.5 billion coalesced from a variety of sources. Yet Eureka is not even an attempt to establish Europe's own technological trajectory, lacking funds, strategy and political commitment.

With the coming offer from Japan we have a programme which puts people before chips. It offers a radical breakthrough in the direction of new technologies rather than the mere incremental — even if extensive — changes offered by SDI.

The issue of intellectual property rights in the Human Frontier Programme has not yet been resolved, but with the Japanese government providing a large part of the funds, this may not go in favour of the participating countries. There is also the opportunity cost of participation that has to be considered. Any funds or research workers that Europe may commit to the Human Frontier Science Programme will not be available to work on specific European programmes.

What Europe really needs is a technology programme which fits certain economic and social criteria; does it enhance Europe's industrial competitiveness; does it create jobs and stimulate wealth; is it environment-friendly; does it help to fight hunger and poverty in the world; does it take into account the need to conserve energy; would it contribute to improvements in living and working conditions; would it reduce regional inequalities?

In the light of these criteria, and the need for Europe's efforts not to be too diffuse, a commitment must be made to a European technology programme which will concentrate on computer science, particularly software, biotechnology, new materials and raw materials. All these are essential to Europe's future industrial effectiveness. Such a programme would align with the Human Frontier better than the United States High Frontier. It would allow Europe to respond positively to the Japanese programme from a position of strength. We cannot allow ourselves to be sub-contractors even in a science programme which encompasses our objectives.

The Guardian, 17 April 1987

37. Le Pen: This Racist Menace should be Banned from Britain

Jean-Marie Le Pen, leader of the French *Front National*, was invited by Sir Alfred Sherman, one-time special adviser to Margaret Thatcher, to speak at a fringe meeting at next week's Tory Party conference in Blackpool.

Sherman, whose views, to put it charitably, border on eccentricity, is on record as saying that Le Pen is neither fascist nor anti-Semitic.

More than this, he has laid into the representative body of the British Jewish community, the Board of Deputies, calling them 'fourth-rate non-entities' because they have dared to question Le Pen's political credentials.

Despite apparent discomfort among the more honourable elements at Conservative Central Office, and the recent advice proffered by Norman Tebbit, the silence of Sherman's former mentor, Mrs Thatcher, has been truly deafening.

Do the Tories know who they are consorting with? If not, it's time the record was put straight.

First, the *Front National* (FN) is an extreme Right-wing organisation whose membership includes outright neo-Nazi elements, some of whom were to be seen parading in Lyon during the Klaus Barbie trial, and openly dishing out literature that claimed that the Nazi gas-chambers and death camps were 'a hoax'.

Some of the FN's members are no strangers to violence and murder either:

- October 1984: Alain Barthes, then leader, shot and wounded an injured car driver who had rung his doorbell for help
- January 1985: Marcel Chivat, an FN candidate, violently assaulted an old couple in their home
- February 1985: Michel Fleurus, an FN candidate, was charged with assault, and grevious bodily harm.
- February 1985: Serge Lopez, FN leader in Beziers, bombed the home of an immigrant family.
- April 1985: Pierre Soraire and Marc Mazure, both FN members, were convicted of carrying hand grenades at a political meeting.
- July 1985: Jean Pierre Chatelain, FN 'security officer' in Savoy, was convicted with three other FN members of blowing an immigrant café to pieces.

To this unsavoury selection of bloody incidents can be added the brutal murder, by FN members, of a Socialist Party election worker during the March 1986 election campaign.

Wherever Le Pen goes, violence follows. And after his recent whistle-stop nationwide tour, there were near pogroms against Arabs, black and Jews in several cities.

In April, after a big FN street demonstration in Marseilles, a Jewish student was shot in the head and severely wounded by an FN goon squad.

Le Pen himself is no angel. He has been accused of torturing Algerian independence fighters while he was in the French 'paras' during the Algerian war. He has a court conviction for touting recordings of Hitler's speeches and Nazi marching songs. He was condemned in a French civil court for anti-Semitism as recently as June last year.

So who is he — and Sir Alfred Sherman, for that matter — trying to kid?

The recent controversy over Le Pen's comments that the holocaust was just 'a detail in the history of the Second World War' was no gaffe.

Boosted by recent FN election successes, Le Pen was testing the water to see what the response would be. Virulent racism, anti-Semitism and the targeting of people with Jewish names are already the stock in trade of Le Pen's weekly rag, *National Hebdo*. Witness the favourable two-page obituary given to Adolf Hitler's henchman, Rudolf Hess, a couple of weeks ago. Le Pen himself has gone so far as to describe the black leader of the French anti-racist movement, *SOS Racisme*, Harlem Desir as 'a half-Jew' and also to have echoed the claim that 'the Americans built the gas chambers'.

Both these statements appeared in last week's edition of the glossy French magazine, *Globe*. The whole group of the European Right of the European Parliament in Strasbourg is tainted with fascism. Among Le Pen's FN colleagues are Bernard Anthony, the author of vile anti-Jewish statements, and Roland Gauther, a French volunteer who fought on the side of the Nazis during the war. Then there is the *Movimento Sociale Italiano*, the FN's Italian bed-partner, which quite unashamedly pays homage to its fascist origins. So it should. Its leader, Giorgio Almirante, was *the* senior official during Mussolini's Salo Republic, and has just had his parliamentary immunity lifted so that he can stand trial for aiding neo-Nazi terrorists.

In fact, the MSI has spawned some of the most murderous terror gangs and individuals in Europe: the Armed Revolutionary Nuclei (which blasted 86 men, women and children into oblivion at Bologna railway station in 1980), Mario Tuti and Stefano Della Chiae, to name a few. One of these Italian merchants of terror is currently a top adviser to the Nazi National Front in Britain.

(Oddly sitting with this lot in the European Parliament is the Ulster Unionist MEP, John Taylor, who threatens to sue anybody calling him a fascist. Suffice it to say that if you lie down with dogs, you get up with fleas.)

It is to be hoped that the Labour movement and anti-racists and democrats generally will build up a crescendo of demands to ban Le Pen from entry to Britain. His presence would be a serious threat to public order. But, more than this, it is time that events across The Channel were given far more serious attention.

Tribune, 25 September 1987

38. Review

James Maxton by William Knox, *J. Ramsay MacDonald* by Austen Morgan, and *Philip Snowden* by Keith Laybourn and David James (Eds.)

This triad of biographies — Maxton, MacDonald and Snowden — has as its subject men who had much in common: they first obtained their political wings in the *Independent Labour Party* (ILP); they were prominent in the Labour Party throughout its early decades; *they all ended their political lives outside of its 'broad church'.* This was not all they shared. These three all showed strong political courage. During the 1914-18 War they all, to various degrees, came out in opposition when such a step required physical as well as intellectual courage. Maxton received and served a twelve month prison term for his anti-War activities and the other two both lost their Westminster seats in Lloyd George's 'coupon' election immediately after the War.

They all blamed the docile acceptance, at best, and wild chauvinism, at worst, for the War, and its consequential horrors, by the majority of Labour MP's upon the fact that they were *placemen*. They were the trade union representatives who lacked either or both the socialist convictions or the courage to oppose what was so clearly an Imperialist War. The result was that 1917 saw the trio as delegates, MacDonald and Snowden were amongst the convenors, to what has been described as 'perhaps the most remarkable gathering of the period', the Leeds Convention that set up the stillborn *Council of Workers' and Soldiers' Delegates*, after the Russian model. Yet as they converged they started to move apart. Their fates were those of the Yogi and the Commissars, even though their similar experiences during the War were to shape their whole pattern of thinking.

The two commissars were MacDonald and Snowden. In January 1924 there was the formation of the first, albeit minority, Labour Government. MacDonald became Prime Minister and Snowden Chancellor of the Exchequer. Less than ten months later Labour lost office as the Zinoviev letter chased Liberal supporters into the hands of the Conservatives. In 1929 Labour had its second chance as a minority Government, and MacDonald and Snowden took the same offices. This time the slump and the inexorable wave of rising unemployment in an environment of collapsing industries worried and harried them almost from the beginning. Snowden, a liberal freetrader almost by religion, refused to countenance any form of protection. MacDonald, virtually crippled by Treasury orthodoxy, was only able to stagger as far as a 'revenue tariff', far short of Mosley's demands for 'Keynesian' economic management.

The consequence was that, when the crunch came in 1931 and the International Bankers demanded the implementation of the 'May Report' calling for a balanced budget to be achieved through massive public expenditure cuts, including unemployment benefit, as the cost of further support for the pound, Labour turned chicken. Although they offered no alternative, half the Cabinet baulked at the logic of their own beliefs and refused to vote such cuts. Snowden and MacDonald saw this as the cowardice of the First World War repeated. They chose to form a National Government with a rump of renegade Labour MP's, the Conservatives and the Samuelite section of the Liberals. National Labour took nineteen years to pass away, while Snowden and MacDonald were both physically dead after six. Politically all three were dead long before. Snowden only lasted in the National Government a year before they betrayed his freetrade idol, and rather pathetically attempted, without success, to rejoin the Labour Party. MacDonald lost his Westminster seat to Manny Shinwell in 1935 and had to creep back into the House of Commons through the Scottish Universities.

Maxton fared a little better. He kept his socialist credentials. Entering Westminster in 1922 as one of the leading *Red Clydesiders* he quickly got himself suspended from the House, and watched the 1924 Labour Government critically from the sidelines. During the Miners' strike of 1926 he ceaselessly criss-crossed the country speaking in support. In the aftermath he produced, with the Miners' leader A.J. Cook, the Cook/Maxton manifesto calling for an end to class collaboration in favour of class war. The second Labour Government he observed from afar. The debacle of 1931 saw him draw the same conclusions as MacDonald and Snowden. Labour lacked the will. The result was a mirror-image. Maxton led the *ILP* out of the Labour Party to the left to pursue a prolonged and respected decline to obscurity by the late forties. Even he found difficulty in convincingly portraying the Second World War as just another Imperialist War. Yet it was Maxton as leader who resisted attempts to re-affiliate and as a result the *ILP's* last major electoral act was to be responsible for Labour's only by-election defeat during the 1945 Government shortly after Maxton's death in 1946.

The two Manchester University Press (MUP) books are both from a new series, *Lives of the Left*, which intends to provide a series of original biographies of leading figures in the European and North American socialist and Labour movements. The two here will certainly serve as valuable introductions to their neglected subjects, although both contain errors of omission and commission — Maxton more than MacDonald. Snowden, in contrast, is a collection of short disconnected essays from a variety of perspectives, inadequate in many ways, but sufficiently evocative to hope that MUP will add his name to their list for attention. All three lives lost to Labour would have proved valuable object lessons to the 'Gang of Four' in 1981. History repeats itself, the first time as tragedy and the second as farce.

Tribune, 9 October 1987

Part 6

1988

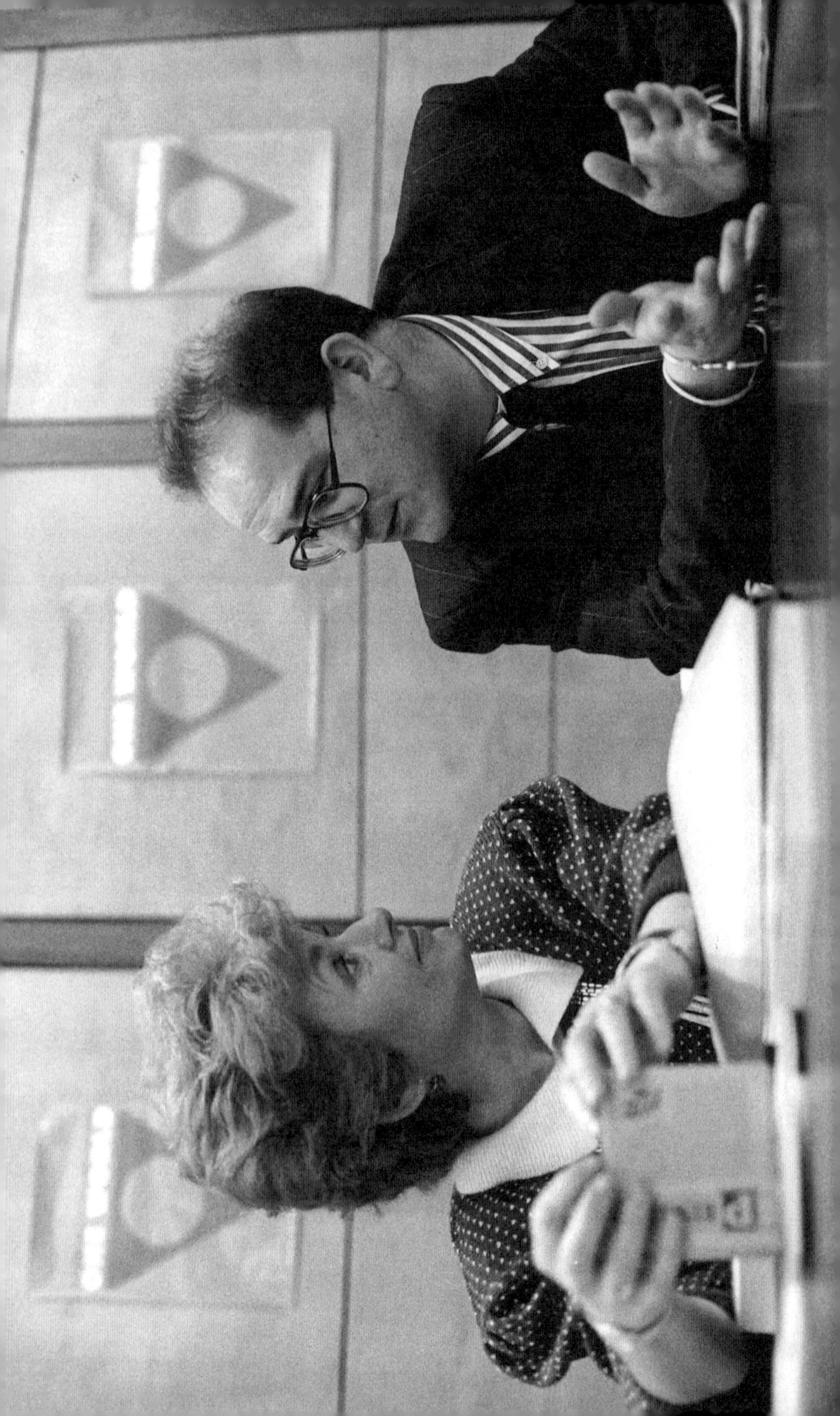

39. Review

Europe without America? by John Palmer

John Palmer has been, with only a brief three year break, the European Editor of the *Guardian* since 1975. In this book, subtitled 'The Crisis in Atlantic Relations', he forecasts the end of Empire — the American Empire. For him American withdrawal from Europe, militarily, economically and politically, will create the space for a Socialist United States of Europe. The political style of this new Europe can be gauged by the touchstones that Palmer adduces; the West German Green Party, the Lucas Aerospace Alternative Corporate Plan, the GLC. 1968 written on a continental scale.

For Palmer, the United States established a hegemonic position in the world immediately after the Second World War and maintained that dominant position unchallenged for more than a quarter of a century. Yet, as with the United Provinces and the United Kingdom before, achieving such a position is only transitory as we wait for Kondratieff to recycle the world-economy. Now this US domination no longer reflects the realities of power. The events of the last month on the world's stock exchanges merely confirm this, even though the deep-rooted historical and political forces that have held the Atlantic Alliance together will not readily disintegrate.

Europe without America? believes that Europe can gain its freedom. To do this will require a cohesive Europe, wider than the current European Community, that has close relations with the countries of Central Europe. To achieve this cohesion, a number of fundamental steps have to be taken. These include the development of an independent and self-reliant European security and defence policy to replace dependence on the US. The creation of a European technological community that would have the resources to tackle Europe's technological plunge. The introduction of an industrial 'counter-strategy' that would replace free trade with planned trade.

These three steps in themselves already establish a daunting agenda for the European Left. In the 1950's British business's confidence of its industrial dominance was as fervent as it was misplaced; today, the same kind of misplaced optimism would be true of Labour's belief in solely national solutions to these problems. Clearly no-one is suggesting that everything must be done at a European level. Many political tasks are best tackled at local or national levels. Nevertheless, it is now clear that the United Kingdom does not have the economic or political strength to avoid

◄ *January 1988: One World's Conference, chaired by Glenys Kinnock.*

the compromises of European Community solutions to these problems. Unpalatable as it may be, states are neither sovereign nor equal.

In some areas John Palmer does not go far enough. To suggest that the excessively modest and rather aimless ESPRIT and EUREKA programmes are even a first step in tackling the lack of European technological competitiveness in the face of the Strategic Defence Initiative and the President's *Competitivity* Initiative in the United States, or the plethora of pre-competitive collaborative research programmes in Japan under the guidance of the Ministry of International Trade and Industry, is to misjudge the scale of the problem by at least an order of magnitude.

Europe without America? is a little like Hamlet where the Prince only gets a walk-on part. The major reason that the US's global domination is at an end lies on the other side of the Pacific. It is the Japanese 'economic miracle' that has hollowed out American industry to a position of total collapse in some sectors. It is Japanese producers who are underselling indigenous manufacturers in Europe and the United States. Historically within capitalism the successor to the power in decline is not the one that has leapt ahead politically or militarily; rather it is the one that less spectacularly but more importantly has won the race for improved productivity.

Palmer's vision, even if flawed in places, is one that cannot be ignored. For as the Labour Party is beginning to come to terms with the European Community its own position is being transformed. The recent appointment of Takeshita as Japanese Prime Minister is a clear demonstration that Japan will take a more assertive role in military and political matters. Europe without America will be maneouvering on unknown terrain. John Palmer has helped to show the future face of the new world economy. The Left now has to develop the conceptual tools and the strategy to help to shape it in our image.

New Statesman, 15 January 1988

40. Review

The Enchanted Glass; Britain and its Monarchy by Tom Nairn

January 1974 saw the publication of the first issue of *The New Republican*, a newsletter whose readers had been recruited from the small ads columns of *Tribune* and similar newspapers. It's message was clear; "A country which maintains an hereditary monarchy, a part-hereditary legislature and an established church is ... a *limited* democracy". It's aim: a British Republic. It's support zero. "Because of the small circulation of this first issue of *The New Republican* I can make enough copies by typing", wrote its editor. Issue 2 was never to appear. *The Enchanted Glass* attempts to explain and bemoan Britain's collective love affair with it's monarchy and the long death of republicanism in Britain, as evidenced by the fate of the last attempt to regenerate a republican spark.

Tom Nairn has a fetish; the monarchy. Asking himself two questions; Why does British politics not have the same features as on the Continent? Why is Britain in steep industrial decline? He concludes by putting history to the question that the explanation for both are the Royal Family and our attitudes towards them. For Nairn, Britain experienced the first bourgeois revolution and thus never fully completed the transition from feudalism to capitalism. While later revolutions elsewhere were forced to go to completion in an attempt to compete with Britain's industrial might, British *sub*-capitalism avoided a forced continuation of its stalled revolution by drawing on the windfalls of its historical priority — Imperialism and Empire. This was the thesis of *The Break-Up of Britain* written in 1977. *The Enchanted Glass* inspects the feudal elements identified in the earlier book and identifies the 'powerhouse' of the whole operation as the monarchy.

It is the keystone of an interlocking set of institutions and practices that form the ideological backdrop against which the media creates a false conscious British nationalism. It has certainly been successful. A survey in 1984 showed that 77% of Labour voters believed that continuation of the monarchy is 'important for Britain'. It functions for them is to create and reinforce a feeling of community and nation.

The Royal Family — the exact membership of which fluctuates with the demands of fashion — is simultaneously 'ordinary' and 'extraordinary'. It is a family of many faces. A third of the population regularly dream about the Queen, usually sharing a cup of tea. As Ken Livingstone said, after the Queen inaugurated the new Thames Flood Barrier at Woolwich, "I have always thought that the Queen is a very nice person indeed. Today confirmed that view". On the other hand they fly helicopters, ride horses and play polo exceptionally well. They have novel and progressive views on modern architecture and are major figures in animal welfare organisations, while spending their weekends with shooting parties that regularly slaughter more birds than there are days in the year. Like any family they have their black sheep and wayward members who have their peccadilloes and get themselves involved with porno-stars, with women who learnt their sexual technique in Shanghai brothels, or who merely abandon relations to life sentences in institutions for the mentally ill. All of this makes them just like the family-next-door and the family in the super-rich 'soaps'.

What purpose does all this serve? It serves to cement together a group of nations in the British Isles against their own best interests. It emphasises nation at the expense of class and it acts as the brakes on the idea of progress. It is the containment strategy to resist coming to terms with the modern world. It protects the *status quo* and *those who benefit from it*. So the strategy of non-participation by the left is profoundly mistaken according to Nairn. The Monarchy can neither be seen as merely ornamental nor too expensive. It is not the feudal icing on top of the common cake of parliamentary democracy, or a rather imaginative con trick on the nation by a family of immigrants. One criminal, quoted by Nairn, admiringly said, "Look at the Royal Family...It's marvellous the way they kid people. Honestly, it's incredible. I watched the Duke of Edinburgh the other night talking about the Royal Yacht. Fucking *yacht*. Fucking *yacht*. It's an ocean-going liner...". Trivial carping about costs *pace* Willie Hamilton distracts from the main problem.

As Neal Ascherson wrote, "It is commonly and comfortably said that there is nothing basically wrong with British institutions, 'the finest in the world', but they are not working well at present because the economy is in such a bad state. The reverse is true. The reason that the British economy does not work is that British institutions are in terminal decay". How has the Labour Party responded to this set of institutions designed to prevent any action being taken to pull the British economy out of the long-term tailspin it is in? With acquiescence at best, and enthusiastic incorporation and sycophancy at worst. The last time Party Conference debated the abolition of the monarchy and the hereditary principle was in 1923 when the Chairman declared the motion lost by an overwhelming majority. The extent of Labour republicanism during the 1964-66 Government was a failed attempt by Tony Benn to remove the Queen's profile from some of our postage stamps. More recently, when the European Community threatened the same, it was a member of the *Campaign Group* that entered the lists to defend Her Majesty and British traditions.

Taken literally *The Enchanted Glass*'s main message that says that the monarchy is *the* reason for Britain's economic failure is far too simple. Both the Low Countries before and the United States now have lost their hegenomic positions in the world without the benefit of monarchy or, for that matter, the rest of the feudal equipment. Japan has managed it's economic miracle saddled with an Emperor that is close to a Deity. What this latest book from Tom Nairn does is to make the thesis of his earlier book, *The Break-Up of Britain* (outlined above), that much more convincing. It's not the monarchy, but the whole feudal apparatus and attitudes that have to be changed. British institutions have to be brought in lines with the realities of late capitalism. The Second Chamber has to be rescued from attitudes towards nation; class and economy have to be transformed. It is probably too much to expect such progressive modernisation, to counter the Thatcherite regressive variety, from the 229 seemingly intelligent individuals who seem happy to endlessly act out some arcane medieval mummers play in the House of Commons.

New Socialist, October/November 1988

Part 7

1989

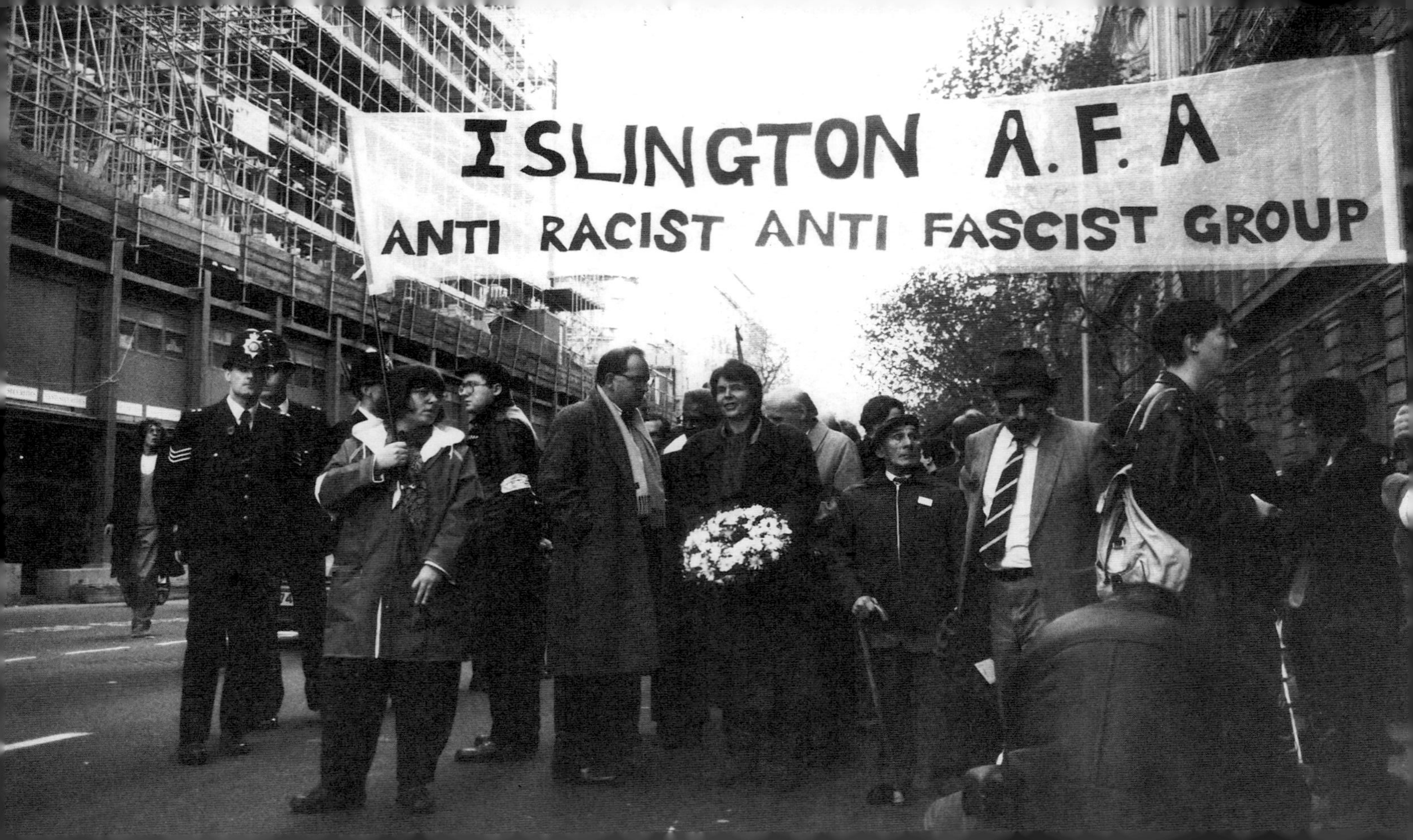
ISLINGTON A.F.A
ANTI RACIST ANTI FASCIST GROUP

41. Review

Unit 731 by Peter Williams and David Wallace

An aspect of *Unit 731* is excessively topical. This book is about Japan's biological warfare division set up in 1935 by Ishii Shiro in Japanese-occupied Manchuria under the cover of a Water Purification Unit. It was here that Japanese soldiers carried out freezing, ballistics and live vivisection experiments on Russian, Chinese, American, British and Australian prisoners to help win the war for Japan with the creation of what today would be seen as the 'poor man's' Atomic Bomb. The topicality lies in the question; *Did the Emperor know?*

500-600 prisoners were consigned to the Unit each year. If a prisoner survived the initial inoculation of lethal bacteria it did not save him. A cocktail of further experiments were conducted until death from infection intervened. No-one ever left the death factory alive. Following anatomical study the bodies of the dead were burned in the Unit's incinerator. The doctors and technicians referred to the prisoners as *maruta*, the Japanese for a log of wood, and that is exactly how they were treated. *Marutas* were tied to stakes while shrapnel bombs were exploded charged with gas gangrene to see how long they took to die. Others were exposed naked to temperatures of $-20°C$ to investigate frostbite, or worked to death in malnutrition experiments existing only on water and Army biscuits. There is much more. For those that want to see more they can now do so. In Hong Kong they've just released *Children of the Sun*, a horror film in full grisly detail of Unit 731's activities. In total almost as impressive a catalogue of man's inhumanity to man as can be found anywhere in time and place.

Certainly most of the Japanese military establishment had a good inkling of what was going on at Pingfan, the Unit's Headquarters, just south of Harbin. So too did the Foreign Ministry and the Cabinet. Both Prince Mikasa, the Emperor's brother, and Prince Takeda, the Emperor's cousin, visited Unit 731. Yet there is no solid evidence that the Emperor himself knew. Hirohito was a biologist, but his interests were in slime mould, micro-organisms far removed from disease-causing bacteria, and he was so isolated from everyday life that most of his subjects could barely understand his quaint court Japanese when he announced Japan's unconditional surrender on August 15, 1945. The only verdict can be the Scottish legal verdict of unproven.

◄ *Remembrance Sunday 1989: Anti-fascists prepare to march to the Cenotaph (photo: Searchlight magazine).*

The real scandal is a different one. Unit 731's unique research data, obtained in some cases from experiments on US servicemen, was secretly traded to the Americans in exchange for war-crimes immunity. None of the major actors were prosecuted by the International Military Tribunal for the Far East, and there was just one brief and unnoticed reference to the fact that Japan had been working on biological weapons. Many of the protagonists went on to make their future careers in medical fields connected with their Mengele-like research. A whole clutch of ex-Unit 731 members became prominent in the highly successful multinational Green Cross Corporation specialising in producing a whole range of pharmaceutical products.

The United States denied all. When the Russians tried twelve members of the Unit they had captured in December 1949 and sentenced them to up to 25 years hard labour it was the height of the Cold War and American claims that it was another show trial were generally believed. The same was true when the *Report of the International Scientific Commission for the Facts Concerning Bacterial Warfare in Korea and China*, drawn by Joseph Needham and five other experts, exposed the fact that the Americans were experimenting with some of the techniques learnt from Unit 731, in that unholy bargain, during the Korean War. As late as December 1986 the Ministry of Defence in Britain was saying that, "we still have no evidence to support allegations that the Japanese experimented on Allied PoW's..." In Britain and the United States hundreds of the victims of Unit 731 are still seeking compensation for their wartime experience. If there is any justice, Williams and Wallace should have removed the last remaining barrier to British Government recognition of the truth of these too long outstanding claims.

Tribune, 17 March 1989

42. European Arms Exports

The present report[1] is intended to portray the present situation regarding arms exports from the European Community and issues related to this, in order to provide a basis for the recommendations on actions which the European Community should take in this field.

Brief History of the Arms Trade

Ohlsson (1987) has described the history of the arms trade since the Second World War in three phases.

The *first* phase from 1950 to the mid-1960s saw the US supplying its allies with military hardware, especially in Europe. From the mid-1950s onwards the US and the USSR were competing for influence in the Third World and were giving away second-hand, often out-dated items of military equipment to allies and friendly nations. Great Britain at this time was also supplying its colonies and countries such as Belgium and Holland due to the great arms producing capacity which it had developed by the end of the Second World War.

The *second* phase from the mid-1960s to the late 1970s saw the commercialisation of arms transfers. Arms were sold rather than given away, often through complex financial deals involving elements of 'counter-trade'. The weapons sold also became more sophisticated because recipient countries did not want out-of-date equipment if they were paying for it. During this period the arms industry of Western Europe had been re-built, which increased the number of suppliers and therefore competition on the global arms market. Markets were found for the new suppliers in the Third World where liberation struggles and cross-border conflicts increased the demand for arms.

The Arab-Israeli war of 1973 brought about a 400 per cent increase in the price of oil which provided the oil-producing states with increased revenues with which they could, and did, purchase arms. This second phase is characterised by a massive increase in arms sales to the Middle East.

The Soviet Union during this period began to use arms exports as a means of obtaining hard currency.

The *third* phase of the arms trade, the late 1970s to the present, is characterised by a significant slow-down in the growth of arms sales. The growth rate for arms exports of the developed world in the period 1981 to 1984 was below one per cent (SIPRI). The prime reason for this is the decline in the price of raw materials which has reduced the revenues available to Third World governments. Commentators have said that 10-15 per cent of the indebtedness of the Third World is due to military purchases. The United Nations puts this figure even higher, at between 20 and 25 per cent.

Further factors have contributed to the slow-down in the arms trade. Many of the Third World governments purchasing in the 1970s have completed their military stocks and now only require updated and replacement weapons. Added to this, some of these governments, such as Brazil, North and South Korea and India, have now started to produce their own military equipment. There are also newcomers amongst the European arms manufacturers, namely Greece, Spain and Austria which adds to the number of suppliers and increases the competition in the market place. However, there is no reason why the global arms market should continue to stagnate. An improvement in the world economy would again give governments increased revenues with which to purchase arms.

SIPRI and ACDA Statistics

It is extremely difficult to obtain reliable statistics on the arms trade. Firstly, because governments are sensitive to public scrutiny of their arms trade, and they are therefore not willing to supply data; secondly it is difficult to define what constitutes a 'military export'; thirdly, the complexity of arms deals involving counter-trade and offsets makes it difficult to assess the total value of exports.

There are two main sources of statistics on the arms trade, the Stockholm International Peace Research Institute (SIPRI) and the American Arms Control and Disarmament Agency (ACDA). The statistics from each source differ significantly, and cannot be easily used for cross-comparison. SIPRI collected data by identifying specific transactions through the press and other sources. Usually a transaction must be reported from five different sources before it can be included in the data. As this method is very laborious SIPRI restrict their collection of data to large items of military aircraft, warships, missiles and armoured vehicles. British Government officials have said that SIPRI data are reasonably reliable.

ACDA collect data on a wider basis than SIPRI. It includes major weapons plus artillery, infantry weapons, military communications and electronic equipment, uniforms, non-armoured military vehicles and the transfer of equipment for the defence industries. However, the data is not collected from independent sources. It is largely compiled from statistics supplied by other government departments in the United States. There is reason to believe that ACDA's arms transfer figures are deflated. In one instance its estimates for France were below figures given to the French Assembly by a ratio of three to one.

Your Rapporteur, for the purposes of this report, therefore, relies mainly on the statistics available from SIPRI.

The Economics of Arms Transfers

Economic analysis of arms transfers is an area which has not been greatly explored. The paucity and unreliability of data in this area makes empirical research extremely difficult. It is also difficult to define what constitutes an arms export as this can include military support services and equipment or training and the transfer of know-how, and non-military equipment can be used for military purposes, for example Land Rovers.

Arms production and export can be seen as goods or a service, similar to any other product and it is now largely viewed by European governments as an area of the economy which contributes to economic growth, higher employment and corporate profits.

It is also claimed that arms can act as product leaders to open markets for civilian goods in the same region.

The pressures on the arms industry to export are twofold. Firstly, the larger production runs achievable through exports reduce the unit costs of the item and, secondly, contracting defence budgets lead companies to look for other markets for their products.

The research and development required to produce modern military equipment is extremely expensive; therefore larger production runs effectively reduce the R&D costs per unit. There are also cost-savings in the learning curve on larger production runs. For example, the McDonnell-Douglas F-15 fighter required 600,000 person hours for construction of the first unit. By the 10th unit this had reduced to 200,000 hours and by the 100th it has reduced to 90,000. Estimates predict that only 40,000 hours would be required for the one thousandth plane.

Production runs in the United States can exceed 1,000 but generally in Europe runs are considerably smaller, which can make European products less competitive on price.

Exports of military equipment can also reduce costs for European governments who can renegotiate purchase prices for domestic military equipment in the knowledge that the unit costs will be reduced by exports. Additionally, companies are stimulated to bid more keenly for defence contracts when they know there is a potential for export. Thus governments can obtain better value for money for national procurement. The export aspect of defence procurement has now become so important that the British Government intends to include in defence contracts specific provisions to cover export possibilities.

The defence industries are generally looked upon by European governments also as a means of maintaining employment. Exports, therefore, function as a means of securing this employment. Figures for exactly how many jobs are involved in the defence industry are difficult to obtain, and they are split between those directly employed in the industry and those indirectly employed in the industry via defence industry suppliers and subcontractors. The arms industry in France employs 4.5 per cent of the industrial workforce and in Italy the industry employs 1.8 per cent of the workforce. Some commentators argue that the contribution of arms industries to employment is insignificant and that exports cannot be justified on employment grounds. However, it has to be borne in mind that employment in the defence industries is concentrated in certain regions; for example, in France most of the industry is around Paris, and therefore cessation of employment would hit some regions very badly. Your Rapporteur, however, considers that this is no different to the effects of the restructuring of the European steel industry, or the steep decline in the shipbuilding industry.

The US Bureau of Labour Statistics in 1976 estimated the employment generated by $1 billion of expenditure for national defence was significantly less than for the state and local government spending $1 billion for health and education.

Defence Industries and Export Policies of Member States

Belgium
Belgium is a relatively small but significant arms producer. Arms sales in 1985 and 1986 were worth $32 million and $23 million respectively. Approximately 95 per cent of production is exported. Half of the exports go to the Middle East and Maghreb. There have been fewer arms sales to the Third World recently and this has not been compensated by increased sales to other industrialised countries.

Companies must have permission from the Belgian Ministry of Defence before they can export military equipment. Before granting permission the government considers four criteria:
- the protection of Belgian economic interest
- the protection of Belgian national security
- international embargoes
- general principles of law and humanity.

The Belgian Ministry of Defence, like many other governments, insists on receiving 'end-use' certificates from buyers. These are guarantees from the purchaser that the weapons will not be re-exported. However, the Belgian authorities have a reputation for taking a liberal attitude towards these licences. Executives of a Belgian arms manufacturer have indicated that end-use certificates have only the strength of a 'moral commitment', i.e. they are not worth the paper they are written on.

Although Belgium is only a small arms producer it is significant as an arms trading centre due to its central geographical position, its importance as a business centre and its permissive legislation on arms sales. Furthermore, it is not against the law in Belgium for private individuals to have arms stores.

France
France has the most aggressive exports policy of the European Community member states. This is partly due to their independent military strategy which requires that they produce a significant proportion of their own weapons. The French Government has openly acknowledged that arms exports are necessary to reduce the unit costs of equipment supplied to their own services and to provide revenue for the high research and development costs necessary for the production of technologically advanced weaponry.

The proportion of French arms sales to the Third World has increased from 71 per cent in the period 1977-81 to 86 per cent in the period 1982-86. However, arms exports have decreased since 1984. The French arms industry tends to rely on major arms deals which makes it vulnerable if these do not materialise.

Official estimates put employment in the French arms industry at 280,000, which constitutes 4.5 per cent of the French industrial force. The industry is largely based around Paris.

France was a major supplier of arms to Iraq during the Iran-Iraq war (1980-1988). French arms constituted approximately 25 per cent of Iraq's total supplies. In the process, Iraq has accumulated large debts with the French ($4-5 billion) which have had to be re-scheduled. The French have been forced to look for alternative markets in order not to become too dependent on the Middle East. To this end they have improved their after-sales service and are now more willing to agree to technology transfer through offset agreements in order to gain sales.

At the same time, France was also illegally supplying Iran with weapons. Iran purchased three Combattante II class missile boats and large amounts of artillery ammunition from the Luchaire Corporation. The French Government claimed that they did not know of such deals, but an experienced arms salesman has commented that it is almost certain that the government was aware of the deals. Muted criticism from the opposition at the time implies that they were aware of and condoned the operation.

Italy
The Italian government encourages arms sales in order to reduce the unit costs of military equipment. There was a rapid increase in Italian arms sales in the late 1970s and early 1980s. This was due to large naval orders from countries in South America, Africa and

the Middle East. Arms exports have declined dramatically in the period 1982-86. Orders for less sophisticated weaponry have declined due to the increased number of suppliers and the efforts of other industrialised countries to produce arms for Third World requirements. Italy is attempting to rectify this situation by developing joint ventures with Third World arms producers, and raising the technological level of arms production by entering into co-production agreements with other Western arms manufacturers.

As in other European countries, there have been moves to make the defence sector more economically effective. A special industry-government committee has been established to make recommendations on how to restructure the arms industry and how to increase exports. FIAT is the company leading these efforts.

Italian companies apply to the Ministry of Foreign Affairs for licences to export arms, but these are subject to approval by the Ministry of Defence. The Italian government generally takes a permissive attitude towards arms exports. It is possible that an Italian port has been used for US shipments of arms to Iran. Subsequently an inquiry into the allegations was established and arms exports to areas of conflict were officially temporarily frozen.

The Italian Foreign Ministry has recently made efforts to prevent the illegal export of arms by tightening up on the procedures for 'end-use' certificates. Under the new laws arms exporters have to give details of how the weapons will be transported, the itinerary, with intermediate stops, and the final destination. The details given by companies are to be cross-checked by customs officials. If there are any discrepancies the customs officials have the power to halt the sale.

Netherlands
The Netherlands has no industrial producers of major military equipment such as fighter planes, missiles and tanks. The Dutch defence industry is based over five major industrial areas: electronics and optical, aerospace, shipbuilding, truck and ammunition. About one-third of defence sector production is for export.

Dutch export regulations prohibit the export of arms to areas of conflict, or political tension, or to regimes which do not respect human rights. There is an upward trend in Dutch arms sales estimated at approximately 10 per cent per year. The Dutch government is increasingly becoming involved in arms transfers by making representations in arms sales promotions and selling out-of-date equipment to ease budget pressures.

Dutch companies involved in the defence sector are actively encouraged to participate in European co-production agreements, through increased government subsidies for military research and development.

Spain
Spain is a relatively new arms producer and exporter. It has low production costs and there are few restrictions of exports. Almost all arms sales are to the Third World, mainly countries in Latin America and the Middle East. Spain has rapidly increased its share of arms sales to the Third World from 0.2 per cent in the period 1977-81 to 1.6 per cent in the period 1982-86. CASA is producing military aircraft for export to Indonesia and Chile.

The export of arms to countries at war is illegal in Spain. However, there is evidence that arms were delivered to both Iran and Iraq by a company via the port of Barcelona. The official destination for the arms was Portugal or Indonesia. *El Pais* (5 February 1988) reported the existence of an arms dealer in Marbella which advertises military goods in defence journals. The Spanish authorities were apparently unaware of its existence. Although there is no direct evidence of illegal arms trading, your rapporteur notes the fact that the company was unknown to the relevant authorities with great concern.

West Germany
Germany prides itself on its restrictive policy on arms exports and has in the past called for a register of arms sales in the United Nations. However they feel that their position on arms exports is somewhat compromised by co-production with countries which have more lenient export regulations. For example, West Germany itself would not have agreed to the sale of Tornadoes to Saudi Arabia in 1987 but was obliged to withdraw its opposition by Britain.

Recently there have been investigations into the violation of West German export regulations. In 1986 two executives of an arms producing company were sentenced for the illegal re-export of military equipment to Argentina, Saudi Arabia and South Africa. Another court case investigated the transfer of missile and electronic parts and engineering support for the construction of rockets to Libya. Furthermore, the state-owned shipyard HDW and the engineering bureau ILD were found to have delivered blueprints of submarines to South Africa. A Parliamentary Commission was formed to investigate the circumstances of the deal. It is alleged that members of the government were aware of the sale and consented to it.

Exports to Iran during the Iran-Iraq war were not allowed under German export regulations. However, floating bridges were sold to Iran, and no export licence was required because they are not classified as military equipment. Nevertheless, it is clear that such equipment would be invaluable in the war effort.

There have been serious breaches of the German export regulations. The fact that they have come to light implies that the German authorities pay serious attention to controlling the arms trade.

United Kingdom

The United Kingdom is another aggressive exporter of arms. Exports are encouraged by the British government for similar reasons to the French, namely that exports help to reduce the unit cost of military equipment and therefore result in better value-for-money in national procurement. British companies are encouraged to consider the export potential of all military equipment which they are hoping to sell to the British government. The implication is that contracts are likely to be awarded to the companies which can demonstrate significant export potential.

The Defence Export Sales Organisation (DESO) in the Ministry of Defence exists to facilitate the export of British Military Equipment. It has four offices abroad, in the United States, India, Saudi Arabia and Malaysia.

The share of UK arms exports to the Third World declined from 85 per cent in the period 1977-81 to 67 per cent in the period 1982-86. This, however, is due to an increase in exports to industrialised countries.

Britain does have some difficulty selling major weapons abroad because they are sophisticated and therefore expensive. The government's emphasis on export potential is aimed at resolving this problem. The Royal Ordnance Factories have now designed a new family of armoured vehicles which can be produced and maintained in Third World countries. SIPRI reports that there is evidence from the pattern of new orders that British arms sales to the Third World will increase.

All military sales require an export licence which is awarded by the Ministry of Trade and Industry, in consultation with the Ministry of Defence and the Foreign Office. There was a formal ban on sales to Iran and Iraq during the conflict but this referred only to 'lethal equipment' that could 'prolong or exacerbate' the war. Britain did sell radar equipment to Iran supposedly for surveillance over its eastern borders but it is obvious that this equipment would have been used in the war effort on the western borders.

Britain also has now resumed exports to Chile where there are considerable human rights violations.

Despite the British government's permissive attitude towards arms exports to the Third World, it maintains a restrictive policy in some other areas. For example, the government does not allow the export of some types of equipment to certain other European Community member states for 'security reasons', which poses a number of interesting questions in relation to 1992, and the political barriers that may be erected to prevent the formation of a common internal arms market.

The Iran-Iraq War

This section of the report looks at European arms exports in relation to the Iran-Iraq War. Looking at a specific region and a specific conflict provides a framework for realising the practical effects of arms exports from Europe.

Iraq has a population of only 16 million compared to Iran's 48 million, and its geographical position makes it much more vulnerable in a war of attrition. However, Iraq did have greater access to the world's most advanced arms suppliers and was able to obtain military technology much more freely than Iran. Not only was Iraq able to obtain more sophisticated weaponry but it has also benefited from a much higher degree of standardisation in its equipment and more readily available spare parts.

Iran began the war with military stocks and skilled manpower somewhat depleted due to the 1979 revolution. Furthermore, much of the existing equipment had been supplied to the Shah from the United States and the new regime was unable to obtain further supplies or spare parts (apart from the transfer of arms revealed in the 'Irangate' affair in which five separate covert shipments of US arms worth $30-87 million were sent to Iran between August 1985 and November 1986).

After the American hostage crisis in 1983 the United States supposedly launched 'Operation Staunch' to limit arms sales to Iran. The Iranian government has been able to obtain some spare parts for its US equipment but was forced to pay extremely high prices for the goods.

Arms Transfers to Iraq and Iran

Iraq benefited from the support of other Arab nations in terms of financial aid and the supply of arms in military emergencies. Kuwait, for example, paid some of the arms suppliers with oil on Iraq's behalf. In 1986 Iraq obtained 55 per cent of its arms from the USSR,

20-25 per cent from France and 20-25 per cent from other sources. During the course of the war France sold more than $5.6 billion worth of arms to Iraq.

Iraq obtained arms through a mix of counter-trade and cash. Iran, on the other hand, had largely to pay cash. Iran had substantial difficulties in obtaining arms and spare parts on the illegal arms market. Armaments had to be routed through middlemen who charge extortionate prices, and there was always the possibility of fraud. Iran, therefore, increasingly turned towards North Korea and China who, although producing arms inferior to Soviet and Western arms, supplied 70 per cent of Iran's arms in 1986.

Iran co-ordinated its efforts to obtain weapons both legally and illegally in Europe from an office in the Iran National Oil Company in London. This, however, was closed by the British Government when its activities became more public.

The Iran-Iraq war, in the words of a SIPRI commentator, 'has demonstrated that national boundaries or political ideology mean little in the boundaries of the arms trade business'. Some reports indicated that private arms dealers purchased Iranians' weapons captured in Iraq and sold them back to Iran!

The war also illustrates that a nation which exports arms has no control over the identity of the party against whom they will eventually be used.

European Arms Deals

The examples below illustrate the deals which were carried out during the conflict.

Iran was able to obtain three Combattante II class missile boats and large amounts of 155mm and other artillery ammunition from French factories. At the time the deals became public, the French government claimed that these were illegal sales made by the Luchaire company. However, one arms dealer commented that it is almost certain that the French government was fully aware of the transactions.

Iran also bought several Chieftain tank parts from Britain. Additionally, it bought Plessey air defence radars, replenishment tankers, logistic support ships and other equipment from the UK. Some equipment shipped in crates marked 'vehicle parts' was justified by the British MOD on the grounds that it did not form part of the 'lethal' part of the vehicle. Exports such as these, although ostensibly legal, were not following the spirit of the law.

Both Spain and Portugal supplied Iran with large amounts of ammunition and light equipment during the conflict. Portugal often acted as a transit point for illegal arms obtained in the US (not, however, the arms involved in the Irangate scandal). Portugal did recall one shipment of arms in Spring of 1987 when the trade was publicly exposed.

Iran obtained grenades, light arms and F-4 and F-5 parts and engines from Greek dealers, although the origin of these is not known. Iran has also bought engineering equipment from West Germany which would undoubtedly aid the war effort.

Embargo on South Africa

The United Nations imposed an arms embargo on South Africa in 1977 in protest at its apartheid policy and its aggression towards other African states in the region. Although the embargo has not been total the result has been to stimulate the development of an indigenous South African arms industry. South Africa is now a prominent world leader in the field of weaponry. In addition to arms and ammunition, a complete range of support equipment has been designed and developed in South Africa specifically for South African conditions.

In 1982 Armscor (the government body responsible for arms production and procurement in South Africa) entered the international weapons market. There are however no details available concerning South Africa's exports.

Undoubtedly embargoes stimulate the development of indigenous arms industries; the Israeli industry developed rapidly as a result of the French arms embargo after the 1967 war. This, however, was by no means a total embargo as Israel was able to obtain arms and military technology from other countries.

Despite these adverse effects of embargoes, they can for a time restrain the military capability of an aggressor. As the effect of the embargo is less as time goes on, it must be combined with intense political activity at the time of the embargo to reduce the aggression.

Apart from the UN embargo on South Africa, there are at present only bilateral arms embargoes. The Member States of the European Community could act more effectively to restrict the arms trade if they acted together through European Political Co-operation, the secretariat for which has now been established.

Acting together to restrict arms sales would:
(i) make the restrictions more effective
(ii) share the immediate economic disadvantages associated with the embargo;
(iii) allow the EPC to work politically for the reduction of aggression.

The Illegal Arms Trade

There is no significant illegal arms trading carried out by freelance arms salesmen without the passive acquiescence of Governments. If they do trade illegally it is generally in small arms which are easily hidden and transported. There is no strict dividing line between legal and illegal arms exports, the reality of the situation being much more complex.

Arms exports are illegal if they contravene national export regulations. However, it is apparent that it is often governments themselves which breach the regulations. An experienced arms salesman has said that governments do, in fact, know about 95 per cent of the so-called 'illegal' arms trading, and make it possible for such exports to take place. There have been recent cases in France and Germany (mentioned above) where allegations have been made that senior members of government were fully aware of specific illegal arms deals.

Furthermore, there are more subtle violations of national export regulations. Neither Britain nor Germany is permitted to export military equipment to Iran, but Britain has sold sophisticated radar equipment on the grounds that it is for surveillance on the Western border of Iran, and Germany has sold floating bridges as civilian products. Undoubtedly, both would have been used in the Iranian war effort. Britain also shipped parts for Chieftain tanks to Iran, justified on the grounds that they were 'non-lethal' parts. However, as British regulations also prohibited the sale to Iran of items likely to prolong or exacerbate the war, such items were still clearly a breach of the law.

It seems that it is relatively easy to obtain false 'end-use' certificates for military exports. Italy however is attempting to eradicate this practice by checking the authority of certificates, and asking for more detailed information.

Arms embargoes appear to be broken so frequently that one might judge them to be an ineffective measure. A private arms dealer, however, has confirmed that embargoes would be effective if governments wanted them to be.

Counter-trade

As the global arms market has become a 'buyer's market' during the 1980s there has been a considerable increase in the number of arms deals involving counter-trade. This is the general term given to deals which involve 'payment-in-kind' or 'barter'. The rise in counter-trade reflects the growing power of the buyer over the supplier who is anxious to sell in a shrinking market. Counter-trade avoids the need for payment in hard currency, which Third World countries find increasingly difficult in the economic recession, and it is a means by which less-developed countries can obtain advanced technology. It is estimated that between five and 30 per cent of world trade is conducted through counter-trade.

Counter-purchase is one type of counter-trade activity. In this transaction the exporter agrees to purchase goods from the arms buyer over a specified period of time. The goods are often not related to the military sector and the company itself has to manage the deal and find markets for the goods which it has obtained. When counter-purchase products are related to the original export, then the transaction is referred to as 'buy back'. However, it is not inconceivable that a defence company in Europe would be left looking for a market for tonnes of oranges, for example. Greece's deal with Libya in October 1984, believed to be worth $1 billion, is to be financed by oil which could be used for domestic consumption or sold on the spot markets.

Offset arrangements usually involve the transfer of technology. Direct offsets can involve the purchasing country in the manufacture or assembly of the components used in the purchased product. This agreement provides employment in the recipient country, and perhaps more importantly, allows the country to acquire advanced technology and the skills required to use the technology, thus creating a more highly-skilled workforce. Indirect offsets are agreements by the sellers to contribute to the buyer's economy. The arrangements usually take the form of a joint venture in advanced technology and do not relate to the original exported product.

Indirect offsets frequently require the assistance of the government of the exporting country in order to plan the offset arrangement and administer the agreement. A case in point is the offset agreement reached between the British government and Saudi Arabia over the £5 billion package agreed in February 1986 involving 72 Tornado aircraft, 30 Hawk trainer/strike aircraft and 30 PC-9 trainers. The British government has agreed to encourage UK investment in joint ventures in Saudi Arabia worth £500m to £600m. This amount is considered to be equivalent to 35 per cent of the value of the British components of the military goods.

It is likely that the Saudi government would like to see most of the investment in the form of 50-50 joint ventures. This way Saudi Arabia has more direct control and gains more technological and economic benefits from the investment. This offset agreement is additional to the part payment of the £5 billion deal in the form of oil from Saudi Arabia. Also included in the offset are proposals for licensing agreements, training in technology and expansion of export opportunities for Saudi companies. The Saudi government has decided to drop its insistence that all joint ventures include advanced technology.

Offset agreements have now become so complicated that it is increasingly difficult to assess the true value of an arms deal to both the supplier and the recipient, thus making the official arms transfer statistics an even more unreliable source of evidence. Private agencies have been established to help companies deal with the complexities of offset agreements.

Cooperation in the European Arms Industry

The European defence industry is economically ineffective due largely to the duplication of efforts on behalf of the national governments. The increasing pressure on defence budgets, and the ever-increasing costs of research and development have forced both government and industry to consider co-operation within the European arms industry more seriously.

Increased efficiency within the European defence sector could reduce the pressure on defence companies to export. It therefore is an issue which has to be considered in relation to arms exports. However, it has to be said that whilst increased efficiency in the defence sector could reduce the pressure to export, there is no guarantee that this would happen. In fact one of the aims of the Independent European Programme Group (see below) in stimulating co-operation is to improve the competitiveness of the European defence industry.

Some commentators believe that the co-ordination of the defence production and the creation of an integrated European defence market should ultimately be the responsibility of the European Community. However, this is not automatic with the present narrow interpretation of Article 223 of the Treaty of Rome which prevents the Commission from dealing with any aspect of national security requirements. In the meantime the only forum for managing co-operation in the defence industry in Europe is through the IEPG.

The Independent European Programme Group

The group was set up in 1976 as the principal European forum for co-operation in the research, development and production of defence equipment. The Member States are Belgium, Denmark, France, Germany, Greece, Italy, Luxembourg, Netherlands, Norway, Portugal, Turkey and the UK. Its aim is to eliminate the waste inherent in the European defence industry where separate national industries are producing similar equipment in uneconomic quantities. Clearly this is a waste of European skills and financial resources.

The IEPG is not intended to develop European co-operation in opposition to the American defence industry. In fact the IEPG have done much work to promote co-operation between European allies and the US in military production. However, NATO procurement favours the American defence industry, a situation which may be balanced by co-operative agreements between European and American companies and the US procuring more European arms. The Defence Ministers of the IEPG meeting in Seville in June 1987 stressed the important role of the IEPG in strengthening the European arm of NATO through the development of an effective and technologically advanced defence industry.

The IEPG in 1987 announced proposals to improve the competitiveness of the European defence industry in the global arms trade. It recommends that competitiveness is achieved by opening national procurement procedures to encourage greater intra-European arms trade and by greater co-operation between both governments and defence industries within Europe in defence research.

Although the IEPG has spent some considerable time investigating the possibilities of transatlantic co-operative programmes, the American government has nevertheless become alarmed at the prospect of European defence industry collaboration. They fear that European collaboration will exclude the US from sales in Europe as well as improving the European competitive position in global arms deals. As a result, amendments to the 1986 Defence Authorisation Act have reduced some of the legal barriers to European arms sales in the United States, and $125m was made available in FY 1986/87 for the support of joint US/European development projects, and the testing of European equipment in the US. These measures will make it considerably easier for European companies to sell military equipment in the US. At the same time concern has been expressed at the possibility that COCOM regulations might be used as a means of slowing European co-operation when the US particularly saw it as being against its own interests.

The IEPG has been made responsible for finding suitable projects for US/European co-operation. By Autumn 1985 six potential projects had been identified. The IEPG have recently looked into the possibilities for co-operation in the aeronautical field. Their survey revealed that all the major aircraft projects planned over the next two decades are to be collaborative. It seems there is the possibility that some programmes will be shared out instead of dividing them into national segments of work. There is also the possibility that a transnational company will be set up to administer programmes in the same way that Airbus Industrie has operated in the civil sector.

IEPG is also concerned to see the industrial and technological development of NATO states which have less developed defence industries (LDDI). European Defence Ministers are concerned that they should become integrated into the European defence industrial community to strengthen the Alliance. They have agreed that

- all countries will examine the possibilities of increasing defence and equipment aid in order to develop the industrial infrastructure of the LDDI countries
- in order to create a more competitive European defence industry certain appropriate industries from LDDI's will be allowed greater access in the national procurement projects of other nations. Efforts will be made to give more orders of LDDIs to LDDIs under collaborative programmes. The participation in joint ventures is also to be encouraged.
- Arrangements will be made to stimulate the participation of the LDDI countries in collaborative research and development programmes in order to give them access to the latest defence technology.

Possibilities for Conversion to Civilian Production

It is not easy to suggest changes in the military industry which would appear to threaten profits and reduce employment. However, this same economic climate is reducing possibilities for export and reducing national defence budgets, and it would therefore be wise to consider structural changes in the defence industries which will secure employment and profitability in the future.

The key question at governmental level is to ensure that resources which are released from defence procurement or military R&D are actually used to help convert the industry to civilian production. Defence needs apart, it has been shown that the economic benefits in terms of output, jobs and research and development, are greater from non-military spending than military spending.

A key factor in considering conversion is the problem that, although a particular industry may not be totally dependent on defence contracts, a particular plant within that industry may be. The plant may also be in a remote area, for missile testing perhaps, and provide the major focus for employment in that area. Any reduction in the defence work in these locations must be carefully planned.

A further problem is that defence technology has become extremely sophisticated: the workers therefore tend to be highly skilled and highly specialised. Their skills may not be transferable to the civilian sector without retraining. Defence workers are usually highly paid compared to civilian workers, which would undoubtedly make them reluctant to transfer to the civilian sector. Furthermore in some countries defence workers have high security of employment. For example in France the 'Military Planning Act' of 1984 gave 15,000 dockers and workers in Brest and Cherbourg employment guarantees for between 10 and 20 years. Workers are unlikely to want to change to civil production as this would threaten such guarantees.

Despite these difficulties, however, governments have considerable power to initiate a change from military to civilian production. Firstly, national governments are virtually the only purchasers of the products of the defence industries. They therefore have considerable power as 'consumers'. Secondly, governments provide much of the funding for research and development in the defence industries and are therefore in a position to redirect military R&D funding to other national priorities. Thirdly, governments themselves run defence establishments and therefore have considerable scope for redirecting military production.

A United Nations study of disarmament and development includes a list of products which could be produced by military industries converted to civilian production.

For example, the industries involved in producing tanks and other armoured vehicles could convert to producing:
- pipelines for irrigation
- heat pumps
- oil spillage pumps
- tidal barrage systems
- wave power systems
- wind power systems
- submersibles and other equipment for marine mineral exploitation and agriculture
- heavy duty pumps for canals
- hydrofoils
- rolling stock
- brewing equipment
- heavy earth moving equipment
- fire fighting equipment

The technical possibilities exist for conversion but the markets for such civilian products is not always strong. Governments, however, could influence the market for such goods by putting increased resources into such areas as development aid, energy conservation, and national industrial infrastructures.

Most economies undergo continual structural change due to such factors as technological change, international trade changes or changes in social habits. It is therefore not unknown for companies to diversify into different sectors of the economy to maintain their profitability. For example, tobacco companies in many countries have had to develop in other industrial areas, such as food processing or retailing. Mining equipment manufacturers have diversified into the electronic sector due to the decline in the mining industry. The diversifying of a company is rarely carried out by diversifying the work at a plant. It is more likely to be carried out by a process of buying companies in the new sector, thereby making the company less dependent on the old sector. This strategy whilst keeping the company viable does not solve the problem of redundancies in the declining sector.

This strategy, applied to the defence industry, would lessen the economic imperatives to export arms. Whilst redundancies cannot be lightly dismissed, there is no reason why redundancies from the defence sector should be considered any different to those brought about by the decline in textiles or the restructuring of the steel industry. It is government's responsibility, along with industry, to establish a retraining system which will allow workers to take part in the growth sectors of the economy. However, this is not an issue to be dealt with by this report.

Large scale change in the military sector has been undertaken on previous occasions. In the United States after the Second World War employment in defence related industries fell from 12 million to one million. During this time unemployment did not exceed four per cent. Structural change on such a large scale was made possible by the upsurge in demand for other industrial goods and services after the war. Also in the UK between 1953 and 1957 the government reduced the military budget by one-third in real terms. At the beginning of this period the unemployment rate was 1.5 per cent rising only to 1.79 per cent in 1957.

There will be no motivation for defence industries to convert to civilian production whilst the military sector remains highly profitable, particularly when contracts are 'cost plus'. As governments are the main purchasers of defence equipment they are responsible for creating an extremely lucrative defence sector. Recent restriction on defence budgets, however, and government efforts to obtain better value for money in defence purchases are beginning to reverse this trend. Such economic factors are pushing defence companies into becoming more aggressive arms exporters, in order to maintain the profitability of the company. In order to lessen the drive towards increased arms exports governments could support the industries in converting to civilian production by helping them to redirect their research and development funds away from military projects and into civil advanced technology R&D programmes such as ESPRIT, BRITE, RACE, EUREKA and equivalent national programmes.

The American Market

European arms exporters who face declining business elsewhere in the world are looking to expand arms exports in the United States. This has coincided with the US government's attempts to encourage collaboration between US and European defence contractors in order to mitigate criticism over the US trade surplus with its European allies in defence goods, and partly to deflect the dangerous drive, as they see it, towards a European Arms Industry.

Arms exports to the US from Europe and Canada reached a peak in 1985/86 of $2.9 billion, although the United States still sold $4.4 billion worth of arms to its allies in the same year. In the year ending 30 September 1986 France was the only country to have a defence trade surplus with the US. Britain overtook Canada as the largest single supplier with sales of £1 billion. Increased foreign sales in the American market and the Administration's attempt to encourage collaborative military projects with its allies have created a protectionist backlash in Congress. For example, the Glenn amendment to the proposed 1987-88 Defence Bill would bar SDI contracts going to a foreign company if there is a competent US company in the field, and the Trafficante amendment would place a five per cent cost premium on any foreign bid competing with a US company in an unemployment blackspot. Possibly in response to protectionist sentiments in Congress, the Defence Department is carrying out a review of the benefits to the United States of the Memoranda of Understanding on defence procurement which it has with 19 of its allies and friendly countries.

It is extremely difficult for arms manufacturers to sell in the American market. The Pentagon bureaucracy delays contracts considerably. Products also have to be 'Americanised', for example the Royal Ordnance in the UK had to make approximately 100 engineering changes to its mortar production for the American market. Production also has to be Americanised as well as the final product. Regulations require that the US produce, or at least be capable of producing, many of the arms used by the American services. To comply with this requirement the Royal Ordnance will provide the Pentagon with a 'technical data package' after it has made deliveries of the goods.

It is generally accepted in the American market that any foreign company with orders worth $100 million or over is obliged to produce the goods in the United States, through licensing agreements with American companies.

In view of the difficulties in selling in the United States market, and the growing protectionist attitude, many European companies are now seeking to maintain a toe hold in the market by collaborating with American defence companies. For example, Royal Ordnance has several gun projects with BMY, and Marconi has collaborated with Rockwell in order to win the HFAJ secure radio contracts.

Taking this strategy further, European companies are also now buying defence companies in the United States. Recent purchases have been made by UK companies GEC, Dowty, Lucas Aerospace and Smiths Industries. This has partly been made feasible by the cheap dollar.

The Pentagon is not keen on foreign companies buying into sensitive defence programmes and consequently there has been an increase in the number of programmes classified as 'no foreigners' and 'black programmes', programmes which are highly secret. Some foreign companies get around this problem by appointing a panel of American 'honorary' directors of the US subsidiary to deal with such programmes.

Japan: The Defence Industry

Article 9 of the Japanese Constitution includes the principle of the non-possession of war potential. This was changed in 1954 mainly due to pressure from the United States, and Japan then began to re-arm for self-defence. The Constitution also limits government spending on defence to one per cent of the Gross National Product. This level, however, was openly breached under the Nakasone Administration, and is likely to rise further. It must be remembered that one per cent of Japan's GNP is a significant sum. In 1988/89 Japan will be the largest military spender after the United States and the Soviet Union, with expenditure likely to reach $40 billion. The Japanese defence sector is small compared to those in other developed nations, accounting for only 0.5 per cent of Japan's industrial output (in the US this is approximately 11 per cent). The large defence contractors in Japan

are the old heavy industry companies:
- Mitsubishi
- Kawasaki
- Ishikawajima-Harima
- Sumitomo
- Fuji
- Hitiachi-Zosen (shipbuilder)

The Ministry of International Trade and Industry (MITI) ensures that in both military research and development and in production, work is spread around the different companies. Approximately 90 per cent of the defence procurement budget is spent in Japan, although much of this is on goods produced under licence from the United States. Japanese companies, however, are now beginning to undertake more of their own research and development, which allows the Japanese Defence Agency to purchase more from domestic suppliers. The money thus saved has been used to fund research and development into more sophisticated equipment.

It is likely that the Japanese defence industry will develop in a similar way to other industrial sectors, viz. the mastering of foreign technology, the development of a large, protected domestic market, leading to a massive concentration on exports.

Japanese defence industries are already looking at the possibilities of exploiting the global military markets in the medium-term (8-15 years). Two major non-defence companies have recently established research operations to investigate foreign military technology. It is expected that at the end of the research period they will have decided which products to develop.

In 1983 the Japanese government decided to exempt the transfer of military technology to the USA from the restrictions on military exports. As a consequence of this, in 1986 the Japanese government authorised two exports to the USA. One concerned a ship-building technique and the other, a seeker technology for shoulder-fired surface-to-air-missiles. There is still a ban on the export of finished military goods.

The US Defence Advanced Research Projects Agency has noted with some concern the increasing use of Japanese technology, particularly electronics, in American military projects. Japan has also exported Kawasaki C-1 transport and small boats to Iran and jeeps to the Nicaraguan military. These have been permitted on the grounds that they were for civilian use, a common ploy used by governments wishing to circumvent their own export regulations.

It is clear that Japan will become a major exporter of military equipment in the twenty-first century in direct competition with European manufacturers. This will have two main effects. Firstly, it

will become more difficult for European defence industries to sell on the world arms market; they should therefore develop strategies which place less reliance on military exports by
  (i) rationalisation of the European defence industry through collaboration;
  (ii) development of civil technologies.

Secondly, Japanese military equipment could become an attractive purchase for NATO and other European countries as it is likely to be cheaper and more reliable than that presently available.

The Arms Industry and the European Community

The Commission does not have specific powers to regulate the arms industry in the Member States. Article 223 of the Treaty of Rome exempts industry relevant to a country's national security from the normal competition rules. It contains a list of items which has not been updated. Some argue that, because this list does not include modern equipment, Article 223 could be circumvented.

The institutions of the European Community have no direct powers to regulate the export of arms from Member States. The Single European Act, however, prevents Member States from taking any action which would endanger the security of the countries of the European Community. The export of arms could endanger European security and therefore could legitimately be regulated by the Community.

European Political Co-operation has occasionally produced a co-ordinated policy on arms exports, for example the embargoes on Argentina during the Falklands war, and the embargo on Libya due to its support of terrorist activities in Europe.

The whole issue of Community involvement in defence is a very confused one. It is now time to clarify the position and decide upon future action.

Conclusions

Collecting evidence on the arms trade is a difficult task because governments are not open about their activities. Governments are, in fact, regularly breaching their own export regulations.

Governments are keen to develop the export potential of their military equipment because this reduces the unit costs. However, unit costs could be reduced by the longer production runs which would be the result of co-operation within the European defence sector. During the 1970s and 1980s the economic aspect of military sales seems to have become more important than their political aspect. Governments must acknowledge that military sales are essentially political in nature and this aspect must be given prime consideration.

The European Community should adopt a common arms export policy through European Political Co-operation. This is necessary for maintaining European security; we cannot tolerate a situation where arms sold by one Member State may endanger the security of another Member State. Adopting a common export policy would also share the short-term economic disadvantages of embargoes, i.e. one Member State will not be tempted to pick up the sales which are not permitted by another Member State. A common export policy would also make embargoes more effective.

Embargoes need to be closely monitored and sanctions against offending companies, or government officials, must be applied. Governments must adhere to the spirit of export regulations as well as to the letter of the law. They must also make greater efforts to verify the details of proposed exports.

Before we attempt to control the arms trade in any way, we must establish what is going on. Firstly, we must establish an EC register of arms transfers. Secondly, the European Parliament must investigate further the nature of the arms trade through a committee of enquiry.

Since this report was originally drafted substantial changes have taken place with the Gorbachev proposals for unilateral conventional disarmament made at the UN General Assembly offering amongst other things arms conversion of three Soviet Weapons Manufacturing complexes for which European suggestions are being sought. These new elements will have to be taken into account.

In attempting to control the arms trade we are recognising that arms are not simply a commercial product — we are recognising that the sale of arms also has profound political and social effects for humankind.

Reference

1. This is the first opportunity that the European Parliament has had to discuss the export of arms from the European Community in detail. Previous reports have discussed exports but only in conjunction with other issues. The Trivelli Report in 1985 looked at arms exports in relation to Third World economic problems; in effect looking at the social, economic and political consequences of European Arms exports.

   The Fergusson Report of 1983 looked at arms exports in relation to a common industrial policy. It urged the development of co-operative arrangements for the production of arms and the removal of trade barriers to create a common defence market in Europe. It noted the Dankert Report on Arms Procurement made to the Western European Union in 1977. This report commented that a common defence market would reduce the pressures to export to the Third World and therefore exports could be limited to those perceived to be in the interest of Europe according to a commonly-defined external policy.

The Committee on External Economic Relations in reviewing the Fergusson Report recommended that: arms exports between Member States of the European Community should be unrestricted; other states could be accorded the same status as Member States; specific arms deals outside these states could be agreed after consultation with national governments within European Political Co-operation and with the European Parliament; exports to other countries should be restricted.

ENDpapers 19, Spring 1989

43. Europe — The Lost Agenda

June 15 is likely to see the same rising tide of apathy for the third direct elections to the European Parliament as characterised the two previous elections in 1979 and 1984, with voting rates running at about one in three. Any enthusiasm there is may be for using the election — like any election — as a referendum on a third term Tory Government's handling of the poll tax and the National Health Service, of the economy and food quality. *Yet this would be a missed opportunity for the Labour Movement.*

Whatever image the European Parliament has with the general public — part justified, part a myth created to feed anti-European sentiment — its growing influence over legislation as well as its budgetary powers mean it can no longer be ignored. Admittedly, the procedures whereby this detailed scrutiny takes place are byzantine; not dissimilar from many national parliamentary procedures. Yet if the process is incomprehensible the product is not. Parliament has exerted considerable influence on health and safety and environmental legislation. It has made substantial progress in limiting the growth of Common Agricultural Policy (CAP) spending and hence provided extra funds for social and regional spending and research. Yet these developments have largely gone unrecognised. Where a parliamentary initiative has attracted major publicity, as with the recent public hearing on fraud in the Community, public interest has been engaged by the information emerging from the event itself about the British Government's role in blocking investigations, rather than turned towards the institution which provided the political platform.

However, the third legislature, which will run until 1994, covers a period which will be of determining significance for the future development of the European Community. It is here that the choice will be made between *Bruges* and *Bournemouth*: between a narrow pinched free market Europe, fit for multinationals, as advocated by Mrs Thatcher in Bruges last September, and the other possible

Europe where social progress marches step by step with economic integration, as outlined in the speech by Jacques Delors, President of the European Commission, to the last Congress of the TUC.

The battle will be around a number of issues. The first will be the creation of the 'internal market' and 1992. It is not a question of whether we support the internal market objective; the globalisation of the industrial economy is proceeding so rapidly that many of the measures put forward just three years ago as part of the market opening package would have had to be implemented anyway by the Member States to keep themselves competitive in the world market. Here the issues are the direction of the national market and the role of public authorities in economic management, the role of trade unions in policy making at a European level, and the scale and power of planning instruments available at local, national and European level.

The European Parliament must determine a far broader agenda for a social Europe encompassing not only minimum standards for health and safety at work, but welfare rights and the management of the internal market. We must continue to fight for women's rights and ensure that the opening of the internal barriers to the movement of labour does not create a white fortress Europe closed to the third world and whose people inside — Europe's thirteenth State — are second-class citizens without the same rights and duties as everyone else. We have to ensure that while tools of economic management have been surrendered at national level after 1992 broader and more powerful weapons exist to intervene in research, training and the regions at a European level.

The second issue will be monetary integration. Socialists in Government have been bedevilled by the vulnerability of national currencies. Further development of the internal market would seem to require a common strategy on interest rates, without which rapid capital flows would have disastrous social consequences. With growing support for monetary union across the political spectrum, the key question for socialists is how it is possible to make monetary integration politically accountable and socially progressive by maximising its authority, while maintaining the rights of national governments to pursue investment strategies that allow broad and frequent interventions in industry.

The third area of dispute will be over the future financing of the European Community. The currently agreed ceiling for existing own resources will probably be reached in 1992. What, therefore, is the appropriate size of the budget at this stage of the development of the Community? Are present methods of financing suitable (now mostly through VAT, customs duties and agricultural levies with top-up contributions from Member States)? Are controls on spending sufficient, with widespread fraud in the agricultural sector resulting from the failure of Member States co-operating together to eliminate it. Strengthening controls should be a pre-condition for increasing the budget.

While recognising that the increased CAP spending has been brought under control, socialists must argue for further cutbacks on a policy that serves neither the interests of the consumers nor producers, with the sole exception of the multinational agri-capital companies. By cutting back CAP subsidies further resources can be released for productive public investment in infrastructure and regional spending, with special emphasis on research spending close to the market which will be the key to Europe's future competitiveness. After the elections the *Framework Programme* of Community research will be under review. This will be the opportunity to press for a re-orientation of Community research to include environmental and social objectives in its remit and the gearing of programmes to Community needs and resources rather than to meeting the preoccupations of Europe's multinationals determined to ape the USA and Japan. *Increased own resources are justified to provide the means for economic intervention in the economy*, but not to fill the ever ready maws of Europe's food stores.

The choices made and the battles fought will start to determine which vision of Europe is going to prevail. The European Parliament is hampered in determining these issues because of the *democratic deficit*. Although its power has increased the Parliament has not filled the vacuum created by the structural inability of national parliaments to preserve their prerogatives. Power has not just seeped from Westminster to Brussels; the boardrooms of multinational corporations, the top tables at Gorbachev-Reagan/Bush summits have made national sovereignty a hollow concept. Increasingly issues are European, if not global; no individual nation state can control Ford or IBM, preserve the ozone layer or insulate itself from Chernobyl.

National parliaments have lost power under the Treaty of Rome and evolving capitalism. Even if they were to scrutinise European legislation more efficiently, they could not mandate their Ministers in the Council without creating total paralysis in Community decision making. Socialists must devise means of overcoming the *democratic deficit*. That may not mean a grandiose new treaty of union; but it must give the European Parliament a stronger role in shaping the future, whether it be structuring the internal market, protecting living and working standards, or pursuing new social goals.

These are the issues that need debating with the electorate between now and June 15; trivialisation and attempts to outbid the Prime Minister in 'little Englander' rhetoric would be a pointless distraction that would fool no-one, let alone the electorate.

Julian Priestley and Glyn Ford, Tribune, 12 May 1989

44. Labour in Europe

Labour is now the Party of Europe. For the first time since the formation of the European Community the Labour Party is now far more committed and enthusiastic than the Conservative Party. This transformation has not taken place overnight. It has come through the slow dawning within the Labour Party of new realities both home and abroad. The era of the small independent nation state has passed on, if it was ever truly with us. Now multinational industrial organisation and worldwide environmental interdependency require transfrontier decision-making. Also, ten years on from the third Tory victory many trade union leaders see the European Commission and Parliament as the only hope for improving the working environment and their role in tripartite social dialogue.

The problem is that this political conversion has been one of politics best kept secrets. Labour has proceeded either with crab-like stealth or undue hesitancy, or both. The decision was made to change Labour's European itinerary at last October's Party Conference. But few could criticise those that missed the formal apostasy for it was drowned in the noise and rancour of the defence debate. What is more surprising is that so few commentators have noticed how this sea-change has started to colour the whole of Labour's policy map.

In contrast, long-term divisions in the Tory Party over Europe are now being paraded in public, triggered by Mrs Thatcher's Bruges Speech. Here she firmly reclaimed the mantle of Enoch Powell and proclaimed that 'Europe' was to be a free trade area and nothing else, a Continent whose sole guiding principles were to be de-regulation and de-control. As she has already abolished 'community' in the United Kingdom with a regal wave, perhaps it is hardly surprising she would like to replicate the same tunnel vision politics at European level. Yet many in the Tory Party are unhappy with this 'fog in the Channel, Continent cut-off' style of politics. Michael Heseltine seems to be offering himself as leader of some kind of guerrilla movement amongst the Conservatives.

Yet faint stirrings of opposition to this reconstituted politics of imperialism, with all its grandeur and all its irrevelance, only seems to confirm how the Labour Party has leapfrogged over Conservative retrenchment to become the one Party that takes constructing a *communitaire* Europe seriously. Britain's imperial pretensions are more likely to provoke a guffaw of laughter than a cry of outrage from Community and third world leaders these days.

Compared to earlier debates over attitudes towards Europe in Britain the ground has shifted. The *European Movement* and the *Get Britain Out Campaign* once fought the issue out on the broad simple plains of principle. Now the tide of history has passed them by, and both are marooned organisations, isolated from contemporary politics, waiting for the passage of time to finally extinguish greying memberships. The debate on principle has been resolved, as it has been rendered redundant, by the pattern of worldwide industrial and environmental development. For the European Commission's plans for 1992 and the creation of a single internal market are a symptom, not a cause, of late capitalist re-ordering. What the debate is about now is the kind of Europe we are going to build. In that regard Mrs Thatcher is totally isolated with her tired Atlanticism and visceral imperialism.

In the March session of the European Parliament a vote was taken on a resolution which covered the free movement of workers, social security rights (including pensions) and supporting the goal of bringing national benefits into line with the best available. It called for a European employment policy based on improving health and safety measures, and giving special help for the weaker members of society. It also backed the Commission's intention to draw up a European company statute with an option to include a clause on worker participation and moves to enhance industrial democracy. When a vote was called, it was carried 238 for to 34 against. With a solitary exception, *all those voting against were British Tory MEPs*. How ironic that, after years of division on the left, it is now Britain's right of centre forces that appear so divided and so far adrift from their potential European allies among Gaullists and Christian Democrats.

The opposite is true of the British Labour Party. Here the Party has signed, almost without reservation, the joint socialist manifesto for the European elections. But what kind of Europe is Labour committed to building? This is now clear. We demand that progress towards the 1992 Single European Market must be accompanied by an *upward* harmonisation of the social wage both here in Britain and across Europe. This means the adoption of a Social Charter to improve *inter alia* training, pay (European minimum wage), health and safety, maternity rights, childcare, and pensions. Trade unions must have a full role in planning this legislation and its workplace implementation. Unless this is done the consequences when the barriers start to fall will be massive social disruption and social dumping as industry ups sticks and peregrinates around Europe looking for optimal conditions for relocation. It is the recognition of this threat that has made Europe's Christian Democrat Parties support the need for a Peoples' Europe. Labour and the Socialist Group would want to go further than them, but unlike the Conservatives we would at least be setting out on the same journey.

Industry requires massive injections of both public and private investment if it is to remain competitive with Japan and the United States. Increasingly this will come from an enlarged European Community R&D Budget. Sector by sector small nation states are no longer capable of competing and beating the world's industrial superpowers. Only in Britain are we sufficiently self-deluding that we believe, as a Junior Minister said last year, that the best way to obtain industrial innovation is by tax relief to entrepreneurs. The Japanese are laughing all the way to the research lab.

Yet, if 1992 is not to suck economic activity towards the geographical centre of the Community, then we need the countervailing forces of substantial and sustained regional spending to plant and nurture new sources of economic activity in those areas suffering from the decline of traditional industry. To achieve this Britain will require a large and well trained workforce. At the moment we train a lower proportion of young people than they do in South Korea. The European Social Fund must be used to boost such training, with special emphasis towards women and ethnic minorities who all too often have lost out in their initial education.

All of this is going to produce a massive restructuring of European industry. This process will have to be managed and will require the involvement of national governments, local authorities and the trade unions across Europe. Labour must organise at the same levels of aggregation as capital, and one key element of that is European.

Common Security is another area of progress. Gorbachev, because of the threatening upheavals in Soviet society, has been forced to offer reductions in military spending to free resources for civilian investment. The resulting INF deal is for Europeans, and Central Europeans in particular, no more than a brief hiatus before continued progress. At the moment, because short-range nuclear forces have been retained, any nuclear conflict would initially be fought out across the two Germanys. Helmut Kohl reads German public opinion well when he comes out against NATO nuclear modernisation. It threatens to unpick the INF deal, while serving

US military interests. European and American industrial, economic and financial interests are beginning to sharply diverge as we see the start of the decline of a Great Power. Europe needs to look after its own interests by becoming a more semi-detached partner in arrangements that put its interests second to those of the United States. In the European Community Socialists want to create the conditions for achieving and maintaining a denuclearised Europe, both East and West, through Common Security, increased trade, and cultural interdependency.

The next decade will see the construction of a new Europe. The choice in front of us is clear. We can reinforce Napolean's dictum that we are a nation of shopkeepers by treating Europe as merely a trading area and nothing else, or we can try to create a Community. We need a Europe where we protect and enhance the quality of the environment and life. A Europe in partnership with rather than dominating over the third world. A community where everyone living in Europe has the same rights and duties, where we look outwards, rather than inwards, where we go forwards together united as all the different colours of Europe.

Glyn Ford and Carole Tongue
Morning Star, 20 June 1989

45. We Can Open a Second Front in Europe

Our pessimism was unjustified (*Tribune,* May 12). The greater turnout in Britain for the European elections sets public participation and interest in the European Community on a higher path, and gives the newly-elected MEPs significantly more authority than before.

For the first time, some serious discussion took place in Britain on European issues: the social dimension *versus* a crude *laissez faire* approach to the internal market; the higher standards of health care and welfare in most Community countries; the 'sovereignty' debate (mostly an internal one in the Tory Party).

The election result — 45 seats for Labour, 32 for the Tories — is the first clear repudiation of 10 years of Thatcherism, and a vote against the whole gamut of government policies from the poll tax to water privatisation and the dismantling of the health service. It is also an endorsement of Labour's more positive approach to the EC, and its attitude towards the social dimension of the internal market.

The swing to the Left in Britain was reflected elsewhere in the Community. The Left gained in Portugal, Ireland and Denmark. In

Spain, no territory was conceded, despite the travails of Felipe Gonzalez' government. Only in Greece and France was significant ground lost. No major change was registered in West Germany, Italy and the Benelux countries.

Now, with 182 seats, the Socialists strengthen their position as the largest single political group in the Parliament. The Christian Democrats come next, with 123. Taken together with the reduced presence of the Communists, the Greens (now strongly represented in the Parliament, following poll successes in France, Germany and Italy), sundry radicals and independent socialists, the Left commands a wafer-thin overall majority for the first time.

This majority is, by its very nature, fragile. The Greens, and on some issues the Communists, are unreliable allies. The French Greens, who make up a significant part of the new Green group, have concerns quite different from those of the socialist tradition. Discipline within the Socialist Group is not strong; it will not be easy to build up a resistant voting force based on several such disparate groups.

It is not just crude numbers that count in the European Parliament; assiduous attendance, participation in committees and the amount of work MEPs are prepared to put in will be of greater importance than ever. The complexion of the Parliament will change by an extent greater than the shift to the Left in its composition.

The British Labour Group now provides a quarter of the membership of the Socialist Group and brings with it the psychological impetus of our victory. It would be a crime if our new found potential for influence was dissipated or abused.

The exercise of formal powers by the Parliament requires it to act by *qualified* majority. To impose its will in the budgetary procedure, to stand any chance of prevailing on legislation, or to throw out the Commission, requires the Parliament to vote by a majority of its *members*, and by either three-fifths or two-thirds of the votes cast.

Despite its improved position, the Left will be forced to seek accommodations with the more progressive elements on the Right if it wishes to exercise power effectively. This need not mean a lowest common denominator approach, or cosy chumming up with the Christian Democrats; but it will act as a constraint on any action by the Left majority.

On the other hand, formal powers are one thing — influences and impact another. The Parliament and the Commission working together can push forward priority issues for the Left such as environmental standards and the Social Charter. The Parliament can cajole, threaten, encourage and ultimately force the Commission to bring forward proposals to make the fairly vague objectives of the Charter a reality. In particular, the Parliament can influence the Commission on the legal base for its social dimension proposals, with only limited recourse to unanimity, thus reducing the opportunities for Margaret Thatcher to veto social legislation. There is Centre-Right support for a social dimension to Europe; we must demand step-by-step progress on social harmonisation alongside the creation of the 'internal market'.

When even Christian Democrats are anxious to attack Mrs Thatcher, we can open a second front in Europe against her.

More broadly, the Parliament will be able to use its rights to initiate action, and its control over its own agenda, to force the pace on a number of Left priorities; peace and disarmament questions, increasing co-operation with Comecon countries; a vastly-strengthened Lomé IV Convention on Third World trade with more resources, and a greater emphasis on the environmental and women's rights aspects of development.

Glyn Ford and Julian Priestley, Tribune, 23 June 1989

46. Testimony to the House of Commons Foreign Affairs Committee on the Single European Act

Examination of Witnesses

Mr Glyn Ford, MEP, Leader of the British Labour Group, European Parliament and Mr Chris Piening, Institutional Affairs Committee, examined.

Chairman

159. Mr Ford, Mr Piening, welcome to you. We thank you very much indeed for coming to the Committee this afternoon to help us with our studies. As you know, Mr Ford, we are looking at the Single European Act and the way in which it has affected our own policy and the stages that may lie beyond it. Would you like to start with a short statement on how you see the scene in the light of those concerns?

(Mr Ford) Thank you very much. We are very pleased to be here, at your invitation, to give evidence to this Committee. Mr Piening, who is the first secretary of the Institutional Affairs Committee of the Parliament, will deal with any detailed questions you have about the operation of the Act. I understand from your visit last week you may have heard enough of the details but there may be some further

questions, and I thank you for the opportunity of a brief introduction. What I want to talk about is some of the further stages which seem to be the most interesting areas in light of some of the recent political developments which have taken place in Europe. From the point of view of the majority of European parliamentarians, there is a view that we are seeing a new, emerging state in an embryonic form, so it is necessary to have a political forum at the same level of economic activity, which is going to be a European one. On a worldwide scale, we are seeing global regionalism occurring with the creation of three major industrial powers — Japan, United States and Europe — and we are going to see competition between those three as to which is going to be the dominant power in the world over the next 50 years. Firstly, we are likely to see the creation of a Europe at an industrial level, secondly, at a financial level and, thirdly, at a security level, if the pattern of past global development is to be followed in Europe. It is therefore vital for us to have democratic accountability, otherwise we will be in a situation where we will be surrendering democratic powers which have been fought for over decades and more. A lot of power has gone from national parliaments, including Westminster. That power has not gone to the European Parliament, it has either gone to the Commission, where it is now very clear the Commission make decisions which at one time were made at Westminster level, or more importantly it has gone to the Council of Ministers, and the Council of Ministers of course meet in secret and are unaccountable. We have to make it clear when we are talking about the need for new powers for the European Parliament, we are not talking about taking fresh power from Westminster. It has been suggested that these powers are not necessary because there is the possibility of a scrutiny committee here in Westminster controlling the Council of Ministers and the Commission. There are two objections to that; firstly it is not viable if it does its job, because if we have 12 scrutiny committees around the European Community mandating the various members of their national governments, then we are going to be in a situation of total paralysis. Secondly, and probably more realistically, I do not think there is very much appreciation of the scale and extent of what is going on in the European Community, which can be exampled by one small story I was told recently about an international public affairs body. Market Access (Europe) Ltd, who did a survey of MPs on the 1992 programme and they listed a set of items of legislation and asked which was going to be most important for Europe over the coming decades: 75 per cent of the MPs — and I presume maybe even some of you — actually replied the harmonisation of weights and measures was going to be the key issue for the next decade. That, as a basis of scrutiny, bodes ill for the United Kingdom in Europe. The European Parliament's power has increased under the Single European Act but it has not overcome the vacuum created by the structural inability of national parliaments to preserve their own prerogatives. It is rather ridiculous that we have the situation now where social matters have to be unanimously agreed in the Council of Ministers and yet single market legislation only requires qualified majority voting. I think the future lies in many senses with the Parliament and the Commission working together and I think it is fairly clear that when the Inter-Governmental Conference commences, which has been promised by President Mitterrand, Parliament will push for further Treaty modifications than the ones which are necessary purely for economic and monetary union, in the areas of the powers of Parliament and in terms of social legislation. Certainly the kind of issues Parliament will want to raise there will firstly be a much stronger right of initiative in the European Parliament, secondly the possibility of selecting the successor to Jacques Delors as the President of the Commission, and the possibility thirdly of individual censure of commissioners. One of the problems with our censorship powers is that they are rather blunt and cannot be directed in particular areas. But we do not necessarily have to wait for Treaty modifications before we make progress, we have the possibility of bilateral agreement with the Commission. I wrote some months ago in an article published in *Tribune* that we should reach a bilateral agreement with the Commission: "Any amendment retabled at the second reading stage, under the co-operation procedure which applies to most 1992 legislation, should automatically be taken on board by the Commission, so preventing the Council of Ministers from rejecting it except by a unanimous vote. Any proposal or common position rejected by Parliament should be withdrawn, and hence killed off, by the Commission. Finally, the conciliation procedure, the three-month negotiating mechanism between the European Parliament and the Council, should be extended to cover all major legislation. These changes require no Treaty change and could be implemented by simple agreements between the two institutions involved. Finally, with respect to the Social Charter, some pressure has been put by Parliament on the current President of the Council that if we can only get an agreement of 11 to 1 we can proceed by inter-institutional agreement which does not require unanimity in the Council to proceed. These are the kind of issues I believe Parliament is going to be raising in terms of the Inter-Governmental Conference and in the Institutional Affairs

Committee, and these are the kind of issues I believe your Committee needs to address itself to.

160. *(Chairman)* Thank you very much. I was interested myself in that reference to inter-institutional agreements. This is just one more procedure between the different institutions in the Community that we would like to learn more about. How do you feel that the SEA has already changed the balance between the institutions, even before any of the agreements you have just suggested have been struck? Do you feel there has been a change already since the Act came in?

(Mr Ford) Yes, it has been a fairly slow but significant change in that the views of the Parliament have to be taken much more seriously by the Commission than they have been in the past. I think it has also changed the operating procedures of Parliament which tended in the past very often to have to hunt around for things to do. We now find our workload has increased significantly and much of our time is spent on Single European Act matters which in the past were not debated at the same level of detail because we did not have the same degree of influence. Generally we find the direct clashes between the Commission and Parliament over these matters are comparatively small. What the Commission tends to do, particularly on the amendments, is to take Parliament's views on board very often and we are finding ourselves now being used as a channel for lobbyists from trade unions and industry in a way we were not in the past, because we can actually have an influence on the final outcome of the legislation where it is not seen as a major political battleground.

161. *(Chairman)* When you speak of the Parliament, of what does the bulk, the centre of gravity, of the Parliament consist? Is it genuinely a parliament or is it in fact the two largest parties, which are yourselves and the Christian Democratic Group, getting together and agreeing on what the line should be and everyone else being left aside?

(Mr Ford) It is a combination of a variety of different factors. Up to now the new Parliament is still settling down, and the committees have not got down to serious work in many cases, but in committee you get a different operation from the one in the full plenary session. In committees it is a fairly open debate with very few pre-arranged deals going on. In the Parliament itself, of course, the weight of the Socialist Group and the PPE can deliver the necessary 260 votes for passing amendments under the Single European Act. Jean Pierre Cot, the Chairman of the Socialist Group, has made it clear that his strategy as Leader of the Socialist Group is to build a coalition of the left before opening out to the centre. That means we do pay more

attention to the two small Communist Groups and the Green Group and Regional Group than we might do purely on the basis of weight of numbers.

Mr Shore

162. I have two questions. One is concerned with your assessment, Mr Ford, of the impact of the SEA on the Council of Ministers and the way that they behave. My second question is one to which I am sure all of us would like to know the answer; it had not been in our minds before you raised it. Can you say more about inter-institutional co-operation as a means of getting around, as it were, the situation in which one Member country does not go along with the other eleven?

(Mr Ford) To deal with the questions one at a time, I do not know whether Mr Piening has anything to add, but at the Council of Ministers level I think they have tended to go along with many of the detailed amendments which have been proposed by the Parliament and accepted by the Commission. I do not know of any particular clashes which have taken place there, so in that sense the Parliament is now becoming a fairly effective amending body over small-scale issues. Maybe Mr Piening has something to add as First Secretary of the Institutional Affairs Committee; he has been following this more closely than I have. On the second point, if you are talking about the possibility of an inter-institutional agreement, there is procedure, as I understand it — I am not a constitutional lawyer — which actually allows the Parliament, Commission and the Council of Ministers to act by joint agreement. We have done this on one occasion in the comparatively recent past where there was actually a solemn declaration against racism and xenophobia. That was approved by the Council of Ministers, the Commission and the Parliament. That was agreed, and according to the lawyers it acts as an addendum to the Treaty of Rome. Certainly, the lawyers who have given answers to questions about the competence of the Parliament now to deal with issues of racial discrimination quote this inter-institutional agreement and solemn declaration. The suggestion was made last week in the debate in Parliament following the Mitterrand speech that the same kind of procedure should be used with respect to the Social Charter, because, as I said before, you do not need unanimity in the Council of Ministers to agree to sign an inter-institutional agreement. I think the more important point to make in one sense is that in the long-term Britain certainly cannot be in a position of being the odd one out of 12 continually, because if you are voting 11-1, 11-1, 11-1 continually,

you find out in the end the vote is actually going to be 11-0, and that is partly due to the fact that Mitterrand promised new negotiations on the Treaty in his speech in Strasbourg which seems to be his way of solving the problem of one country trying to block progress in a whole series of areas which are considered important for the other eleven.

163. *(Mr Shore)* Does the inter-institutional agreement allow you to go beyond, as it were, a declaration? Can anything be based upon it without the consent of all twelve which would have legislative effect inside the Community?

(Mr Ford) You may need to talk to somebody who is better qualified in law than I am, but I understand that once you have the agreement you can proceed into law subject to the Treaty base. With regard to the Social Charter, you can use 118A as a basis for making progress in a series of areas which would fall within the broad remit of the Social Charter. We would hope that 118A would be used and interpreted on its widest possible basis. I understand that to challenge the Commission's interpretation of the legal base requires unanimity in the Council, which we are not likely to get, or some legal action by a Member State concerned which is going to take a considerable period of time, so with the necessary will-power, which may or may not be there, the Commission could make substantial progress on Social Charter issues.

Chairman

164. Would Mr Piening like to say a word on the particular issue of inter-institutional agreements?

(Mr Piening) Thank you. I would like to make perhaps a couple of points. First of all, Glyn Ford referred to the joint declarations which have been made in the past: the example of racism and xenophobia was one. There are in fact now two which are possibilities within the next few months. One would be a joint declaration by the institutions and those Member States who wish to be party to it on the Social Charter. The President of the European Parliament is keen himself to put his signature to such a joint declaration, and there is a feeling in the European Parliament, and certainly in the Institutional Affairs Committee, that such support by the Parliament as an institution should be given to the Social Charter, or a declaration on the Social Charter, regardless of how many Member States actually sign the Charter, so if only eleven out of twelve signed, it would not be seen as an impediment by the President of the Parliament to his putting his own signature to it. Another area where there is an attempt being made by Parliament

to have a joint declaration is on the declaration of fundamental rights and freedoms which Parliament itself adopted earlier in 1989. Ultimately, the Parliament would like to see this appended to or incorporated in the Treaties. The declaration of fundamental rights and freedoms is not the same as the declaration on social rights, which is another way of describing the Social Charter, but would in some ways duplicate the Convention on Human Rights of the Council of Europe. This would be something which could only be put into the Treaties provided all the Member State governments agreed, so it could not be the subject of an inter-institutional declaration. It would give it sufficient weight that subsequently when Treaty amendments were being discussed in the forum of an Inter-Governmental Conference a decision could be taken at that stage to append it to the Treaties. Another example of inter-institutional agreements is the conciliation procedure, which I think in any case is a rather interesting example of co-operation between the Parliament and the Council. The conciliation procedure applies at present only to Acts having financial implications; it applies particularly to Article 203 of the Treaty and the budget itself, but can also apply to research or environmental measures, for example, where spending is involved. The European Parliament is saying this conciliation procedure should be extended to cover other areas of legislation where at present there is no room for discussion between Council and Parliament on the content of possible legislation, so very often the proposal which is before the Parliament has to be voted on without the benefit of some discussion or exchange with the Council on the substance. A conciliation procedure extension could be agreed by inter-institutional agreement and would therefore provide more of an opportunity for Parliament to discuss specific legislative matters before they come to vote, and could possibly remove many of the misunderstandings which at present are at the basis of differences of opinion on Single European Act legislation.

165. *(Chairman)* So, in all these ways one out of line with the other eleven could simply be bypassed?

(Mr Piening) I do not think it is correct to say that in actual legislative decision-making inter-institutional agreements can bypass the eleven. Where laws are being decided in the Council there is no way an inter-institutional agreement can, for example, circumvent the necessity for a qualified majority, if that is what is required, or unanimity, in cases where that is required.

Chairman: let us turn to something slightly different to do with lobbying.

Mr Canavan

166. Presumably, the European Commission has stepped up its efforts to lobby Members of the European Parliament, either individually or collectively, in groups or parliamentary committees, to explain its draft proposals in some detail. How much of an increase has taken place in that type of lobbying and communication on the part of the Commission?

(*Mr Ford*) It is difficult to measure exactly but certainly there is a degree of willingness to talk to and meet with members of the European Parliament that seems to be stronger now than has been in the past. Certainly, for example, members of the socialist group dine monthly with the socialist commissioners and I have noticed the attendance of the commissioners has increased rather remarkably over the last few months.

167. (*Mr Canavan*) So is it done mainly through wining and dining? No formal meetings?

(*Mr Ford*) There are formal meetings with members of the Commission, normally with small groups of MEPs from relevant committees. It tends to be done at committee level. There is strong contact between various political groups and the cabinets of various commissioners and there is a willingness to provide information to MEPs which would be remarkable in British parliamentary terms.

168. (*Mr Canavan*) And there has been a marked increase?

(*Mr Ford*) There has been an increase. I would not want to go as far as 'marked'. It is difficult to measure. Obviously since the election, interest in the socialist group and even the British Labour delegation has increased because of our increased strength and necessity of having us on board if they want certain things to go through.

169. (*Mr Canavan*) What other effect has the Single European Act had on the Commission and its role?

(*Mr Ford*) A willingness to take on board some of the detailed amendments. In the past the Commission was always reasonably sympathetic to proposals from the Parliament, now they want to pick the ground on which they have major battles, and are prepared to make concessions on some of the less important issues from their point of view, which may be very important from the point of view of trade unions, industry or other pressure groups. In that sense the Commission clearly want to accommodate the Parliament as far as it reasonably feels it can, and only select a small amount of items on which to try to over-throw Parliament's decision.

170. (*Mr Canavan*) Are you satisfied the discussions you have with the Commission are full and frank?

(Mr Ford) It varies from commissioner to commissioner, but it seems to me generally the Commission tends to try and be as helpful as possible within the limits of its own political position and its collegiate role.

Chairman: Can we turn now to future developments, which you have already mentioned in your opening statement.

Mr Rowlands

171. You did describe to us quite fully some of the changes you would like to see in the functional roles of the European Parliament, particularly the extension of the co-operation procedure into other areas. I do not know whether you would wish to elaborate on that, or more particularly on the greater role you might envisage the European Parliament having in financing and revenue-gathering processes, which I do not think you included in your opening statement?

(Mr Ford) In terms of co-operation procedures, if we are going to extend them much wider than we do now, there would need to be an agreement made by the Commission and the Council of Ministers, possibly through Treaty amendments. In terms of financing and revenue, I do not see that being something which is likely to come in the near future. At the moment we are having discussions in the Parliament — and I make it clear I have a lot of sympathy for increased power for the Parliament, but I do not necessarily support all the proposals which are likely to be put forward in these matters. I wanted to alert the Committee to some of the proposals which will be pressed by those members of the European Parliament that are markedly more federalist than the British delegation would be on both sides of the political spectrum.

172. *(Mr Rowlands)* In the spectrum of degrees of federalism, where does the group stand?

(Mr Ford) The group has not established a formal position on the matter, so it is a question of feeling. I would think that apart from the Danes, the British Labour delegation would still be the least federalistic group within the socialist group.

173. *(Mr Rowlands)* There is a major Inter-Governmental Conference coming up. The agenda will be about EMU but there might be other items on it or you might wish to see other items on it. Have you any thoughts to offer us on that?

(Mr Ford) In terms of the Inter-Governmental Conference, the European Parliament would certainly be pressing for some representation there. That has been clear from a number of statements which have been made by leaders of various political

groups and the President of the Parliament feels he should be represented there in some way. The point I made earlier was that one of a number of issues we would want to have on the agenda which went further than monetary and economic union would be the powers of the Parliament. There seemed to be some hints in President Mitterrand's speech to the European Parliament last week that he saw the agenda being wider in that way as well.

174. *(Mr Rowlands)* That the future powers of the European Parliament would be an item on the agenda itself?

(Mr Ford) Yes.

Chairman

175. Would that not be a contradiction in terms if this is an Inter-Governmental Conference — that the European Parliament should be represented on it? Is that not rather a puzzling mixture?

(Mr Ford) I have not reached the exalted heights of the Presidency of the European Parliament but I understand that certainly at summit meetings in the past there has been representation and observer status for representatives of Parliament, namely the President. It would seem to me there is therefore some custom and practice for allowing some input from the Parliament on these matters.

(Mr Piening) At the last Inter-Governmental Conference which discussed the Single European Act and decided on that, the Commission as another Community institution was present throughout the discussions, and as Mr Ford says at certain meetings, members of the Parliament were present. Article 236 of the Treaty is in that sense one of these difficult things because it does say specifically that any Treaty change must be decided by representatives of the Member States, in other words by the governments; so if one were to want to change the Treaty to allow institutions to take part in Treaty amendments, you would first have to modify Article 236, but you cannot do that with the participation of the Parliament or the Commission. So in the past, as I say, the Commission has been present, with Parliament present on an unofficial basis, and the European Parliament would regard that as being a precedent which would or should allow Parliament to participate on a fuller basis in any future Inter-Governmental Conference.

Mr Rowlands

176. Returning to one specific aspect about the future role and functions of the European Parliament, the powers and influence of

this place, Westminster, historically were built on scrutinising and exposing maladministration and corruption. Both seem to exist in the European Community but the European Parliament has played virtually no part in exposing or revealing them — I have not got the impression they have played a significant role or part. Have you any thoughts on how the European Parliament might play what is one of the more traditional functions of a parliament?

(*Mr Ford*) Firstly, the Parliament has played some role in investigating certainly the issue of fraud; we have a budgetary control committee which has a reputation in the European Parliament for being fairly hard on some of these matters, and I believe the budgetary control committee has not got the publicity it deserves for the role it has actually played. Secondly, I have to say from my experience as chairman of the committee of inquiry into the growth of racism and fascism in Europe, it becomes very difficult to conduct such inquiries, or inquiries into fraud by analogy, without the right to demand the presence of witnesses. I think if we are talking about how Parliament could increase its powers in this regard, it would be essential to have witnesses and people in attendance who otherwise might wish to decline.

177. (*Mr Rowlands*) So is that a part of your agenda?

(*Mr Ford*) It is certainly not one which has been discussed a lot but it seems to me those people who are concerned with the budgetary control committee would be very keen to have powers like you have in the House of Commons, to demand the presence of witnesses. At the moment the problem is if anybody is going to have a particularly rough time on the budgetary control committee, apart from the staff of the Commission or the Parliament, they do not attend.

Chairman

178. Have you any views on the likely timing of when this great conference might get going and when it might run to and what might come out the other end?

(*Mr Ford*) My preference would be fairly quickly. President Mitterrand seemed to indicate the first meeting may be next September.

(*Mr Piening*) If I might add something, according to the Madrid Summit, the Inter-Governmental Conference, if it is convened, will be convened after the beginning of the first stage of the Delors procedure, which is next July, so theoretically it could start at any time after next July, but there was also an agreement that full and adequate preparation would need to be made, and it is a matter of definition by the governments involved as to when those preparations are complete.

179. *(Chairman)* So, we are assuming, to take your words, that the first stage of the Delors proposals, including the provision that all Members of the European Monetary System participate in the exchange rate grid, is up and running by July of next year, and that the conference will start?

(Mr Piening) That is my understanding of what was agreed at Madrid, though the agreement did not necessarily insist that all Member States should be participating in the Exchange Rate Mechanism by the time that first stage begins. It is during the first stage that all Members would be expected to join.

Chairman: Could we now turn to European political co-operation?

Mr Welsh

180. Mr Ford, in 1992 European political co-operation is to be reviewed. Do you have any views yourself on any desirable changes in the machinery or scope of it? Do you want a bigger secretariat, for example, or do you think there should be more scope for this to deal with other parts of Eastern Europe, or on the other hand are you satisfied just to leave it as it is?

(Mr Ford) My own view is that it is becoming increasingly important that the European Community speaks as often as possible with one political voice. Therefore, it may imply a bigger secretariat: I suspect it does. Certainly, with respect to Eastern Europe, it is important that the Community as a whole approaches the matter with a set of common aims and objectives. Clearly, the Eastern European dimension will be an important one for us over the next decade. Now the Soviet empire is dissolving in front of our eyes day by day, the Parliament is increasingly paying attention to what its relationship might be in the future with respect to Eastern Europe. There are already talks about associate membership of the Community for Hungary and Poland. We already have a situation now where the German Democratic Republic, though not in name, is in reality an associate Member of the Community in terms of its trading relations with West Germany. I think the Community's future will depend very much on the attitude that is taken. I do not think that at this particular stage anyone knows what the answers are going to be.

181. *(Mr Welsh)* Are we saying that if there are negotiations the Community should be the catalyst, that Eastern countries should not be dealing with individual countries which make up the

Common Market but should be dealing with the Common Market; that should be the catalyst of all the negotiations?

(*Mr Ford*) My view is that the European Community as a whole has to come to some agreement or accommodation with the countries of Eastern Europe. I believe that if there is to be any progress towards German reunification, for example — it is one of the very topical issues of the day — that is likely to take place in a wider European Community rather than separately from it, so I would not endorse the line that one should go slow on European integration; otherwise, one will stop the prospects for German reunification. I think it is an encouragement for us to go ahead rather than slow down.

Chairman

182. When this Committee was in Brussels recently there was drawn to our attention the process by which the European Political Co-operation Group issue communiqués on views which have been reached, these communiqués being put out in the name of the Presidency of the Community, because the Presidency of the Community is occupied by someone who is chairing the European Political Co-operation Group. There is room for some ambiguity about whose voice one is really hearing. Is it the Community's voice, the collective EPC's voice, or is it just the Presidency's voice? Does that ambiguity worry you, or do you feel quite relaxed about all that?

(*Mr Ford*) As far as I understand it, there have been no major problems where anyone claims to have been confused about whether it was the Presidency, the EPC or individual Member States speaking. I can see there is a potential problem there, but it is not one which has actually arisen as yet. When it arises I presume something will have to be done to resolve it in future.

Chairman: Finally, could we turn to other very current issues relating to British policy towards the European Community.

Mr Jopling

183. You will know that over the years it has been a somewhat familiar situation that the British delegation has found itself in a minority of one. I can remember John Silkin coming back here month after month in that position, and Peter Walker found himself in that position when he protested about the extravagances of the Common Agricultural Policy, and we are likely to find ourselves in that situation, we are told, over the Social Charter and over the question of economic and monetary union at Strasbourg. Without going into the merits of those things, I wonder if you could comment

on how you see in general terms Britain conducting its point of view, whether you agree or disagree, within the Community? Do you believe that we have an inherent inability to put our presentation more positively, that we do not co-operate enough with our allies or could it be that we do not have the correct approach in negotiating, for instance, our refusal to accept unpalatable generalised statements which are favoured by other nations or indeed our failure to look far enough ahead at future developments? I would like to have a general comment on the philosophical approach we have to situations which so often seem to leave us in a minority of one.

(Mr Ford) Obviously I think Britain's historical position and its current position in the European Community has been deeply influenced by our own geography, after all we are separate from the Community; by our own history, we were one of the major global powers until comparatively recently; and by our Atlanticism, Britain has never seen itself, for all those reasons, as an integral part of Europe and the European Community. One likes to quote: 'Fog in the Channel — Continent cut off', a headline from *The Times*; there has been a little of that attitude about it. I also think psychologically many of the other Member States have demonstrated that they can get their way if they want to fight over two or three issues which are important to them rather than having block opposition to large numbers of different issues. If one looks carefully over the last five years at the voting records of various national delegations in the Parliament, the British group on both sides, both Conservative and Labour, do not have the worst record. It was the way we approach it which gives everyone the impression we had the worst record in terms of voting with everyone else. Let me also be very clear that I certainly would be seen now as a pro-European, that does not mean to say I support some of the absurdities which go on within the European Community. I like to quote Nietzsche — "Madness is rare in individuals and common in parties, groups and organisations" — which is amply demonstrated by the Common Agricultural Policy as far as I am concerned. So all those reasons make a contribution towards Britain's isolation within the Community, which is hopefully changing at the moment. Certainly recent events in terms of the Labour Party's own perceived shift in position on the European Community has led to the Labour group within the Socialist Group being seen as central ideologically rather than (as previously) semi-detached on one fringe.

Chairman

184. M. Jacques Delors has a view which he has shared with some, including this Committee, that the whole process of European integration and European union should now be accelerated, in order to lock in the Federal Republic of Germany in some way and prevent it, in his view, being diverted too much in its relations to Eastern Europe. Is that a view you subscribe to, and do you happen to know whether your German Socialist colleagues buy that view, or do they think it is unsoundly based?

(Mr Ford) It is not a view I automatically subscribe to. One cannot be sure at this stage what will be the best response. My own view, as I expressed it earlier, is that certainly one should not slow down the process of integration. I see German reunification as eventually coming through the European Community rather than outside it. I think the German Socialists would accept that view at the moment, but things are changing so rapidly over there that I am not sure whether they or anybody else will have the same view on this matter in six months' time as they have now.

185. *(Chairman)* That really leads me to the final question, which I was going to put on the basis of raising our sights a few years ahead. However, as you say, things are happening so fast it may be only a few months. First, you have answered the issue about how you see the Community handling relations with Eastern Europe. Secondly, can I expand that and ask: What about the handling of the enlargement question? There is a long queue of people forming to join: Austria, Cyprus, Turkey, Sweden, Norway, Malta, and no doubt a few others as well. What do you feel about the way the Community should handle all that, and what role will the Parliament play in that?

(Mr Ford) First of all, the Parliament will play a crucial role because the Parliament needs to deliver 260 votes for any new accession to the Community, and there are a number of examples where those votes will, I suspect, be impossible to deliver, certainly in the present political climate. For example, in relation to the application by Turkey, no matter what the Commission says — but I do not think they are likely to have a different view from ourselves — the combination of human rights and anti-Turkish racism in Germany would mean it would be impossible to deliver 260 votes for Turkey's accession any time in the next several decades. I think that is very clear. The general attitude, with the exception of some of the states very much on the periphery of the Community, like Turkey and Morocco — which has talked about applying to join — where there are particular political problems, would depend on

your view of what is happening in Europe. My view is that the 1992 process is a symptom and not a cause. What is going on is that industry is aggregating itself at a new, higher level, so therefore the 1992 process is about trying to assist that. The view some people would take — and it would seem to be implicit in the statements made by people like Jacques Delors — is that we are actually doing something which would not otherwise happen, and so we need to wait for the process to be completed before we can see any further enlargement. Taking the former view, that it is a natural process that we are only marginally altering, then my own view is that we can actually contemplate enlargement rather earlier than we might otherwise. In terms of assimilating the Austrians or Maltese or Cypriots or Norwegians, I do not actually see a major problem, because I believe we are part of that natural process. The major problem is going to be how to deal with the third issue I mentioned after industry and financial integration: security integration. One of the major battles which is going to take place in the Parliament, and maybe amongst Member States, is whether we want to allow the admission of any further neutral state apart from Ireland, because that is going to have implications for the whole super-power relationship in Europe for the next decade, and certainly there is a strong resistance in some quarters to the accession of any such neutral state, no matter what its economic or industrial base or the possibility of its ready and safe assimilation into the Community in other regards.

Chairman: That is a very interesting reply. Speaking personally, I totally share your view that politics is the outcome and not the cause of social and industrial change, but that is opening up wider issues.

Mr Rowlands

186. Just pursuing the issue of neutrality, when we were in Strasbourg last week one Member of the Labour Group more or less laid it on the line that he saw defence and security as fundamental features of the Community, and therefore Austria appeared to be beyond the pale because of its neutrality. I am rather concerned that you seem to be sharing that view?

(Mr Ford) I am sorry; I do not share that view. To make it very clear, my view is that it is inevitable in the next decades that Europe is going to have to take on a security dimension. My own personal view of the kind of shape it should take is one which would welcome the addition of further neutral states into the membership of the European Community.

187. *(Mr Rowlands)* Compromising their neutrality?

(Mr Ford) My own view is that I would like to see Europe having a defence voice without the Americans. I think it is inevitable in the long run. Maybe we need to have a much longer hearing than this, but I see that because there is going to be a sharp divergence of trade and industrial issues between Europe and America, a continued close Atlanticist position is one that is not tenable on either side. Therefore, it means that Europe will have to look after its own security interests without the Americans. So you can have the first view, there needs to be European security, and that either leads to the conclusion it needs to be an independent one or the conclusion you need to compromise the neutrality of countries like Austria. I take the former rather than the latter.

188. *(Mr Rowlands)* There are huge implications in terms of military manpower if you envisage the withdrawal of the manpower of the United States from Europe. Is that what you are envisaging?

(Mr Ford) I am happy to discuss this! I did a report for the European Parliament on European Common Arms Production and Procurement, and the estimates, which were approved by Parliament with very few people against, were that we could save something like 10 billion ECU a year in terms of wasted resources currently by having common arms production and procurement, and that would offer some incentives to a number of Member States moving in that direction. Secondly, in view of the developments in the Soviet Union, partly because of the threatened revolt of the Soviet consumer against the lie that the Soviet military machine has been living for the last 30 years, we have a situation where there offers to be much further progress on negotiations in nuclear, biological, chemical and even conventional disarmament than people anticipated even a few years ago. I think our major problem is not finding additional manpower for Western European armies but dealing with the problem of arms conversion.

189. The connection with enlargement will be if you push down this road or this road develops, would it not make it harder rather than easier for states like Hungary to at least increasingly associate with the EEC?

(Mr Ford) I think I will end by quoting James Maxton who said: "If you can't ride two horses at the same time, you shouldn't be in a bloody circus!"

Chairman: On that comment — you are whetting our appetites on issues which run at the edge of this inquiry and indeed issues which this Committee has been reporting on over the past year in other inquiries — I think we must call a halt, because otherwise our time and your time will run away. I thank you very much, on behalf of the Committee, both you and Mr Piening for answering our questions very patiently and frankly. It has been very much appreciated.

1 November 1989

Part 8

1990

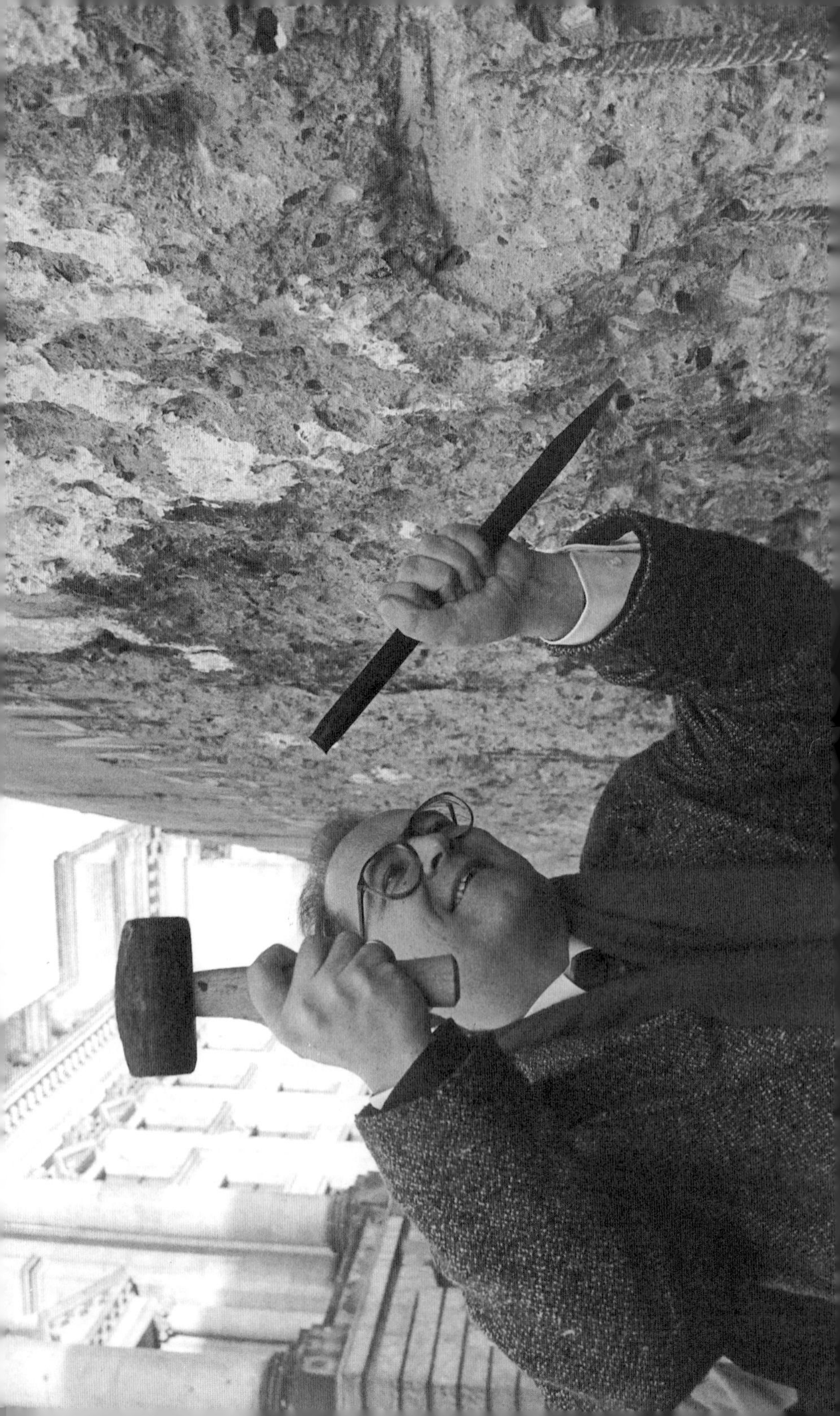

47. The New Europe: A Socialist Vision

The development and completion of the Single Market is part of the logic of capitalist development in an increasingly competitive global economy. Because it is an inevitable development, there is no reason to await its 'completion' before embarking on other steps. In any case, completion of the Single Market will not be achieved by 1992, nor for many years to come. The Single Market is a programme, not a date.

Our concern as socialists is with the consequences that will follow from unbridled development of the Single Market which, in Darwinian fashion, will continue to favour the strong 'core' states and regions over the weak 'peripheral' and 'semi-peripheral' areas. If the present sea change in the Community is truly to mean a better life for all the people of the Community — women as well as men, ethnic minorities as well as the white majority — and an equalisation of interests within and between states, then the capitalist system must not be allowed to find its natural level of (im)balance. Change must be managed in the interests of people, instead of being allowed to roll over people.

It is, therefore, essential that development of the Single Market is *accompanied* — not merely followed — by development of the Social Community. As we explain in more detail later, intervention by the Community to set high social standards throughout the Community is vital to Europe's economic development as well as to the welfare of individuals.

But the Community's development must also be guided by the 'Europeanisation' of Europe. Just as there is no reason to slow down implementation of the Social Charter, so there is no reason to postpone enlargement of the Community until the Single Market is completed. As we develop closer relations and new forms of association, leading to full membership when appropriate, with the new democracies of Central and Eastern Europe, we can look forward to a European Community which, by the year 2000, is truly becoming 'our Common European Home'.

Above all, we have to understand and recognise Europe's place in the world economy dominated by the 'triad' of Japan, the USA and Europe. Europe's political future rests on its economic strength. But at every turn, Europe is being out-performed by the USA and Japan. Our low level of investment in science and technology is only one indicator of our relative industrial decline. With the secular decline of the USA, the question is whether Japan or Europe can replace it as the world's dominant economy. Central to our vision

◄ *Early 1990: at the Berlin Wall (photo: Niels Leiser).*

of the New Europe, therefore, is an industrial strategy which can enable us to compete and succeed in the modern world.

If Europe is to succeed in an increasingly competitive world economy, then we have to make a qualitative leap in our ability to use modern technologies, production processes and telecommunications. Europe cannot succeed by trying to compete by cutting costs. Europe can only succeed by producing high-tech, high-quality, high-value-added and environmentally benign goods and services — not merely to defend our own markets, but also to penetrate the growing markets of the rest of the world.

The Single Market — together with intensified global competition, of which it is in part a product — will force massive industrial restructuring in Europe. The subliminal message of the Cecchini Report is that the profound shake-up necessary to modernise European industry will initially have high social and regional costs. If, however, we fail to restructure and modernise, then declining global competitiveness will have social and regional costs which are just as high — but even longer-lasting.

But if industrial restructuring is left to the 'free market', then it will victimise millions of people throughout the European regions. The purpose of a socialist industrial, regional and social policy is to manage the process of change in order to create a society which is both prosperous and just. That can no longer be done primarily at the national level; it requires a socialist, European strategy.

In this process of modernisation, science and technology are the leading force. Europe is falling behind, particularly in comparison with Japan and other countries of the Pacific Rim. The European Community has a vital role to play here, increasing European investment in science and technology; promoting joint ventures between companies and countries; reducing duplication; investing in technology transfer and diffusion; and raising the standards of basic science and technological education in schools, colleges and universities. We must concentrate resources on the priorities we select, giving preference for instance to near-market research designed to improve Europe's industrial performance.

We must not make the mistake of thinking of science and new technologies as some natural, neutral given. We can and must question our science and technology: will it destroy or create jobs? Will it protect or pollute the environment? Will it enhance or undermine individual autonomy? We have a *choice* of technologies.

A distinctive European technology must also be driven by the needs of civil society, not those of the military. The skills and resources now employed in defence R & D and armaments production should be a driving force in Europe's industrial modernisation.

Improving Europe's investment in education and training is, therefore, vital to our future economic success. National efforts are, of course, needed. But a European strategy is also essential to promote the development of a highly-skilled workforce in the 'peripheral' regions and to develop language teaching within an increasingly integrated European workforce.

Europe cannot and must not pursue industrial modernisation and growth regardless of the environmental consequences. That would be self-defeating, not only because of the damage to our own environment, but also because Europe must fulfil its own environmental responsibilities if the Third World is to be enabled to develop without further damage to the global environment.

Nor can environmental protection be tacked on to the end of industrial development. Ecology and economy must go hand in hand. The issue is not 'growth or no-growth'. As Poland vividly illustrates, no-growth can be environmentally disastrous. The issue is how to achieve quality growth. Environmental modernisation is therefore an essential part of a socialist strategy for industrial modernisation. We have to ensure that European companies 'get ahead of the game', investing in clean, safe and environmentally benign processes and products that will meet the demands of consumers and environmental regulators throughout the world.

Similarly, environmental requirements must be integrated into science and technology policies. We can and should *choose* to promote environmentally aware and responsible science — as well as to prioritise investment in environmental science itself.

We propose that the Community should adopt a European Environmental Charter, bringing together and building upon existing provisions for environmental protection. In promoting the environmental transformation of industry, we need to use all possible policies — environmental taxes and charges as well as regulations. There may, for instance, be scope for a 'green VAT' as part of the harmonisation of indirect taxation.

Growing European integration has gone hand-in-hand with the growth of regional, sub-national movements. Both reflect the declining power of the nation state to control modern economic forces. It is essential that development of the Single Market does not compound regional inequalities and thus lead to massive emigration from poorer regions and inefficient 'overheating' in richer regions. Our goal as socialists must be to equalise interests and opportunities across Europe. Trade imbalances within Europe are a constraint on growth throughout Europe. The German surplus, and corresponding deficits in every other Community country except Ireland, represents a structural problem for the entire Community. Growth in the richer regions will be assisted by the development of the poorer regions of Europe — just as, on a global scale, it is essential to end the 'reverse transfers' of wealth from the poorest to the richest countries of the world if the world economy as a whole is to prosper.

We therefore envisage a far greater role for European structural funds to promote industrial development and modernisation — including education and training, transport and telecommunications — in the regions. Priority should be given within the science/technology strategy to regional centres for technology transfer and diffusion and to skill training in the regions.

The Common Agricultural Policy should be gradually scaled down, thus releasing resources for industrial and regional investment. A restructured CAP must also take proper account of the interests of the Third World.

Our new European Industrial Policy must create incentives to capital to invest in the peripheral regions of Europe, by creating the right environment for modern industries. High-speed transport and telecommunications — the fast movement of people, goods, information and ideas — are vital, as is the development of a highly-trained workforce capable of using the new technologies.

Europe must be a Community for people, not merely a Market for business. The Single Market will take place in any event. What requires concerted European action is the creation of a 'social space' in which individuals, communities and regions can enjoy a better life. But 'Social Europe' is also vital to the *economic* success of the New Europe. Without high social standards throughout the Community, the Single Market will encourage companies to continue trying to compete by cutting costs — moving to the areas with low wages, low environmental protection and low skills — instead of pursuing the only strategy which offers success in the global economy, that of high-skill, high-wage, high-quality production.

Our commitment as socialists to the Social Charter, therefore, is based on our economic analysis as well as our determination to give individuals equal life-chances. But the Social Charter has been seriously weakened in the process of bargaining which preceded its adoption — particularly because of the opposition to all of its provisions from the Conservative Government in Britain.

We therefore envisage a 'Stage 2' when the Social Charter will be widened and deepened. Widened to include groups — particularly pensioners — who are omitted from its present provisions. Deepened in terms of the protection which it offers those included. Future provisions must, for instance, include effective strategies against racism and sexism as well as the guarantee of a minimum income as well as a fair wage. The first priority is to complete the current work programme, ensuring the most effective possible legislation to implement the Charter's provisions. But Stage 2 should begin by 1992, when the present work programme will be complete.

The social strategy must therefore include full rights for employees, including the right to information and consultation about their company's plans, particularly when a take-over or merger is planned or threatened. It must include stronger protection for workers' health and safety, so that industrial modernisation is not pursued in ways which damage working people's own environment.

It must include, too, measures which enable women *and* men to combine satisfying paid employment with family responsibilities, personal leisure, education/training and community involvement. Shorter working hours and a shorter working lifetime have always been central to the Labour movement's demands. Today, the challenge is to create working time arrangements which give individuals far greater autonomy in their own lives, including the opportunity of lifetime learning. Support for families is particularly vital, including better maternity, paternity, and parental leave, and high-quality child care provision.

Europe's workforce must not be a divided workforce. We are proposing a European Residents' Charter, guaranteeing equal rights and equal duties to every European resident. Without this floor of basic rights and duties, the danger is that migrant workers — from Central and Eastern Europe as well as the traditional sources of 'guest workers' — will be used to undercut the conditions of working people in the Community. At the same time, creating common standards for every individual throughout the Community is a vital part of our campaign against racism and xenophobia.

The map of Europe has been redrawn. The Cold War has ended. Europe must now rethink the assumptions, as well as the armaments, on which our security system has rested for over forty years. As America increasingly looks across the Pacific rather than across the Atlantic, pulled by economic and trading imperatives, it is all the more important for Europe to find and speak with a European voice on security and peace. NATO's role increasingly will be to help manage common security within a Helsinki framework. The procedures for European political co-operation need to be brought within a process of democratic accountability, if they are to be made even more effective.

The transformation of Europe has profound implications for the defence industries. Progress on nuclear and conventional disarmament negotiations will mean substantial cuts in European — and especially British — defence spending, with many defence contracts being cancelled. Left to the 'free market', defence contractors will either try to sell more arms to the Third World — perpetuating a disastrous misallocation of resources and dangerous instability — or they will close factories and sack workers. Instead, it is essential to manage disarmament on a regional, national and European level by intervening in and assisting the process of defence diversification.

As stated earlier, shifting defence industries into civilian production is vital to Europe's industrial modernisation. The Community can and must ensure that employees are retrained where necessary, that workers and managers together are enabled to develop alternative, civilian production strategies for their firms, that investment in R & D is shifted from military to civilian purposes.

The shift in decision-making from nation states to Europe is an inevitable consequence of economic Europeanisation and internationalisation. The debate about 'sovereignty' is often misconceived. As Europe's economy has become more integrated, more power has inevitably moved to Europe and will continue to do so. 'Stop the world, I want to get off' — or 'Stop Europe, I want to get off' — is not an option for any European country, including Britain.

We are Europeans and our future is in Europe. But we know what kind of Europe we want: and we must make sure that our voice is heard and heeded in the building of the New Europe.

The direction is clear: it is towards greater and greater European integration. But there will still be important debates about the form of European decision-making, and the relationship between political accountability at a European and a national level. The central problem is not that power has shifted from national governments and Parliaments to Europe, but that it has shifted towards the Commission and the Council of Ministers, who are not effectively accountable to democratic bodies.

Correcting the democratic deficit is vital to Europe's future. As people increasingly realise that decisions are being made which directly affect their daily lives, but over which they have little or no influence, they will demand more say — for themselves and for their elected representatives. If European institutions do not respond, the European project itself will be threatened. It is essential, of course, to get right the levels at which decisions are made, on the basis of the principle of 'subsidiarity'. It is also vital to enhance the role of the European Parliament, giving it an effective power of co-decision within the Community.

Enlargement of the Community makes it even more essential to have a more efficient, as well as a more democratic, structure of decision-making. Without majority voting on a wide range of social and environmental issues, for instance, an enlarged Community will simply not be able to function.

The debate about whether the priority is to 'deepen' or 'broaden' Europe is sterile. We need a wider, deeper — and faster — Europe.

By the year 2000, the European Community will be very different. It will include Austria and other EFTA countries. It will include not only a united Germany, but also Hungary, Czechoslovakia and possibly others of the new democracies — at least as associates if not yet as full members. We can truly imagine that the Community will be close to becoming 'our Common European Home'.

We have a vision of this New Europe. We are determined that, by the year 2000, Europe should have reversed its relative economic decline and begun the investment in science and technology, in transport and telecommunications, in education and training which alone can enable it to compete and succeed against the rest of the world.

But even that will not be enough. Economic success for Europe as a whole could still mean poverty and backwardness for millions of our people. Only a socialist strategy of intervention and investment — locally, regionally, nationally, and at a European level — will achieve our goals: economic success, a better quality of life for all our people, a just and peaceful society.

Glyn Ford MEP and Carol Tongue MEP
European Labour Forum, Autumn 1990

48. Our Common European Future

Following the British Government's decision to enter the European exchange rate mechanism, the media and parliamentary politics have been preoccupied with the issues surrounding economic and monetary union, the single European currency and the establishment of a central European bank.

Tory policy on the issue of Europe is in a complete mess. Our partners in Europe already consider Britain to be out of the game, relegated to the sidelines. A cosmetic change in the leadership of the Tory Party will do nothing to change that.

The British electorate could be forgiven for failing to recognise that economic and monetary union is only one part of the development towards European union. Britain should have been shaping the process rather than merely adapting to changes made by the other 11 member states.

The current Government has chosen to reject proposals, obstruct change and stand in the way of progress in Europe. The reality is that our European partners are determined to achieve political union, if needs be without us.

Within the Labour Party we now have a much wider and far-reaching approach to Europe, based on goals and priorities we have worked out in partnership with other socialist parties in Europe.

Economic and monetary union is a vital component of this policy and will be a necessary and inevitable development. But our understanding of Europe also includes the wider issues of political union which is about rights of citizenship, institutional reforms, democratic accountability and the community's relations with the external world. A common foreign policy is an integral element of such a political union.

The problem is that the European response to the Gulf crisis, although more co-ordinated than previous foreign policy actions, still took place under the auspices of European Political Co-operation (EPC). A policy was agreed on by the 12 Foreign Ministers which involved no binding commitment.

Neither the European Commission nor the democratically elected European Parliament has any input and, to all intents and purposes, states can choose to undermine an agreed common position. This can hardly be described as the community speaking with one voice.

There is both scope for and a need for the community to consolidate a common foreign and security policy. The Single European Act now includes in its jurisdiction European Political Co-operation. The Martin report called for the two Intergovernmental Conferences to include EPC and also for a common foreign and security policy to be included within the community framework.

In April this year the Kohl-Mitterrand initiative on political union echoed demands for a common foreign and security policy.

Next week, in pursuit of these aims, a historic meeting will take place in Rome. The Assizes in Rome will draw together elected delegates from national parliaments and the European Parliament to express their views on the new goals of economic and monetary union; the need to strengthen democracy in the community; the division of competences between the member states and the community; and foreign policy relations with other states and institutions for example the Western European Union, the Council of Europe and the Conference for Security and Co-operation in Europe.

Designing a common foreign and security policy for the community is not an easy task, particularly because of possible incongruent membership following a future enlargement of the community.

How could a common security policy be forged to include the sensitivities and interests of the NATO member states, the neutral and the former Warsaw Pact states? Yet it is inevitable that the community will have to develop a common policy in this area.

The former communist states have already been attracted to the higher standards of living and the democratic traditions of the European Community. This is part of a natural process of identification with and desire to be joined up with the Western European states.

Since 1989 the queue for membership has steadily increased. Austria, Malta, Cyprus and Turkey have applied for membership while Norway, Sweden, Czechoslovakia, Poland and Hungary have all declared their interest in membership.

A united policy and cohesive approach is the only way to respond to the challenge of potential new adhesions and new association agreements.

Political union, in all its dimensions, underpinned by majority voting on all the major issues, is crucial to provide a supranational structure. This will help to eliminate risks and threats to security in Europe, emanating from renewed ethnic and racial tensions in the East.

The united Germany has already found its *raison d'etre* within the community and European political union.

A common community foreign policy is already taking shape. The commission single-handedly co-ordained the Group of 24 western aid programme to Central and Eastern Europe and has also gone a long way towards building political economic and cultural bridges to the East. The European Free Trade Association has been pulled into the community orbit through the creation of a European economic space and many trade and co-operation agreements have been signed with third countries.

A policy of constructive aid which makes provisions for the Soviet Union has been all the more urgent, given the failure of the Group of Seven at the Houston Economic Summit, to come up with a rescue plan for the Soviet Union.

The Soviet Union has, in a short space of time, been transformed from the Darth Vadar of the Evil Empire to become the Mad Max of the Third World.

In the Labour Party we believe that it is not in the interests of world security to perpetuate either of these myths.

We would like to see the Soviet Union supported in its attempts at democratic reform. The Thatcher Government has chosen to side with the United States and Japan in refusing to extend aid until more reform towards democracy is evident while the German and French Governments are pleading for assistance to prevent the Soviet Union from complete collapse.

In past years the Community has managed to achieve some unity in action in foreign policy. During the Arab-Israeli conflict, the community chose not to fall in line with American policy and again in 1981 the community came into conflict over the transfer of technology to the Soviet Union for the construction of the Siberian gas-pipe line which was to provide an alternative source of energy for Western Europe. The member states did not accept American restrictions on the transfer of technology and the deal went ahead.

Security policy is potentially a more difficult area. The rigid patterns of behaviour and the remnants of the cold-war mentality continue to hamper new advances in this area. Pooling policy on security also raises the political red herring, which has continued to plague progress on general political union: the issue of national sovereignty.

Clearly the issue of sovereignty is not just limited to the control of national currency and setting interest rates. It also applies to security in the next century in an age of mutual vulnerability and economic interdependence can only be guaranteed by regional and global security solutions.

National borders in the community have become and are becoming increasingly obsolete. To date the only attempts being made to get action on security have taken place within the highly dubious Trevi and Schengen agreements.

These agreements which have been devoid of all democratic control seek to police national borders and control immigration and prevent the spread of international terrorism. They are not an acceptable model on which to build the security of the New Europe. The new situation requires us to adopt "the new thinking" on security policy pioneered by the West German Social Democratic Party and advocated by Mikhail Gorbachev.

One aspect of this is to view foreign and security policy as an indivisible whole. Security is not, then, just about negative peace that is absence of war. It is about creating positive peace, forging new contacts, trade economic and cultural and political ties which bind the future of states so firmly together that war becomes inconceivable.

This kind of co-operation between the West Europeans has been the basis of the enduring peace which has reigned in Western Europe. The community has been making some progress on this aspect of promoting security. This is the real essence of the policy of common security.

It is a policy which has at its core the maintenance of security as a seamless web stretching across the globe. Partnership and co-operation is not limited to arms control and disarmament but goes further to include co-operation on the environment, ecology and economics.

If the community were to adopt the principles of common security as a basis for a new security policy, this would also circumvent the problem associated with incongruent membership of NATO states, neutral states and former Warsaw Pact members.

This may create dilemmas for some states which would have to abandon independent nuclear capabilities due to their incompatibility with the principles of common security.

This policy of common security is based on a low-key defence capacity, the doctrine of non-offensive defence, and the gradual elimination of nuclear, biological and chemical weapons.

With the practice of arms conversion policies, defence could be cheaper and more efficient while at the same time resources freed through savings could then be used to promote human development for health education and the environment.

Arms conversion policies funded at EC level could also provide the resources, the people and the material to put into hi-tech investment and help the community to compete with Japan and the US.

It would have the added bonus of allowing the Community to control and regulate the export of military hardware to the Third World and so contribute to global security. In this way a common foreign and security policy would give the community the strength to be a more valuable partner to the developing nations.

With the drive towards European Union gaining momentum, a common foreign and security policy along with the dynamic of global regionalisation will become a *fait accompli.*

States can hope to have any impact on the future only if they function as a member of a regional entity. The consequences of

1992 and the peace dividend will continue to bring fundamental changes to the region. These provide us with the opportunity to create a truly pan-European security community in the long term. NATO and WEU cannot possibly go far enough towards meeting the new challenges of the nineties.

The European Community is, and will continue to be, an important linchpin of any future security arrangement in Europe and an important pillar of the 35-nation Conference for Security and Co-operation in Europe process.

It is therefore imperative for the community to set its own agenda and delineate its own priorities. These will not always be compatible with American security interests. The new policies would have to be a true reflection of the new Europe pending and following community enlargement.

Security policy would not be created with a view to setting up a new military superstructure in Europe. It would be a broader agenda based on the principles of common security.

The current Gulf crisis, coming as it did hard on the heels of the end of the cold war, has reminded us of the fragility of world security and the need to present a common united front.

The Community would then be in a position to play a positive role on the world state. This is its major future task.

If we can achieve that unity of action the Community will not only be able to keep in step with the rapid pace of change in the next century but ensure that it is a truly European one.

Glyn Ford MEP and David Martin MEP
Tribune, 23 November 1990

Part 9

1991

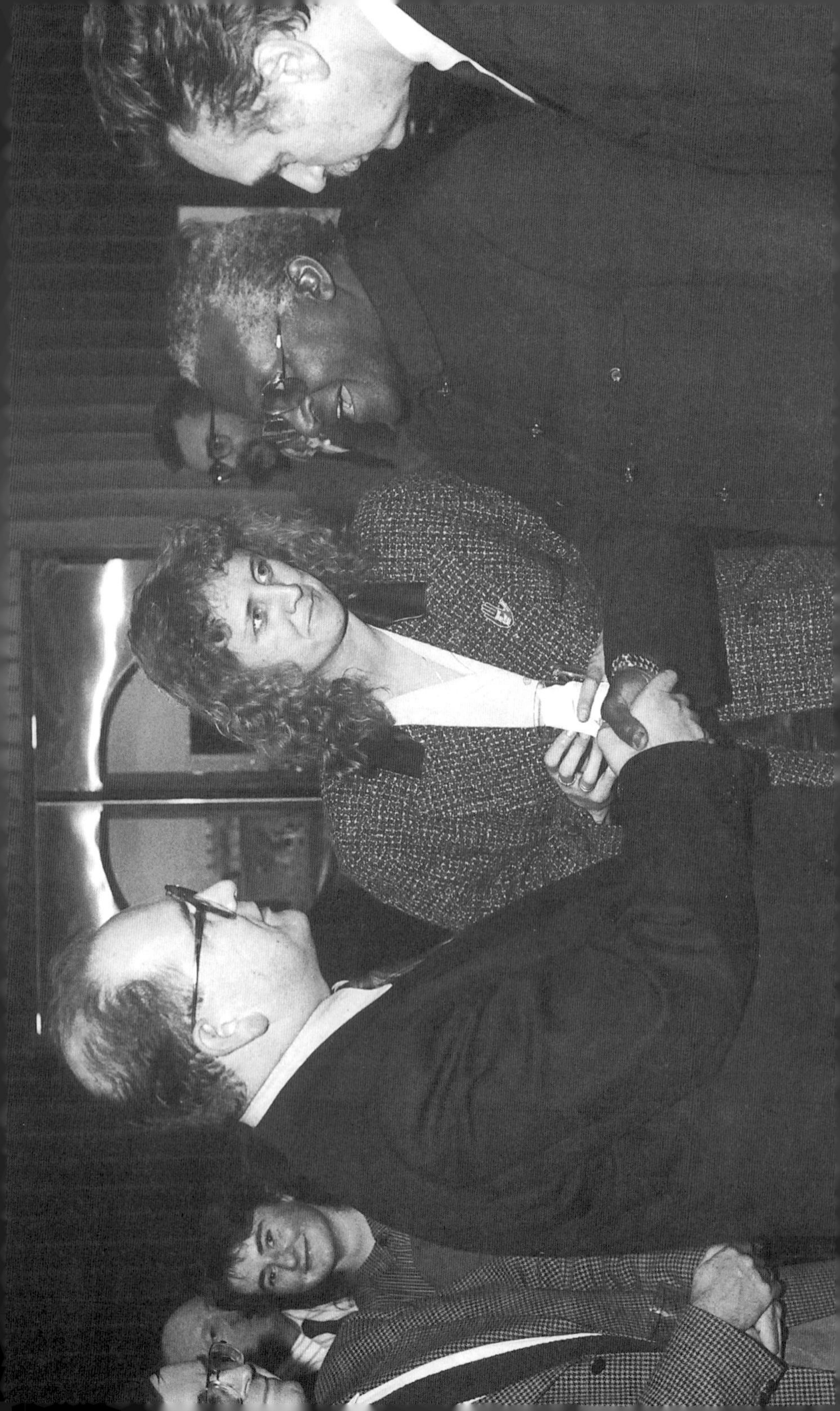

49. The European Parliament and Democracy

There are many states from northern, eastern and southern Europe lining up to join the European Community (EC). The fundamental qualification for membership is that the applicant must be a democracy. If the EC were to apply to join itself, it would be turned down on the grounds that it does not pass this test.

The reaction of the old anti-Common Market Left to our recent article on European political union (*Tribune*, November 23, 1990) and to Phil Kelly's progressive editorial, 'Leading into Europe' (*Tribune*, December 14, 1990), has been revealing.

Responses varied from that of Hugh Macpherson, who rightly complained about the paucity of democracy in the European Community but seemed to think that it was somehow impossible to achieve democracy at that level, to our colleague, Michael Hindley, MEP, who actually argued that the European Parliament should not be given democratic control because we might make the wrong decision (*Tribune*, December 14, 1990). How can a tribune of the people argue against the institution which houses directly elected representatives being made responsible for legislation and accountable to the people?

This is dangerous and irresponsible talk. Not giving the European Parliament democratic control is more likely to lead to the right-wing dictatorial nightmare scenario posited by Hugh Macpherson at the end of his column (*Tribune*, December 21/28, 1990).

The member state, in the context of the EC, is now both too small and too large to deal effectively with the geopolitical changes taking place in global and local economies.

As early as 1984, sales of the top 200 companies alone amounted to over £2,000 million: more than one-and-a-half the total income of the Third World. The capacity of many multinational companies to plan and to take action is now far greater than that of the average Ministry in most individual member state governments. But there is no effective political way to control multinational companies from a member state perspective.

If we look at the proposals being made by the European Parliament for European union of a federal type and at proposals from Scotland, Wales, Catalonia, Bavaria and others for a 'Europe of the regions' we will see that they contain mechanisms for moving power upwards and downwards. Most importantly, they make sure that power is democratically controlled.

◄ *Archbishop Desmond Tutu visits the European Parliament.*

It is time to open the door to our new European future. The key should be democracy. But there is no foregone conclusion that the resolution of the tensions caused by the shift of economic power from the national to the European level will result in a democratic, let alone a democratic socialist, solution.

Politics is about power. Power is quite clearly shifting to the European level.

The only way in which we, as democratic socialists, can gain power is through the Socialist Group's control of the European Parliament. But the European Parliament does not have enough power to give it democratic control of the European Community.

As we have seen, there are some comrades who do not want us to acquire that power, although they do not support 'an unrealistic cry to withdraw'. How, then, do they propose to put their agenda into practice?

Hitherto, the problem with the old anti-Common Market Left has been that it has used its position in the European Parliament only to ridicule the Common Market; the point, however, is to change it.

We on the new progressive European Left are prepared to rise to that challenge.

The European Parliamentary Labour Party is now the largest party inside the biggest group (the Socialists) in the Parliament.

Following the victory of the Left at the European elections in June 1989, the Socialist Group made a priority of its bid for the crucial 'Institutional Report on the Inter-governmental Conference (IGC) in the context of the Parliament's strategy for European Union'. IGCs are the only mechanism for reforming the treaties which govern the EC.

Three reports (known as the Martin Reports) have now been passed with overwhelming majorities in the European Parliament. Their main priority is in addressing the 'democratic deficit' — the fact that, although many areas of legislation have passed from national parliaments to the European arena, they are not under the democratic control of those people elected on a European mandate.

It has been estimated that 80 per cent of economic and social legislation will be adopted at community level by the mid-nineties. This legislation is a particularly entrenched form of legislation in that, once approved by the Council of Ministers, it overrides national legislation and cannot be amended or replaced by any national parliament or by the European Parliament.

The Council of Ministers adopts this legislation behind closed doors. Thus, the legislative powers that national parliaments have delegated to the Community are exercised by the executive branch of the member states meeting in secret.

The European Parliament's remedy to this is to propose that the EC's legislation should be subject to co-decision making between Parliament and Council. Thus the approval of both bodies — the Council of Ministers representing the national governments, and the European Parliament, representing the electorate as a whole — would be required.

This would not enable Parliament to impose on member states legislation that they did not want, as the Council's approval would remain necessary. It would, however, mean that the Council's decisions could only enter into force once approved by a public vote in an elected assembly.

Another frustration inherent in the *status quo* is the inability of the elected representatives of the people to put into practice the programme on which they were elected. The European Parliament has no power to initiate legislation. That right lies solely with the unelected European Commission. That cannot be democratic.

The European Parliament is also seeking the right to elect the President of the Commission. At present it is only consulted on this matter. The Commission's important political responsibilities require the democratic legitimacy of the European Parliament's endorsement. It would also enable the people to bring the executive to heel.

These three modest but specific demands, if backed in the IGCs and written into the new treaty, would bring EC legislation under democratic control and open the door to a people's Europe.

Glyn Ford and David Martin
Tribune, 1 February 1991

50. Europe, The Gulf and The New World Order

Only a year ago Europe was celebrating: the end of the Cold War; a peace dividend; the dawning of a New World Order where international relations would be based on economic co-operation and political dialogue, with collective security a surrogate for military might. The celebration was premature. We have not yet found global security based on common security rather than mutually assured destruction.

History is not ending, it is accelerating. Regional conflicts threaten global stability. The Iraq-US war is not just another Middle East conflict. It is already threatening to widen to include peripheral NATO states, like Turkey, and to engulf Israel and maybe even to justify clashes between Egypt and Sudan. It will almost certainly precipitate a world economic recession, devastate the environment and poison political relations for years to come. The potential for escalation should not be underestimated.

What is going on in the Gulf? The conflict is being described in mutually exclusive ways. For Daniel Ortega, former Sandinista President of Nicaragua, it is a war of North versus South, with the forces of the first world pitted against those of the Third. For President Bush it is the US as global policeman stepping in to stop one of the big boys bullying a small neighbour. Neither of these caricatures is remotely close to the truth. Both seek refuge in simple ideal images of the battle between good and evil. We don't live in such a convenient world where moral choices are made for us. Instead it is much more complex. Some would argue the best analogy would be that of an imperialist war — between *two* imperial powers. One old, tired and in decline, almost forced to fight to maintain its global reputation, and the other new, headstrong and aggressive, only able to attempt to impose its will by force.

It is scarcely necessary to rehearse the fact that the US is hardly a paragon of virtue: the Bay of Pigs, Vietnam, Nicaragua, Chile and Grenada are the sins of commission. The sins of omission are even longer, including Palestine, Cyprus and East Timor. Iraq has given us a police state horrifically outlined in Samir al-Khalil's *Republic of Fear*, internal political terrorism on a scale probably only exceeded by Iran; genocide against the Kurds and the horrors of Halabja. It has murdered Palestinians. August 2 was not the first or the finest example of Iraqi enthusiasm for military solutions to economic problems. The 1980 invasion of Iran had at its root ideas of a Greater Iraq that in comparison made expansionist ambitions by the further shores of Zionism seem modest. Here one might say the choice is between the bad and the worse.

The commencement of hostilities in the Gulf on January 17 was unnecessary while sanctions and/or diplomacy were not exhausted. Neither offered a route to avoid military action, even if Saddam Hussein seemed determined to reject all final attempts at negotiation. The US driven by the spiralling cost of the military intervention, the climate and eroding public opinion tried the short-cut. It is already clear it will not be so easy. The video-game war played out on our television screen may look spectacular, but the blood spilt is real and the bedrock of the Iraqi military machine remains. The land operation will be long and savage if Iraq is to be completely subdued. Our short term objective must now be to achieve the swiftest possible end to hostilities with the liberation of Kuwait. An immediate cease-fire without Iraq agreeing to complete and total withdrawal from Kuwait would be a victory not only for Saddam Hussein and his terrorism, but also a green light to the other expansionist powers in Africa, Asia and South and Central America. The likes of Belize would disappear into the maws of its neighbour within months. Such a state of anarchy would be an unacceptable basis for a stable and democratic future. We have then at this current juncture no alternative but to support the continuation of military action as the lesser of two evils. But our concept of democracy and need for democratisation must also include the future development of the occupied state. Feudal Kuwait must be freed to move towards democracy in the interests not only of its wealthy but of the rest of the world.

More importantly we must win the peace. This can only be done by strictly limiting our war aims to the liberation of Kuwait while no-one would benefit from an immediate cease-fire except Saddam Hussein. What lessons can be drawn from the Gulf crisis for the future of Europe? It has been said that Europe's economic and political destiny and the road to European Union is doomed, largely because Europe's impotence has been highlighted by the conflict. Another oilshock and the prospects of world economic recession will have a devastating impact on Europe's political and economic regeneration. There is a fear that Europe may be tempted to become isolationist and seek to put its own house in order. This is a charge already levelled at some of our European partners. Britain for its part may drift further away from Europe, strengthening and consolidating its transatlantic relationship in a revived London-Washington war-axis.

Yet the writing is on the wall. Never have the signs been clearer. Europe now has to speak with one voice and define its own foreign and security policy regardless of how difficult or impossible that task may at first appear.

The dominant parameters to political action are no longer bipolar. With one Superpower in terminal decline and the other thrashing around in the Gulf desperately trying to restore peace and democracy to a troubled region there is most definitely a role for Europe as a world power. Over the decades we have witnessed how far US and European interest have diverged in major policy fields, not least after the experience of the security policy in the 80's, and more recently in the Uruguay GAAT round. We can no longer tolerate a situation where the US is leading the dance and running the world to comply with its own interests for these are not, and will not always be, compatible with ours.

We have a responsibility to the world and to ourselves as Europeans to begin preparing the peace in the Middle East. The US and the UK as a sole actor, due to the burden of its past in this troubled region, cannot be seen as an honest broker. The role then automatically falls to the European Community. The fact that so far Europe is seen to have responded in a disjointed and disunited way to the crisis is as much to do with the lack of the procedures and mechanisms available as with the political will for a common stance. Hence European political union and a Common foreign and security policy becomes vital to enable Europe to act as a positive and stable bulwark in what is increasingly an anarchic and unstable international environment. As a cohesive united force Europe could then throw its weight behind the UN.

One role Europe can fulfil is to limit and scrutinise arms transfers to the Middle East. In extending such a policy to the Third World in general, it could actively promote peace by denying states easy access to weapons of mass destruction. An essential component of a common foreign and security policy must be to make progress on a common arms procurement policy by removing the imperative of small national arms manufacturers to export.

The European parliament has called for the convocation of an international conference in the Middle East to find a lasting, just and negotiated solution to the crisis. The Palestinian problem lies at the root of many of the major flashpoints in the Middle East. While we have rejected Saddam Hussein's direct linkage between the Kuwait occupation and the Palestinian problem, there is nevertheless a burning sense that as long as the people of the *dar al-Islam* see this as axiomatic to the cause of peace in the Middle East the issue will have to be addressed — with or without a Saddam Hussein. A united Europe can play the role of honest broker and help with the setting up and organisation of a Conference of Security and Disarmament in the region, coupled with a comprehensive strategy of arms control regimes and disarmament initiatives.

Europe already plays an important function in providing aid for the refugees and displaced peoples in the Middle East. But it is now urgent that Europe dons the mantle of statesmanship and starts to act in a manner commensurate with a world power. For too long Europe has been content with the economic stature of a giant, the political stature of a dwarf and, in foreign and security policy, the profile of a garden worm.

Rassegna, 18 February 1991
(The weekly magazine of the Italian Communist Party)

51. Neitzsche was Right; Twice

In *Beyond Good and Evil* Nietzsche wrote, "Madness is something rare in individuals — but in groups, parties, peoples, ages it is the rule". Today looking at Science and Technology Policy in the European Community it is only too clear that he was entirely correct. 1992 and the coming of the single internal market is not some invention by Brussels bureaucrats to provide out-relief for the mobile middle class in the European theatre, rather it is a gentle attempt to direct and channel the 'natural' evolution of modern industrial society as it transits to a new level of organisation at a sub-Global rather than national level. Industry has been way ahead of Jacques Delors in the race to Europeanise its operations. The iron law of competitivity drove it mercilessly along the only path available. To compete with the United States and, more importantly, Japan the domestic market had to grow. Europe was the answer.

It is equally clear, despite much wishful thinking to the contrary, and the occasional human sacrifices of sections of the workforce in certain declining industries to propitiate the gods of the free market, that managing high technology industry is a hands-on partnership involving Government in quite intimate ways. In Japan the infamous Ministry of International Trade and Industry (MITI) uses 'entrusted research' and 'research cartels' as weapons of competitivity to boost rates of initial innovation and levels of post-innovative performance in the economy. In the United States defence spending and defence specifications act in their own very inefficient contemporary way to underpin a hurting industry. Even the most sceptical supporters of *Star Wars*, or the Strategic Defence Initiative (SDI) as it was more formally known, who were incredulous of its claims to offer an invisible but impenetrable dome over the United States that would protect it from incoming ballistic missiles, saw clearly its economic and industrial spin-off.

Yet in Europe we demonstrate our madness. We do this in two ways, quantitatively and qualitatively. In a Community whose future lies in competing with Japan and the United States in high technology industrial goods we spend something between a half and two-thirds of the Community budget on Agriculture. Leaving aside the facts that half of this budget is spent on initially storing then destroying food, that the food produced is very unhealthy, and that current advances in biotechnology threaten to turn the flow of surpluses into a flood, it is still insane that expenditure on Research, Development and Demonstration (RD&D), and the necessary ancillary activities such as training, are an order of magnitude smaller than Agricultural expenditure. When Jacques Attali suggested to President Mitterrand that Europe needed a co-ordinated response to the SDI program, what did we get? Eureka, a project named after a science exhibition put on in Paris' *avant-garde* George Pompidou Centre, that embraced almost all the countries of Western Europe, was almost totally non-selective and non-interventionist and to cap it all had no funds in terms of global technology. Xavier Fels, the Secretary-General of Eureka, estimated that the total *new* funding was between 0-400 million ecu (1 ecu = £0.70). Unfortunately the same failures are to be found almost across the board with the European Commission's technology programmes.

There is a lack of selectivity, concentration, and evaluation, built on top of a failure to make technological choices and work close to the market. The first barrier is defence. The essential problem is that Europe fails to work close to the market in terms of RD&D. The competition rules are used to tie at least one and possibly more of Europe's arms behind its back. In defence *Article 223* of the Treaty of Rome is used to exempt the military industries from the few mildly interventionist and rational elements of European competition policy. In the civil sector the self imposed and implemented bondage of the competition rules ensure that Community RD&D is kept well away from the market place. Japan's post-war high technology success has depended not on basic research, but on work close to the market directly feeding industrial innovation. Yet we congratulate ourselves that we have now succeeded in persuading the Japanese to increase their emphasis on pure rather than applied research. Two wrongs don't make a right.

In terms of sources of innovation it seems clear that in the United States Small and Medium Enterprises (SMEs) are central. In Japan they are irrelevant. In Europe there is an assumption that we follow the American paradigm with precious little empirical evidence. We continue to feed large amounts of resources into direct research in Institutions like the Joint Research Centre at Ispra whose measures of achievement are woeful, whose revitalisation is always tomorrow, and whose main *raison d'etre* is self preservation, instead of encouraging direct, serious and long-term Industry-Academic partnership.

Even at a European level we cannot afford to do everything, we have to make technological choices. Is the SDI or the Japanese *Human Frontier Science Program* closer to the technological trajectory of the future? Even when these choices are made it is necessary to go further. Science and technology are risky activities.

Europe needs to participate in taking those risks. Yet to use resources in the best way a line has to be drawn somewhere. Ongoing evaluation has finally to say enough is enough from time to time.

Finally, if we are to escape our madness, we have to recognise our situation. Europe in the coming decades will face a long struggle to obtain a position of economic strength in the world. The key determinate will be the success of European industry, whose motor will be RD&D and the associated families of innovations whose descendants will provide the wealth and the employment. Science and technology are central to the European enterprise. It must be given the place it deserves, but this requires politicians and scientists to stop believing anyone deserves a free lunch and instead recognise that the process of triage is necessary if one is to concentrate on the essentials.

New Scientist, 8 June 1991

52. Review

Neo-Fascism in Europe, edited by Luciano Cheles, Ronnie Ferguson & Michalina Vaughan

This book is a collection of nine papers from a conference on neo-fascism held at the University of Lancaster in November 1987, with three additional chapters on Portugal, Greece and "Women and the National Front" commissioned to cover the lacunae discovered during the initial conference. The twelve chapters plus introduction cover the extreme right in the European Community reasonably comprehensively with two chapters on each of Italy, Germany, France and the United Kingdom, and one each on Spain, Portugal and Greece, rounded out by an introduction on "Concepts of Right and Left" and a chapter looking more generally at 'Holocaust Denial' literature in Europe and the United States.

The best single chapter is Sheelagh Ellwood's "The Extreme Right in Spain: A Dying Species?" which looks at the so far unsuccessful attempts to modernise the atrophied ideologies and practices of Spain's Francoist parties. The attempt by Blas Pinar — Spain's only post-Franco extreme-right MP — to link up with the French *Front National* home and away produced no electoral success but the telling comment "Spain, however, as successive post-Francoist Governments have not tired of reiterating, is in Europe; and in Europe, there can never be room for complacency."

Other useful chapters include "Nostalgia Dell'Avvenire" — a study of the hidden fascist imagery and iconography to be found in the Italian neo-fascist *Moviemento Sociale Italianio's* recent publicity campaigns by Luciano Cheles, one of the editors, and Vassilis Kapetanyannis's piece on "Neo-Fascism in Modern Greece", a very neglected subject. Finally, Roger Eatwell's "The Holocaust Denial: A Study in Propaganda Technique" makes some astute observations and asks some important questions. How does one deal with academics or semi-academics who actually believe in the truth of their work?

But overall, the book suffers from its origins and its timing. It is a collection of views with no coherent philosophy or position running through the whole, ranging from highly academic analysis of "Concepts of Right and Left" to Gerry Gable's summary of *Searchlight*'s recent work. It is dated; Eastern Europe, the main growth point currently of the extreme right, is still behind the wall and the curtain, and Michael Kuhnen, Germany's neo-nazi Fuhrer, has died of aids. Finally, despite three editors, it required better editing. Opinions may differ, but 'facts', even small ones, should stay the same between chapters. For the bookshelf rather than the political rally.

Tribune, 14 June 1991

53. Interview on Racism in Europe

Mr Ford, you were rapporteur for the Parliament's Committee of Inquiry into Racism and Xenophobia. From your investigations, what general conclusions did you draw about the treatment of immigrants to the European Community?

First, let me say that I have been heavily involved in both of the Parliament's inquiries in this area. There was a Committee of Inquiry from 1984 to 1986, of which I was Chairman, which produced a report on the growth of racism and fascism in Europe. In 1989, I was appointed rapporteur for a second Committee of Inquiry into racism and xenophobia and was responsible for drafting the report, which is going to be published in its final version next session in September. One of the recommendations was that there should be an annual debate in Parliament and that is likely to take place in October.

In terms of the conclusions, I think the broad one would be that there is a problem of racism throughout the European Community.

The victims differ according to the country but the problems are essentially the same. In Germany it is the Turkish guest workers; in France, the people from the Maghreb; in the UK, the Afro-Caribbeans and the Asians. There is a rising tide of racism sweeping across Europe although its extent, and the extent to which it is increasing, does vary from country to country.

I am not very keen on drawing up tables but I think it is fairly clear, just from reading the European press, that it is unfortunately something which is on the increase. And I believe we need positive action to tackle it. I don't accept the idea that if we just sit on our hands, the issue is going to go away.

One of the problems we have is over a European policy on immigration. There clearly needs to be such a policy if the internal barriers are going to come down, and we are in favour of that. The Committee of Inquiry and the Parliament, which adopted its recommendations, believe that the Schengen and Trevi Groups, which are both inter-governmental bodies, should be abolished and that competence in the matters they deal with should be brought within the remit of the Commission and the Parliament.

At the moment, we have this bizarre agenda for both Schengen and Trevi which covers control of international terrorism, drug trafficking, immigration, the right of asylum and prostitution. Now that is a very illiberal agenda. It is suggesting that they are the same kind of problems and they are not — at least not for me and I think not for the rest of the Parliament. I think it is important that we see issues being brought under Parliamentary control. Maybe, if that happens, we won't have the kind of outcome I would like to see, but at least it would have some democratic accountability. At the moment, decisions are made behind closed doors with no accountability to anybody.

Looking at the question of visas, we are talking now about having a common policy in this area. I am in favour of a common visa policy but not one that says that if there is any country in the European Community that currently requires a visa for someone from a third country, then everybody is going to need it. This would mean moving — and the figures change week by week — from a position where about 25 countries in the world require a visa for all 12 Member States to one where 115 countries do. That is not harmonisation, that is illiberalism. So there has to be a happy medium between the two.

As regards asylum policy, what they are now talking about is that anyone refused from any one Member State will automatically be refused from the other 11. The danger here, and I use not my terminology but terminology that is used outside, is that the state which is the 'softest' will have a flood of applicants. As a result, their barriers — their admission criteria — will be raised and the flood will be diverted elsewhere. With this ratchet effect, we are going to have a situation where Europe becomes a fortress to those people who want to flee here from persecution, death threats and so on. I am told that a very small percentage of the world's refugees — perhaps 3% — actually come to Europe. I think we have a responsibility to take them and we should not confuse asylum policy with immigration policy.

Another problem area involves Hong Kong and Macau. The British government made a decision that only something like 250,000 people from Hong Kong will be given British passports that will allow them admittance to the UK. Portugal has adopted the position that any resident of Macau can have a Portuguese passport. I visited Macau before I was elected to the European Parliament. The second language of the territory, after Chinese, is not Portuguese but English. With free movement inside the European Community, which we support, we are going to have a situation where many of these people are going to end up in Manchester, Liverpool or London. I am not against that, but it seems rather anomalous that we actually have Portuguese citizens being allowed into the UK, whereas people from our own colony of Hong Kong are being refused admittance. We need to have some common system otherwise it is going to become absurd.

As regards immigration, I have to say that I am not personally in favour of an entirely open-door policy, but what we do need is to have a policy which is non-racist. At the moment our immigration policy isn't non-racist. Taking the UK as an example, I have got people in my constituency who have been waiting 17 years to be reunited with their children. We have a situation where genetic finger-printing has proved that some of the children refused entry to the UK because they 'were not the children of the parents', were actually the children of the parents after all. They are now being refused entry because they are too old! As far as I am concerned, that is a racist immigration policy.

What do you think are the principal underlying causes of racism and xenophobia in the Community?

It can be tackled at a number of levels. I think partly it is a fear for the future. What you have is a small group of people who have always been with us, and unfortunately I suspect, always will be, who are intellectual, ideological racists and neo-fascists. I do not think there is very much we can do about them as a small group.

They deserve to be pushed to the margins of political society. Unfortunately, in the right sort of political climate, these people can crawl out of the margins and affect much broader swathes of politics. I think unfortunately the climate at the moment is a bit like that.

As I said, one of the underlying concerns is the fear for the future. A lot of people are very concerned about all the changes that are taking place, they feel that their jobs, their livelihoods and their way of life are being threatened, and they are actually blaming it on 'black people'. I think they are wrong. I am in favour of blaming the fascists, because it is their fault, but I think it is wrong for us to assume that anyone who ever votes for an extreme right wing candidate or makes a mild racist statement has to become a leper. We need a programme that actually educates people into understanding that they are in the same situation as many of the black people. Very often, they are the victims and not the problem. This is why, in the Committee of Inquiry report, one of the key recommendations which was accepted was that all European residents should have the same rights and duties. Racism is nonsense scientifically as well as being morally wrong, but most important of all, it is politically dangerous. If you have groups of second class citizens inside the Community then they are inevitably going to be exploited as regards hours of work, rates of pay, health and safety conditions and so on. If such exploitation happens, standards of living generally will suffer, so it is in all our interests to make sure that everybody has the same levels of treatment.

Following from our demand that all European residents should have the same rights and duties, there is, of course, a need to ensure the right of free movement around the Community for all residents. In other words, someone from Iran who has permanent residence in Germany should have the right to move freely around the Community. The same would apply to someone from India who lives in the UK. Look what would happen otherwise. For instance, if you get a job as a long distance lorry driver in England, you are going to be discriminated against if you do not have the right of free movement. Would you take on someone who has got to get a visa every time they go to France? No you would not, you would take on someone who does not have to. If you are an executive working for a company selling abroad, are you going to take on someone who, every time they fly to a meeting at the European Commission, has to get a visa. No you would not.

Perhaps more importantly, on a general level, is the fact that after the 1992 process is complete, there will be *de facto* free movement around the Community, but *de jure*, there may not be. What is going to happen is that unemployed immigrants are inevitably going to be attracted to centres of economic activity, where there are jobs. But if they are from France and they go to Frankfurt, where they are actually 'illegal', they are going to be open to exploitation with all the problems that flow from that.

I think there is a coherence and a consistency to the Committee of Inquiry's recommendations. Unfortunately for the moment, most of the talk about a Europe without barriers is only seen as applying to European citizens. Either they are going to keep the barriers, which makes a nonsense of the whole thing, or we are going to get the situation that I have just outlined which means that we are going to have a pool of second class citizens around, who are 'illegal' at least in a mild form. That illegal status will mean that they are going to be exploited and everybody will lose out as a result. Europe's future is about having a high wage, high skill, high technology economy. It is not, as a few people think, a matter of trying to out-compete the third world by keeping wages down.

About the European Resident's Charter which you said has been accepted by the European Parliament. What do you think the prospects are of it being adopted by the Council?

At the moment, I have to say quite frankly, not very much. If anything, we are on the defensive with regard to these issues. The Council as represented by its Member States appears to be increasingly racist at worst and unsympathetic at best. If one looks at recent statements that have come out of France — for example, the statement by Edith Cresson about 'putting them on planes and sending them back' — this is not the solution to the problem. If you want to understand what is going on, you should try to provide employment and help people to integrate — rather than this inhuman travel agency of putting people on to charter planes.

Looking at Germany, there may still be one or two people who think that the Russians are going to come charging across the borders in tanks but more and more people imagine that they are going to be arriving with suitcases. It is quite fascinating, I have now been to the Soviet Union twice with an 'eminent persons' delegation from the Student and Academic Campaign for Soviet Jewry to talk to people about the plight of Soviet Jews. When I went 18 months ago, I was there with British Conservative MPs — this is essentially a British activity — who were demanding the right for all Jews to emigrate. At that time, the Soviets were being difficult. We were there about 6 months ago, and the Conservative MPs had stopped making that demand. They were starting to realise that they now had a situation where up to a million people were going to emigrate and they did not want to let them in — so where were they going to go? We have now a slightly peculiar position in that the Soviet citizens have the right to leave but nobody wants to take them. It has finally dawned on some people that there is a slight inconsistency here. It is very convenient to beat the Soviet Union round the head and rightly so too, for refusing to allow people to leave, but the consequences of having a million people who are allowed to leave is that someone has to be willing to receive them. It is obvious that we are going to have to deal with the issue of migration from Eastern Europe.

Equally, we are going to have to look at the problems of movement from the south — particularly from the Maghreb — to the north. There are elements of political instability in North Africa, and the increasing emergency of Islamic fundamentalism is likely to lead to a fair number of people becoming political refugees. I would not want to live in an Islamic fundamentalist state if I had been brought up in Algeria in a fairly Western way. I say frankly that they are entitled to make their own choices as to what kind of government they want, but equally I can see that it might be very unattractive for some people who currently live there.

There is obviously some concern, which you have already briefly touched upon, over the direction currently being taken by some of the mainstream politicians in the Community over the immigration issue. How do you view this development?

One of the things we have to do is to tackle the problem head on. In 1984 when I was first elected, we tended to see Jean-Marie Le Pen as a symptom and not a cause of the problem. Mr Le Pen did not change his politics dramatically between 1979, when he stood in the European elections and got 0.3% of the vote, and 1984 when he got 10% and ten members of the Parliament. What had changed was the climate. I have to say that my position has evolved in that I think that Mr Le Pen, for example, is now part of the cause. He has established himself sufficiently and now has a political presence. He is not there because people are looking for a protest vote. He is there because people are unfortunately, in some numbers, supporting his ideas, and the danger is that other politicians on the right and now on the left are actually allowing Mr Le Pen to set the agenda. If you allow him to do this, you inevitably start supporting his arguments, because he ends up setting the terms of the debate. You get embroiled in the numbers game. Mr Le Pen says there are a million immigrants too many and you find yourself saying that there are perhaps half a million or a quarter of a million too many.

We actually have a situation at the moment where the French, for example, simultaneously, complain there are too many immigrants and about the problem of the falling birth rate. If you put those two things together, you actually have a situation where they appear to be complaining that there are too many black people: nothing else. You go round Paris and you see big adverts suggesting that French women should have more children and yet, at the same time, some French politicians are saying: 'hang on, the blacks are flooding in'. The two put together clearly indicate racism. There is not a genuine problem in the sense that France is getting overcrowded. If anything, projections indicate that France is going to have fewer people in the future — the problem seems to be the colour of the people.

Historically, we have had massive movements of peoples around Europe. I am not necessarily in favour of it. I would like to encourage people to stay where they are, but I don't think we can pretend that those movements have stopped. One of the ways we can try and deal with the problem — I am not in favour of banning people from moving — is to give more aid and assistance to the Third World, including of course the African, Caribbean and Pacific countries (ACPs). The second area is Eastern Europe which clearly needs aid and assistance. One of the most effective ways of keeping people in Poland, Czechoslovakia, Hungary, and the Soviet Union is for them to have decent jobs and decent standards of living. That is going to come by us giving them technical aid and assistance. The more we help them, the more we help ourselves.

Can I ask you, finally, about the Community's development policy, particularly in the context of the ACP countries. It is probably fair to say that one of the underlying aims of the policy has been to help maintain populations in their countries of origin. Does the increase in the number of migrant workers point to a failure of development policy at both bilateral and Community level?

Coming as I do from the United Kingdom, I think that the aid policy of the Community, as expressed through the ACP programme, is in advance of that of some Member States. In other words, I don't want to be seen as totally critical of EC policy. It has certainly been more progressive. But there is a problem of quantity. It seems to me that we must put more money into the aid budget. That is something which was true before developments in Eastern Europe, and before some of the more recent developments in the Third

World. It is even more urgent now. There is also a problem of quality. I don't accept all the arguments that are made about the inefficiency of the bureaucracy, but there have been some bureaucratic failures in terms of emergency aid. More importantly, what we should be doing is giving aid and assistance to help countries develop in their own way and I think that that has not always been the case. We have not always given appropriate technologies. For instance, in the energy area, we have tended to pass on what we have used up or what we have spare, rather than making sure that the technologies were designed for the country in question.

Finally, I should say that I think it can be liberating for people to move around the world. I don't think that just because some people come and want to work, it is necessarily a failure of the policy. After all, we are encouraging people to move around the European Community and I don't see why we can't encourage people to move around the world as well. What concerns me is when it is forced on people for political or economic reasons. We have to be careful in the way we measure these things and we certainly shouldn't be saying 'we must be succeeding because no people come here any more'. We do want an exchange, but clearly at the moment part of that exchange is an involuntary one. That is a failure and I think we should be doing more about it by continuing to shift our priorities.

One of my favourite quotes is Nietzsche's 'madness is rare in individuals but common in parties, groups or organisations'. Any community which manages to spend two-thirds of its budget on agriculture, half of which is on storing and destroying food, proves that Nietsche's dictum is entirely correct.

Interview by Simon Horner, The Courier, September/October 1991

54. Europe's Baltic Dilemma

The heavy fortifications which still surround the parliament buildings of Lithuania, Latvia and, to a lesser extent, Estonia are a mark of the continuing sense of insecurity in the Baltic states.

A few months after the three states were accepted as members of the United Nations, the Russian military remains camped on their soil and is in no hurry to leave, fuelling fears of another coup. Fear of the KGB is still high: in Lithuania it is blamed for almost everything that goes wrong and conspiracy theories are widespread.

But the Baltic states' main problems in the future will be internal rather than external, economic rather than military. The three new democracies, each smaller than Wales, are engaged in a race against time to unlock themselves from the collapsing economy of the former Soviet Union. They are still dependent on the rouble, which is currently depreciating at more than 10 per cent a week. Former Soviet markets cannot buy the Baltic states' exports; in return, the Baltic states are being starved of imports of medicines and fuel. Latvia and Lithuania are now suffering serious energy shortages; Estonia has less of a problem, although it does have to face the environmental consequences of oil shale production.

The three states are not going to be able to solve their problems alone. All are desperately short of trained technicians and managers, and there is little room for the three to co-operate together: their products are competitive rather than complementary. They need help: emergency fuel and medical aid, medium-term technical assistance, training in market economies and, crucially, greater trading opportunities outside the old Soviet bloc.

The European Community's decision to press ahead with agreements on trade and economic co-operation is good news for the Baltic states. But the EC will not allow dumping of yet more unwanted food on to its food mountains. The only possibility is triangular trade, with EC grain feeding Baltic dairy and meat sales to Russia.

This of course requires modern agricapital industry, not inter-war peasant farming: any attempt to revive small-scale peasant agriculture, as currently advocated by many who hark back wistfully to a 'golden age' of independence in the twenties and thirties, would be a disaster.

The strongest card the Baltic states have to play is their traditional links with the Nordic countries. Led by Denmark, the Nordic countries have already developed long-term programmes of assistance, and the Nordic Bank is proposing that a Baltic Investment Bank be set up. A close relationship with the Nordic states could well be an easier route towards future applications for EC membership than simply joining the queue behind Hungary, Czechoslovakia and Poland.

If they are not to jeopardise the economic help they need from the West, however, the Baltic states will have to resolve their political problems. The states' desire to re-establish their national identities has brought into sharp focus the question of how, after 50 years of Russification, they intend to treat their national minorities.

In Latvia and Estonia a debate is now raging over new citizenship laws. In Latvia, ethnic Latvians represent only 52 per cent of the population and fear that they could be 'swamped' by Russians. The draft citizenship law proposes that citizenship is restricted to those who were citizens in 1940 and their descendants. All others will have to fulfil a 16-year permanent residency qualification, pass a language test in Latvian and have no known connection with the KGB or the Soviet military or military-industrial complex. Given that voting, property-ownership and even employment rights depend on citizenship, this is clearly an attempt to drive the Russians out.

The proposed Estonian law is less draconian, requiring only two years' residence instead of 16. But the language qualification is similar, and the Estonian language is notoriously complex. In the north-east of the country, there are hundreds of thousands of Russian-speaking ethnic Estonians even using the Estonians' own proposed definition of nationality. It appears that their future is bleak, at least linguistically.

If these laws are ratified, the EC would have difficulty in signing trade and co-operation agreements, let alone in considering future Community membership.

In Lithuania, the problem is different — the hasty pardoning of Nazi war criminals responsible for the massacres of Lithuanian Jews. The Lithuanians took the view that the Soviet courts which made the convictions were merely tools used to subjugate the Lithuanian resistance against Soviet occupation; all those convicted were either innocent or heroes.

In the past couple of months international pressure on Lithuania to reconsider this position has been immense, particularly from United States Department of Justice officials who are currently in Vilnius, the Lithuanian capital, examining the files. President Vytautis Landsbergis gave us a clear commitment that any individual cases brought to his attention would be investigated by a special court. Our confidence in his promise was, however, severely shaken by an MP who suggested that the 100,000-plus Jews killed had all been working for the KGB.

The next few months will be critical in determining whether the future in the Baltic states will be one of open democracies welcoming all willing fully to commit themselves or one of ethnic conflict, matching Estonians and Latvians against stateless Russians, with Boris Yeltsin watching carefully from just across the frontier. The West needs to put pressure on the Russian and former Soviet authorities to withdraw troops and to ensure that what remains of the KGB is reined in, but it also has to make it clear that racist policies are wholly unacceptable.

Glyn Ford and Gary Titley
Tribune, 29 November 1991

55. Review

European Union: Fortress or Democracy? by Michael Barratt Brown

A wide ranging book that covers everything from the New Global Order to countertrading between producer co-operatives in the Third World and First World. It accepts the effective end of the medium-sized nation state as an entity capable of controlling its own destiny, and therefore acquiesces, and does not glory, in the need to create a new Europe integrated successfully in industrial and economic policy, political and security policy.

Michael Barratt Brown explains in the opening chapter the inexorable technical and political developments that have driven him to the conclusion that there is no alternative to membership of the European Community. Britain must play a full and active part in creating a Europe that will be a centre of global power.

But the title contains the message *'European Union: Fortress or Democracy?'* The author wants to ensure that the New Europe created is open, democratic and prosperous. This means that the necessary institutions need to be built: from an effective European Parliament to European Political Parties; from a European Trade Union Movement to transnational networks of Consumers, Socialists have to build in their own image at all levels. The tradition that the technological trajectory is fixed to ensure that the return to capital holds sway over the return to labour must be reversed. We must recognise that, while one of the most powerful drives to creativity is individualism — the wheel was not discovered by a committee, or Citizen Kane directed by a group — it must be balanced by a measure of planning and control in the interests of public welfare. It is only taking both into account that we can flick a switch, and thousands of people work for us around the world.

With the events in Central and Eastern Europe, and the subsequent political fall-out, we have plenty of time. Democratic socialists have been tainted by regimes that borrowed our name, and by our own comrades that confused the rhetoric and the reality. In Central and Eastern Europe it will be a generation and more before planning and freedom will be re-balanced after almost half a century of communism equalling planning plus bureaucracy and nepotism. Michael Barratt Brown produces a detailed schema as to how we can increase economic democracy through interlocking trading networks, like multilayered spiders webs, spanning industries and the world, based on his work as Chairman of Third World Information Network and Twin Trading Ltd. In places, the detail swamp the ideas as the author answers questions few would ask. These ideas are certainly part of the New Europe that *European Union: Fortress or Democracy?* calls for, that simultaneously accepts and transforms the logic of emerging global capitalism, but there are many battles to be fought and won on the way.

European Labour Forum, Winter 1991-92

Part 10

1992

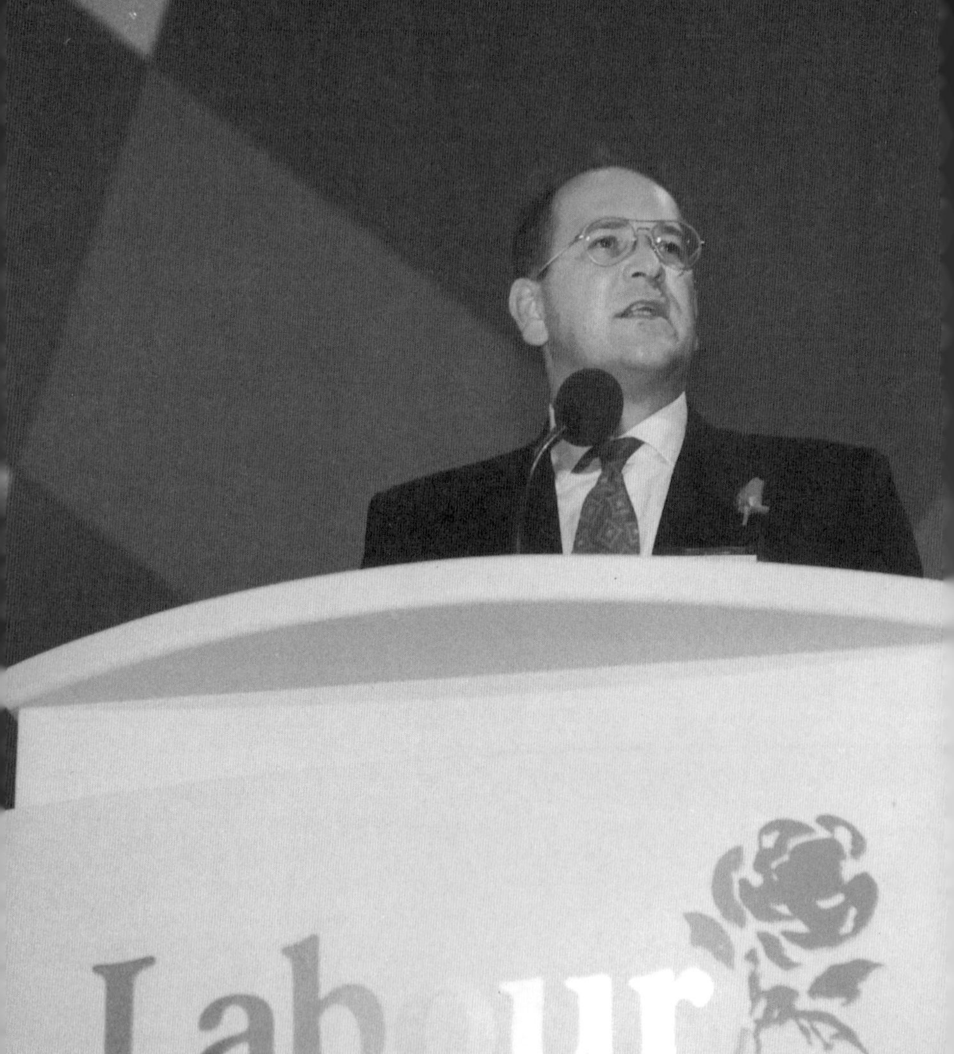
Labour

56. Maastricht: The Lost Opportunity

The Maastricht Summit has been described variously as a watershed in the life and times of the European Community, and as the single most important event in its history since the signing of the Treaty of Rome in 1958. For the European Parliament, however, it has not been the turning point it had hoped for in solving the problem of the democratic deficit.

The importance from the point of view of the European Parliament would have been the principles, put forward at the Rome meeting of Community Parliaments in November 1990 (the Rome Assizes) namely full-co-decision. The outcome at Maastricht has been to create procedures of almost absurd complexity, and quite simply to shut out the 'embarrassing witness' — the Parliament — instead of including the Parliament as one of the key actors in European Union.

While the Commission was allowed to participate, Parliament was merely an observer, and was conspicuous by its absence from negotiations. Over the last year, Parliament has worked ceaselessly behind the scenes to ensure that both Political Union and Monetary Union were dealt with on a parallel timescale, although not as one package. Had the Council of Ministers been left to set the agenda, economic and monetary union would have been taken solely and political union left in abeyance to be dealt with at some future date convenient to Member States.

The usual practice of horsetrading between the Member States of course meant that the terms discussed at Maastricht were actually all stitched up in advance. Mr Lubbers was widely celebrated in the British media post-Maastricht for his masterful diplomacy in ensuring the eleven would not jeopardise the entire Treaty reforms by allowing Britain, the hesitant and reluctant European, to have the final word — 'No, No, No.' He was fully appraised of Mr Major's improbable balancing act at home, leading a Party in total disarray generally, but particularly on Europe, by the contents of a video of the House of Commons pre-Maastricht debate. His sympathies evidently aroused, he then provided Major with the brown paper and string, and Mr Kohl provided the balsa wood, so that Mr Major could fly his kite all the way home.

While on social policy, John Major found a friend in his Conservative ally Chancellor Kohl. Negotiations were interrupted while the two came to a gentleman's agreement whereby Britain would not be opting out, but rather that the other eleven would be

◄ *October 1992: Party Conference (photo: Pat Mantle).*

opting in, thus preserving Major's ability to return home, Attlee-like, declaring 'peace with honour'.

As regards opting out of Economic and Monetary Union, the Bundesbank's 0.5% increase of interest rate this week underlines the fact that economic sovereignty lasts all of twenty minutes. While the idea of Economic and Monetary Union is to create a stable framework yielding benefits to Community Members and adding to harmonious regional development with the aim of reducing economic inequalities. Britain's unwillingness to participate means not only as a nation do we become marginalised, but as workers and citizens British people — both native and visitors — have only duties but no rights. The reality of a 'two speed Europe' is the creation of a Europe of first and second class citizens.

While at the social level the nightmare has just begun. It may have been totally unpalatable for respectable Conservatives to see social provision improved by external imposition, but the spectacle of British Ministers leaving the room when social matters are discussed in Council will be just the ominous starting point. This week German MEPs have called for all British MEPs — Labour and Tory alike — to be excluded from any discussion of social matters. If we can't endorse the policy, we are not allowed to make it.

It is embarrassing for Britain's MEPs that on two of the key issues the United Kingdom has arranged special protocols sidelining itself from the vision of the 1990s and beyond. British citizens, and indeed any other EC citizens living and working here, will find that they have been sold short on economic, financial and social issues; an ever widening gap will open up between the one and the eleven. Most embarrassingly, Major has been negotiating not for the sake of Britain in Europe but in keeping the Conservative Party together, with Major at the helm of the ship, cast adrift from mainland Europe, bobbing out of sight and out of control.

This transitional phase will be dragged out for as long as the Tories can stave off the next election. Labour's real commitment to sign up for the Social Charter, to being a full and participative member of the European Community, is the only vehicle by which to ensure social cohesion and a Europeanisation of Britain. British citizens must be truly bemused by a government which, while promising a Patient's Charter, a Tax Payer's Charter and a Parent's Charter, finds the only Charter it cannot sign — the one which can guarantee all of the above and commits the government itself to action — is the Social Charter.

This is all the more astonishing in the light of the initial draft of the Dutch Presidency. In the short first three months of the Dutch Presidency of the Council, the Dutch stood down from the moral highground of their original *Communitaire* vision and reverted totally to the Luxembourg blueprint, which advocated a continuation of the inter-governmental approach to European Union.

Is the final Maastricht deal in its current form acceptable to the European Parliament? If we ask the question, were we successful in ridding the institutions of the democratic deficit, in enhancing Europe's role as an international actor, and in creating a genuinely democratic people's Europe, then the answer is 'No, No, No.' Progress towards European Union is not keeping pace with change in Europe, but going forward in a series of small steps.

As the only democratically-elected European forum, Parliament had hoped to see its powers upgraded to at least have co-legislative powers. In many areas, indeed, Parliament's powers have been downgraded, with even more power concentrated in the Council of Ministers.

Following the Gulf War and Europe's poorly co-ordinated response to the Yugoslavian conflict, the move towards Europe speaking with one voice has simply reiterated the principle of a common foreign and security policy, but the procedures remain unchanged. As Jacques Delors has pointed out, these procedures are unnecessarily complex.

Member States will now decide by unanimity in the Council of Ministers on common areas of action, and then further decide by unanimity whether to apply qualified majority voting to the implementation of common foreign and security policy.

Moves towards common European defence, promoted primarily by France and Germany, were modified by Britain to ensure that all we get are common defence policies — again Members can reserve the right to go it alone if it is in their national interests. Indeed, Britain's inclination is toward an *à la carte* Europe — you pick off the menu only the items you want. On Economic and Monetary Union, Britain's position is to put off the day of reckoning. Afraid of missing out, they have decided that they will opt in, but later, and on their terms.

Rassegna, 10 February 1992
(The weekly magazine of the Democratic Party of the Left in Italy)

57. Review

Paradigms Lost edited by Chester Hartman and Pedro Vilanova

In the past three years our world has turned upside down. The United States won the Cold War more finally and comprehensively than the Gulf War. The fall of the Berlin Wall was the swallow that brought a summer of collapsing authoritarian and totalitarian economies throughout Central and Eastern Europe. The chaos of the free market swept all before it. From a social viewpoint the problem was almost worse. Hidden deep within most socialists was the view that even the degenerate Workers' States of the Soviet Empire had something to teach. Now we know. The fiercest critics of these regimes never managed to portray the sheer awful ordinariness of state repression in Romania and East Germany. The combination of Stalinism and efficiency means that *1984* became the reality.

Now socialists have some explaining to do, both to themselves and the rest of the world. Were the events of the last three years the inevitable failure of a system flawed at its very heart? A system that could only unwind in this particular manner. A political philosophy out of time, doomed to be replaced by the neo-poujadism sweeping much of continental Europe in the guise of Le Pen, Haider or the Leagues. Or, instead, was it a temporary setback? A less than perfect construction failing under intolerable pressures, whose errors need to be identified and rectified allowing rebuilding on similar but stronger foundations.

Paradigms Lost takes the second view. The dozen or so authors are all associated with the Transnational Institute in Amsterdam, or the Institute for Policy Studies in Washington, both well-known radical think-tanks. Dan Smith argues the need for a new European Security framework based on the ideas of collaboration rather than confrontation; ideas such as 'common security' and 'defensive deterrence' and the need to insist that we harvest the peace dividend. If this is to happen it will require a new European Institutional Architecture with democratic accountability built right into the foundations.

Pedro Vilanova and Fred Halliday in separate pieces try to confront the problems of nationalism. The phenomenon that time and again has proved its power against the iron logic of internationalism. Currently it seems to be in the driving seat again, whether in Scotland or Estonia, Ossetia or Kurdistan. We have no choice but to ride the tiger. Yet in its own heart are the seeds of its destruction. Industrial and state capitalism has stirred too well the races on the global palette. Minorities cascade down the finest dividing lines. 'Little fleas have lesser fleas upon their backs to bite 'em, and so *ad infinitum*'. But the process can be painful. The fact that genetic variation within races is almost as enormous as that found within the world population doesn't stop the British National Party in Rochdale or the Serbs in Yugoslavia.

Other contributors look at the way the Cold War is being replaced by the Drug War; Military Intervention in the Third World;

Sustainable Development in the 1990's; Third World Labour. *Paradigms Lost* is not coherent enough to provide a new framework within which to think. It's far too early. Nevertheless there are a good many building blocks that we should try to incorporate in the future structure. Two in particular stand out. One is old, the other new. The first is participatory democracy. Michael Shuman demonstrates how peace campaigns and asylum campaigns at town, city and state level have counterbalanced and shifted government policies. Second, Susan George makes the point that the annual turnover of the Top 200 transnational companies equals 30% of the Gross World Product. Many are more important that medium-sized nation states. Those 'citizens of these landless states', the employees, should fight for the right to vote. Develop that and you would certainly have a new way of thinking and seeing.

Tribune, 13 March 1992

58. The EC and Japan: The New Agenda

Within the European Community, attitudes toward Japan have been characterised by admiration for the achievements of the Japanese economy, its performance in the world economy, high rates of productivity and efficient exploitation of new technologies. Simultaneously, and as a result of this high performance, relations have been characterised by a distinct irritation at Japan's chronic surplus and what are perceived to be unfair trading practices and protectionist policies. For the most part, then, the EC-Japan relationship has developed primarily in the economic context. On balance, this has been dominated by disagreements over trade and mutual recriminations about protectionism.

Hitherto the structure of the European Community has been such that external relations were confined to external economic relations, with the individual member states responsible for conducting international diplomacy and foreign relations on a bilateral level. Understandably then, for as long as the Community had not taken itself seriously, Japan continued to view Europe as a highly fragmented region and not as a cohesive and effective regional actor, preferring to deal with states on a bilateral basis. In addition to this, since 1945 Japan has generally pursued a policy of cultural and linguistic isolation, parochial self-interest in the international arena, with no evidence of a world view or sense of global responsibility for the burning political questions of the day other than the drive for global economic penetration.

Yet the advent of the so-called 'New World Order' has given Japan new political priorities. Foreign policy *per se* has been elevated to the top of the Japanese policy agenda which calls for new responses from the European Community.

Two major events have awakened Japan's interest in Europe. In 1986 Europe's decision to create the Single European Market shifted Europe to the top of Japan's foreign policy agenda. This was to a great extent guided by the fear of being excluded from what was increasingly seen to be the development of a 'Fortress Europe'.

The Community's 1992 programme and the opening up of Eastern Europe represented the further consolidation of Ohmae Kenichi's vision of the emerging triad power system in the global economy with Japan, the US, and the EC as the three leading industrial powers. But, according to Ohmae's regional globalisation theory, the globe was to be carved into three slices of the pie; Japan was to extend its influence over the Asia-Pacific region; the US was to expand its dominance across Latin America, and Europe was to have Africa. The opening up of Eastern Europe, however, presented Europe with a new set of opportunities which Japan was eager to cash in on. The watershed in Europe in 1989 with the revolutions in the eastern half of the European continent was a further turning point for Japan in its attitude to Europe. The end of communism in Eastern Europe signalled for the Japanese the renaissance of the European continent as a politically and economically significant region. Japan participated in the EC-organised G-24 group in November 1989. At the same time, the Prime Minister's office announced the East European Doctrine. This was followed by a second aid programme and Japan's 'New European Doctrine' announced by Nakayama Taro in Prague in the Spring of 1990.

The wish not to be excluded from the economic opportunities for investment and new markets which this, too, would offer is not the only reason for Japan's keen interest in Europe. There have also been signs that Japan is interested in a greater and more active role in the international political system as seen in attempts to get involved in the CSCE process; the search for a permanent role in the UN and its willingness to use aid diplomacy for exerting influence.

The Hague declaration of July 1991 was to put EC-Japanese relations on a firmer basis. It was a commitment by both the EC and Japan to strengthen what has long been the weak axis of the triad system and was a codification of the recognition of the mutual importance of both actors on the world stage. It was politically significant as an attempt to achieve a more equal balance among the three leading industrial groupings following the Brussels-Washington Transatlantic declaration of November 1990.

While the EC-Japan declaration stressed reciprocity in trade, it set an important precedent for more frequent diplomatic contacts where both areas of disagreement could be discussed and where new areas of co-operation could be opened up. The Prime Minister of Japan will in future meet annually with the EC Presidency and the EC Council.

As crucial as EC-Japanese trade relations are to the functioning of the world economy, this must not be allowed to determine the relationship to the exclusion of all other ties and contacts. Europe should deal with economic and trade tensions pragmatically. It is not, in my view, constructive to complain about Japanese protectionism when we have after all our own form of protectionism in the CAP.

It is then equally justifiable for Japan to look after the interests of its own rice farmers. The real issue is that we are being outcompeted by Japan in our home markets and this is felt most acutely not only in the automobile sector and in electronics but even in areas where Europe has a strong tradition. In pharmaceuticals and biotechnology we are also falling behind. Yet this aggressive approach to trade only serves to create further division and distortion in world trade patterns and leads to what Immanuel Wallerstein perceived to be a three-tier system of strong 'core' states and regions and weak 'peripheral' and 'semi-peripheral' regions.

The trade deficit is not insignificant standing at some $18 to $19 billion. More important is that it is set to increase and that it is exclusively concentrated in the key industries, cars and electronics. This imbalance in trade between Europe and Japan has been aggravated by the hard line approach which the UK has taken. The arch proponent of free trade philosophy has persistently accused the Japanese of unfair trade practices and responded with protectionism and so Japan has instead turned its attention to the EC. In order to gain a foothold in 'Fortress Europe', Japan has been pushing actively with inward investment. In some states it is welcomed. Britain is the world's second largest recipient of Japanese foreign investment receiving 40 per cent of total Japanese investment within the EC. Wales and the North-East have benefitted greatly and overall it has been favourable for the UK trade performance. In other states, France for example, Japanese foreign investment is seen as the Trojan Horse where it will end in the decimation of European industries and total foreign ownership. This only serves to aggravate the lack of a cohesive and rational

European policy towards Japan, and allows Japan to play off Paris against London. It does not change the fact that Japan is a chronically persistent surplus country. Attempts to reduce the trade surplus by making Japanese goods more expensive have backfired by increasing the profit margins of the large electronics multinationals such as Sony. The demand for high quality reliable products is such that this measure did not have the desired effect. The need, therefore, is to encourage Japan to open up, improve market access for European products and expand domestic demand. Europe, too, needs to start to conquer Japanese markets in consumer goods.

On the economic front it will be critical to combine competitive policies with more co-operative ties with Japan in order to avoid misunderstandings and misperceptions. The signal which Japan is receiving from Europe is that their concern over 'Fortress Europe' is unjustified and that, as the internal barriers come down, the EC will not be erecting a hard external shell. This is, of course, far removed from reality; nor does this kind of misrepresentation facilitate good relations. The fact is that as Europe comes together in an effort to achieve the critical mass which will allow it to compete effectively with its triad partners as a strong regional bloc, it will certainly engage in protectionism on a sectoral level. There will not be a massive fortress of Europe *per se* but a series of small fortresses. This will be transitional, temporary, and operational only in certain sectors. It is, I believe, the only way to get the Single European Market off the ground. For politicians the priorities are clear. They have a duty in a time of great change to engage in damage limitation. They have a responsibility to their electorate to protect jobs and industries. Without a minimal and transitional phase of protectionism, the European project would fail. For as Europe restructures and streamlines its industrial sector, its vulnerability to outside competitors is more acute. Opening up would be akin to forcing a chronically ill patient to run the marathon. As borders come down, there is more scope for US and Japanese penetration, which brings us back to the Trojan Horse thesis. But Japan is already operating in Europe and has moved a number of its manufacturing plants to Europe. Inward investment and job creation are to be welcomed. But Europe will not in the long term benefit from screwdriver plants. It needs, instead, to benefit from the expertise of Japanese R&D, which should ideally constitute a firm component of Japan's commitment to Europe, bringing with it facilities and using and developing indigenous research potential.

Europe's inability to compete effectively with Japan is due to our lack of flexible manufacturing processes, and of investment commitment, capacity and partnership which the Japanese system demonstrates and which would allow us to compete with Japan on an equal footing. It is these failings which are the main obstacles to gaining the leading edge in new technologies and in post-innovative performance. If we are to attempt to compete with Japan then we need to do so on Japanese terms. Just as Japan has recognised that the route to wealth and prosperity is to invest more in R & D and education and training, we also need to concentrate on these fundamental elements.

In the European Parliamentary Labour Party's policy document, 'The New Europe', we have acknowledged the changes underway in the global arena, which require more co-operation as well as competition with Japan and the US. This manifesto illustrates our clear commitment to building up our strengths in R&D, to committing more financial resources to education, training and, above all, for the government to guide this process and see future goals and targets along with our European partners. In Britain, we are all too aware of the failure of *laissez-faire* economics where we have paid the price in economic performance.

Socialists in Europe have been impressed by the Japanese approach to investment, their concept of partnership and commitment to human and capital investment. Equally we have admired aspects of the Japanese approach to science and technology, with Japan's managed interventionist policy and the application of new technological developments to production processes and to work organisation. We are not, however, uncritical of some aspects of work practice. The success of the Japanese automobile industry is no less due to the long hours of overtime and low wages. In France, for example, the average worker may clock up overtime of 98 hours a year, while in Japan the figure stands at 55 hours a month, while wage levels at Toyota are almost 50 per cent of levels offered at Peugeot. As democratic socialists we are interested not just in flexibility of work processes and modern production systems but in the ability of the worker to influence these processes and to benefit from flexibility in work patterns.

In the past, the direction and priorities of Japanese science and technology policy have provided ideas for a future European joint and concerted technological programme. While the US concentrated its R&D on the Strategic Defence Initiative and the development of dual technologies which would then benefit the civilian sector, the historical legacy of Japan was such that they have concentrated on civilian technologies. The Japanese response in 1987 to SDI was to concentrate on political and human needs through the development of the Human Science Frontiers Programme, the key components of which were to conduct research into neuro-biology, heredity, growth differentiation, immunity, endocrinology, metabolism, and energy conversion. This project also included elements of international collaboration, although Europe on the whole continued to co-operate closely with the US. In practically all fields, co-operation and collaboration with Japan remain at a low level.

In the European Parliament the importance of Japan is not reflected in our contacts. Many of us have informal links but, for the most part, contacts are developed within the barely functioning all-party EP Japanese delegation.

This is a deficit which will rapidly need to be dealt with and considerable efforts need to be made to upgrade relations with Japan. Japan already follows the developments within the EP with keen interest and may even give it more attention than some European member states do. Europeans also need to be more aware of the changing internal structures in Japan, for this has a decisive impact on the conduct of Japan's external relations. In the last few years the result of these changes has been to produce a much more self-confident policy; a less self-effacing and much more nationalistic Japan, which recently has crossed the taboo line by increasing military expenditure, and passing new legislation to allow the posting of Japanese troops in non-combatant roles abroad. In Europe, we should be supporting Japan in its attempts to emerge from its self-imposed isolation. For this helps Europeans not to fall into the trap of navel-watching and Eurocentrism while stronger Euro-Japanese relations in the political and economic spheres are a good counterweight to US dominance.

In a changing world, the political imperatives for dialogue and co-operation are stronger, and the latter is a critical factor in mutual understanding and confidence in each other's intentions and policies. Interest and contacts should not be confined to the economic arena nor to S&T co-operation. In an interdependent world it is no longer possible to deal separately with trade, business, and foreign policy.

The future question is what roles the EC and Japan are destined to assume in the so-called New World Order. Here, both have a lot in common: they are both seen as economic giants and political pygmies. These roles were, of course, determined by the reconstruction of the post-World War Two order when the US, as the economic giant and world policeman, set the parameters and introduced the *Pax Americana*. This situation has been reversed with the US, however, still wishing to exercise global leadership on the basis of inadequate resources, and Japan and the EC possessing the resources, but lacking the political will to be able to have any leading role in establishing a peaceful and prosperous global order.

For the brief period of hostilities in the Gulf War it looked like the New World Order was rapidly reverting to the old with the US in the driving seat. In the wake of the Gulf War, the US renewed its claim to global leadership, Japan was reviled for refusing to deploy armed forces overseas — while in fact it was only adhering to its American-drafted constitutional constraints — as was Germany. Europe as a regional power was accused of providing a patchy and uncoordinated response, and so the triad-power world was stillborn.

Less than two years ago there was much rejoicing at the prospect of breaking out of the strait-jacket of the military bipolarity which had dominated the European continent for over forty years and constrained the emergence of Europe as a world actor in its own right. These changes were also coupled with the vision of the downgrading of the role of the military factor in the conduct of international relations. Yet even Japan, which has long rejected a dominant military role, is worried about the stability of the 'New World Order' and, if the US were to withdraw from the Pacific, may feel obliged to fill the vacuum.

Japan is a classic example which contradicts the myth of the demilitarisation of international politics and reinforces the reality of a world where arms sales and transfers continue unabated. Japan is even beginning to distinguish itself as a major arms exporter and in the twenty-first century is destined to be a major competitor for the US and Europe in arms exports. Its industrial performance and efficiency make it a more reliable source of weapons. Japan then has also begun to add to the overcapacity in the defence industries, presenting yet another sector where Europe will be out-competed. It has also become increasingly clear that Japan's R&D priorities are in flux. More resources are being committed to the military budget following the decision to raise military expenditure above the constitutionally laid down level, 1 per cent of GNP; in any case, even 1 per cent of a vast GNP is not an insignificant amount. In the period 1980-1988, Japan was second only to the US in terms of military expenditure growth and in terms of real military expenditure (in US $mil!) it came fifth after the US, France, Germany and the UK. It is the leading importer of weapons in the industrialised world. In the same period it was the major importer after India and Iraq and, in 1989, was the second largest importer, surpassed only by India. Japan also has the sixth largest army in the world. The contradictions are all too apparent; there is, on the one hand, a reluctance to play a military role and, on the other, evidence of an increasing military build-up and an increased role in the arms trade. All the indications point to Japan throwing off its reputation as a timid Titan, but in many ways Japan will remain a 'semi-Gulliver' constrained by its past, tied down by the mistakes of history and its suspicious neighbours, but having outgrown its competitors in economic strength and, by implication, potential political influence. It is important for Europe to cultivate cultural links and political ties with Japan in order to reform attitudes which are for the most part framed by fear and ignorance. Socialists in Europe need to encourage Japan to develop a more vigorous and vocal role in international fora which contributes to a more balanced and just world order. Japan's performance at the London G-7 summit was not indicative of this type of approach, and this only reinforces the need for progressive forces in Europe and Japan to link up and create more elbow room for global progressive politics. The arms trade is one area where Europe should encourage Japan to get involved in attempts to achieve a global arms export control system under UN auspices. Japan, with its industrial management expertise, should also be brought into initiatives for working out arms conversion models.

In the final analysis the world as it stands in 1991 is a complex mix of stability and instability, of integrating and disintegrating structures. The only way to deal with the new challenges, threats, and opportunities which arise is to engage in polycentric steering in which Europe, Japan, and the US will have critical roles to play. Both Europe and Japan in the past have taken a backseat and will need to adapt to this new role. Their contribution would be much more effective and balanced if, in the light of the changed international environment, they were to consolidate their economic, political and cultural relations.

Japan Forum, April 1992

59. European Socialisms in Crisis: the Rise of Radical Right Populism

Labour's defeat on April 9th was a terrible shock to us all, if only for the rising expectations that the campaign engendered, with opinion polls and party workers colluding together in imagining that we would achieve the largest anti-Government swing for almost half a century. The reality was that a result, in terms of seats gained, that would have ousted the Tory Governments of 1951, 1955, 1970 and 1979 was not enough in 1992. We failed. Already a multitude of reasons have been advanced for the primary causes of this failure: John Smith's Shadow Budget; the triumphalist Rally in Sheffield; Register Refugees, lost Labour voters fleeing from the electoral register in an attempt to avoid the Poll Tax; Torremelinos Tories voting from tax-exiles in the sun; the *Sun*. All partly true, and one could add to the list: racism in South Yorkshire; the gender gap amongst young men and older women; the created myths, accepted even by our own supporters as historical fact, around the last Labour Government.

Yet all this avoids the central failure. To explain what was happening in Britain, in Europe and in the world. To learn from it, provide an alternative vision of the future *and* convince people that it could, and would, be delivered. This failure is only too well illustrated in the post-mortems. We arrogantly imagine that our failure is unique. Our insularity, the inward looking nature of British politics, means that we don't see the connections between what is happening in the United Kingdom and in the rest of Europe, let alone take it into account.

The United States won the Cold War. The Soviet Union and its colonies were finally driven into political and, more importantly, industrial bankruptcy by the American defence establishment continually pushing up the ante in the poker game of superpower mutual deterrence. The house of cards collapsed revealing a misery of human existence in East Germany, Romania and the Soviet Union that went beyond even the dismal portraits painted by right-wing commentators in the West. Like Oscar Wilde's *The Picture of Dorian Gray* the outward façade remained while massive corruption destroyed from within. All to be revealed, like Dorian Gray's picture, as the fall of the Berlin Wall echoed around Europe signalling the End of Empire.

On the Continent the Social Democratic Left has been tainted by this heritage. Partly unfair, but there were enough Fellow Travellers to give the lie to claims that socialists had no truck with these miserable failed and flawed regimes. The result is that in Eastern and Central Europe the antique Socialist and Social Democratic Parties emerging from almost half a century of repression have been rapidly driven to the margins of politics as the reaction against 'socialism' gathers pace. In the West the political fallout has damaged the German SPD and the Italian PDS (former Italian

Communist Party) directly and poisoned the environment for all those ideas associated with the legacy of Totalitarianism: State Control; Public Ownership; Centralisation; Bureaucracy.

Another facet of the same phenomena that pre-staged the collapse in the East, but has since resonated with it, is the explosive growth of Extreme-Right and Right-Wing Populist Parties, and even Green Parties, across Western Europe. The post war political frameworks are seen to be not delivering either an acceptable process or product and voters search for non-Left alternatives. Le Pen's *Front Nationale* in France and the *Republikaner* in Germany, Jorg Haider's *Freedom Party* in Austria and the *Vlaams Block* in Flanders. But also the populist parties in Scandinavia and the *Leagues* in Italy, which in their way are even more dangerous. History rarely repeats itself.

Traditional fascist parties are making progress, but those like Le Pen and Haider prepared to cut their past with contemporary populism do better, and those like the *Leagues* untainted by history threaten to make xenophobia respectable again. At least superficially, all these have agendas that are against the traditional centre and its accompanying bureaucracy and corruption, prefers private to public, and wants to restore peoples right to make choices over the decisions that directly effect them. This political seachange is the one the Tories sell in Britain repainted in the colours of our culture and history.

This is the environment in which April 9th came and went. Labour was now electable. The voters didn't want to elect us. Labour was seen to be old-fashioned, backward looking to a world of the past, the world that has gone forever. We said, 'It's Time for Change'. It wasn't the kind of change people wanted. Our failure was revealed most poignantly by the fact that we lost the young men. We now have a gender gap amongst under twenty-five year old males. It is not that the building blocks aren't there in our policy documents. The problem is that the framework in which they are presented has deep within it the burden of the past that the Tories have jettisoned.

The Labour Party as a European Party — along with its sister Parties in Europe — has to learn how to organise and fight on this new terrain. It is not a terrain that we would pick if we had a choice. *History and economics don't let us choose.* Isolationism isn't the answer either. It's worse than the disease. The Single Internal Market wasn't invented by Jacques Delors. It is the product of thousands of decisions made over decades by European industrialists in an attempt to safeguard their own futures as work process innovations demand new and wider structures. The European Community is attempting to direct and channel this ongoing process in a way that both allows European industry to improve its productivity and competitivity while safeguarding the interests of workers and consumers today and tomorrow. Opting out on going forward just leaves others in the driving seat.

We, the Labour Party, have to absorb the new spirit of the age, distil its essence and use it to lubricate the creation of contemporary policies that will benefit the many at the expense of the few, that will create more wealth from less, that will ensure that those that can help those that cannot and, most importantly, liberate and empower individuals to shape their own development, community and future.

We have to acknowledge that an era has passed, the world is changing. We will have to operate in a new framework of ideas and realities that owe little to the old superpower polarisation of the post-war settlement and instead is a multi-polar world where Japan, the United States and Europe have similar roles. A world where medium-sized nation states are simultaneously too large and too small. A Europe that continues to walk the tightrope towards increasing industrial, economic and political integration and yet where simultaneously real regional autonomy is created.

Labour must offer a positive vision of hope and fulfilled aspirations where indigenously created and controlled technologies offer high skills and high salaries in an environment safeguarded for the future. A society where people and communities, wherever possible, make decision for themselves. Where everybody, all residents, are involved as equal partners, and are empowered to intervene at all levels of society. Where from a position of strength we help those in need locally, nationally and on a global scale. All we have to do is to convince the Labour Party. In the context of the current leadership elections, we need to start a long march.

Tribune, 22 May 1992

60. Jamboree Starts Race for the White House

Madison Square Garden in New York is where I saw a Labour Party Conference after another election defeat. It was the Democratic National Convention, that four-yearly re-assembly of the Democratic Party, that had moved onto Broadway. It was not so much a Party Conference, more a Busby Berkeley spectacular, with dancing girls and an orchestra, choreographed to the last Hurrah for the hungry TV cameras.

The Chair thanked one speaker for coming on 'our programme'. Everything — almost — was pre-ordained by those producing the show. One speaker, the student leader Li Lu of Tiananmen Square fame, rehearsed his one minute intervention three times in the empty hall before his final appearance. No wonder the convention was only in session between five and eleven at night.

The state delegations assembled around their red, white and blue totems waving the current recommended banner 'Bill Clinton — Putting People First'. 'We love Mario', a reference to Mario Cuomo, Clinton's nominator, or 'Al Gore'. Sprinkled amongst them were the last outposts of opposition, Tsongas and Brown banners. Apart from Brown, everyone else capitulated. Jesse Jackson preached a message of support for the next President of the United States, Tsongas wanted unity and asked his supporters to vote for it. Only Jerry Brown tried to spoil the party. With four million primary votes he claimed he deserved a hearing. Instead he was allowed to speak. During his twenty minute intervention, the majority chatted and his supporters shouted, whooped and cheered. The organisers got their revenge. As he finished speaking, the band struck up with the theme from *Monty Python's Flying Circus*.

That was the style, but what about substance? The revisionists swept all before them. The left was destroyed. In the United States the Democrats have waited a long time since Jimmy Carter limped away from power, impotent in the face of the Iranian hostage crisis. The passage of time has seen the Democrats become hungry for office again. They are prepared to make sacrifices of politics and principle. They had their April 9th four years ago.

Dukakis came out of the Convention seventeen points ahead of George Bush. The Republicans, masters of negative campaigning, struck back. First they tied the label 'Liberal' around his neck and then they turned it into a millstone by a series of attack advertisements, including the infamous Willie Horton ad, which drove the final nails into his political coffin. Willie Horton was a convicted killer and rapist, released on a parole programme agreed by Dukakis, who killed and raped again, and who from his jail cell endorsed the Democrats. These tactics ensured that by November Dukakis was sunk without trace.

This time around they plan no such mistakes on law and order or fiscal liberality. Clinton's not going to spend money he does not have. As Governor of Arkansas he has balanced his last eleven budgets, we were told by almost every speaker who made it to the podium. Clinton will protect the neglected middle-class with better use of the tax dollars already available, rather than raising new ones. Loans to go to college and continued welfare payments at a price. For the former you have to work for the State for two years, and for the latter take any job that is offered. Imagine Labour Party reaction if John Major threatened to introduce the same. Organised labour fared little better. Arkansas is a 'right to work' State where you can be sacked for going on strike.

All of this illiberal agenda, only mitigated by Clinton-Gore's pro-choice position on abortion, topped by lashings of semi-isolationist xenophobic pro-Americanism, and crowned with saccharin family values with Barbie doll wives and unreal children, challenging Barbara Bush to 'cookie bakes' and videos that make 'Kinnock the Movie' look like hard-hitting investigative journalism.

Can Clinton win? It is neither automatic nor impossible. Bush is currently flagging badly. Yet there is a worry that in the end 'time for a change' will still run second to maintaining the 'status quo'. Clinton's next four months will not have been helped by H. Ross Perot's withdrawal from a race he never formally entered. Beforehand we were told Perot's candidature was a definite plus for Clinton. The Democrats were seeing the battle in World War Two imagery. Clinton was the Allies, Bush the Axis, and Perot the Soviet Union helping the Allies to split German resources by opening up a second front. On July 16th, Clinton lost Russia. Immediately the spin-Doctors stood on their heads. Perot's people want change. They would join the 'Comeback Kid's Crusade'. I'm not convinced. They are Conservative, anti-Government, for more spending and less taxes. The Democrats run Congress and an overwhelming majority of State legislatures. Preventing the Perot people from seeing the Democrats as a central part of the problem between now and November will not be easy with the Republicans constantly reminding them.

Yet if Clinton does win, the major impact will be a partial American withdrawal from the world in an attempt to nurse their self-inflicted internal wounds. I'm not sure this programme has any chance of more than slowing American global decline. Nevertheless, the inches of difference between Clinton and Bush may well be important space for the rest of the world to live in.

Oldham Evening Chronicle, 5 August 1992

61. The Choice is Stark: Maastricht or Nothing

Maastricht must be ratified. It offers some protection against the ravages of the unregulated single market with an upwards harmonisation of social and environmental provision. Ratification is endorsed by the European Trade Union Congress, the Trades

Union Congress, and the 16 socialist parties in the European Community.

Of course, in Britain John Major is offering 'Maastricht Minus', with opt-outs on the Social Chapter and Economic and Monetary Union, and a half-threat that he will stuff the new Committee of the Regions with junior ministers and civil servants. Nevertheless, the Labour Party can opt into the Social Chapter and Economic and Monetary Union, and democratise the Committee of the Regions — if Maastricht is ratified.

The choice is stark: Maastricht or nothing. Rejection cannot lead to renegotiation and a new, more socialist treaty. The political balance of forces is shifting the other way. The French 'No' campaign in the referendum did not boost the position of dissident socialists within the French Socialist Party — it boosted the racism and xenophobia of Jean Marie Le Pen's National Front.

In Spring 1993 the French Socialist Party will go into opposition as it is crushed in the general election. In Germany the Social Democrats are in crisis over asylum policy changes. In Italy the former Italian Communist Party — the Party of Democratic Socialism — is only just starting to rebuild, while leading figures in the Italian Socialist Party are either in jail or engaged in internecine warfare to be Craxi's successor.

The arguments against Maastricht relate to sovereignty, economics and citizenship. On sovereignty, so-called internationalists weep over a loss of power from the House of Commons and House of Lords, those still unreformed and semi-feudal relics of the English Civil War and first industrial revolution.

Power has been shifted not by Brussels or Maastricht, but by senior industrialists reconstructing their sectors from national to European level. No one had the nerve to inform Queen Victoria that women could also be homosexual, so homophobic legislation only victimised men; likewise, no one has the nerve to tell MPs that power has already shifted to the European arena with democratic powers fought for over decades being meekly surrendered to bureaucrats, the Commission and the Council of Ministers. Maastricht starts to redress that democratic deficit.

On economic policy, we are told that Maastricht is profoundly deflationary. While it is true that the Treaty of Rome was written in Keynesian language and the Maastricht treaty in monetarist terms, it is determinism of the worst kind to assume this inevitably leads to deflation. And Maastricht does not stop increased spending. It just limits the difference between spending and taxation. Hardly a frightening concept given the prudent financial policies of John Smith's Labour Party.

The most important consequence of Maastricht is the Delors II package for doubling the Regional Fund, Social Fund and Research and Development Fund, plus a new Cohesion Fund for the four poorest member states of the Community. Public expenditure is needed and welcome, whether it comes from Brussels or Whitehall. Maastricht is a brake, not an anchor here.

Finally, we have been told by Ken Livingstone and sections of the Anti-Racist Alliance that the citizenship sections of Maastricht are racist. Nonsense. They replace a totally inadequate system with a poor one. Groups like Schengen and Trevi, whose 'liberal' agendas of terrorism control, drug-trafficking, prostitution, asylum and immigration are drawn up behind closed doors, will have to come out into the light, consult with parliaments and have their reactionary ideas moderated by public opinion. It is the current system that has given us the Air Carriers' Liability Act and the Immigration and Asylum Bill. It is the new system that will give us a European Race Relations Act.

Maastricht has to be built on rather than demolished. The sooner we start building for a 'Maastricht Plus', with a central plank of a European Programme for Jobs and Recovery, the sooner we will start to shift the balance of forces towards the left again.

redgreenradical, December 1992/January 1993

Part 11

1993

THE BRITISH OLYMPIC BID
MANCHESTER 2000
ACHIEVEMENT
FACILITIES

62. Part of or apart from Europe?

The year 1993 is one of decisions for both Britain and the United States. In the thirties, America was beset by an isolationism that was only broken by Pearl Harbour. The Japanese attack was a military disaster and a political godsend. At the end of this month, a new President will take office who may be driven down the road to isolationism for the first time in more than half a century.

America is bankrupt. Its industry is dead and dying. During the election campaign, Bill Clinton made much of President George Bush's over-emphasis on foreign affairs at the expense of domestic intervention. He argued chauvinistically for America first, last and always, and promoted the creation of the North American Free Trade Area to provide an enlarged domestic market for American industry. He realised that, at the same time as America was winning the Cold War across the Atlantic, it was losing the industrial revolution across the Pacific.

Japan's cascade of process and product innovations ate out the kernels of American industrial might. It left the bureaucratic husks of today either administering Japanese inward investment labelled with the body-tags of dead American manufacturers, or marshalling the hapless survivors in the few remaining autonomous production enclaves waiting to be overrun by the barbarians in the retreat from American industrial hegemony.

To identify the problem does not guarantee delivery of a solution. Clinton has to find the nerve and will to invest in America's future and make America pay for it; a labour made doubly difficult with history kicking away the only ideological crutch supporting government intervention — defence spending to deter the Soviet menace. If he fails, America will have no alternative but to close in on itself and pray.

In Britain our problems are not dissimilar. Our history has ruined us. We believe our own propaganda, always a most dangerous position to adopt. Our industry is almost as battered as that of the US, our coffers are almost as empty, and our economy is buffeted to and fro by the decisions of the Bundesbank.

Yet the Tory Right dreams again of empire and refuses to contemplate loss of sovereignty as events conspire to strip us all of autonomy. Did John Major have the ability to maintain the value of the pound in September? Better dead than fed, to paraphrase Richard Nixon.

Yet the Labour anti-Europeans are as bad: a heady mixture of Little Englandism, arrogance and isolationism. On Maastricht, which

◄ *September 1993: Promoting Manchester's Olympic bid at the selection meeting in Monte Carlo.*

is not without its problems, they quickly dismiss the fact that ratification is supported by all 16 socialist parties in the Community and the socialist parties in Austria, Finland, Sweden and Norway.

They decry the rising tide of racism and xenophobia in Europe, and use it to imply that we should put up the shutters to the continent rather than express solidarity with those fighting against the neo-fascists in France and Germany, Belgium and Italy. They don't believe that socialism in one country is possible any more, except in England. They won't realise that we have to build socialism in Europe, not instead of England.

Now that Denmark is no longer the decoy, the Left has to decide whether it runs with the hare or hunts with the hounds. Are we to be a part of Europe or apart from Europe? This will be the year of decision.

Tribune, 1 January 1993

63. Images of Science and Progress

Looking at Labour's attitude to science and technology over the past eighty years, one can almost be forgiven for believing that this whole area of political debate is a non-issue. Publicly, Labour's view of science has consisted of long silences broken by brief bouts of enthusiasm for the 'white-heat of the technological revolution', rationalising industry, or introducing micro-electronics. This public face is misleading, for it conceals more than it reveals. The Labour Party is not indifferent to science and technology — apart from its brief excursions for electoral purposes — rather, the reason for so little debate is that, to use Kuhnian terminology, there is a central view or 'image' of science that is a key element in the paradigm within which Labour's leaders have thought and operated. This central view is one that has a number of elements. The prime ones are notions of science itself as *neutral;* technical progress as inherently *progressive;* and a consequent view that answers to problems of political choice lie with increased access to 'scientific expertise'. This has always been politically disarming, with the threat to limit politics to the management, for better or worse, of industry and the economy, and leaving the practice of 'liberty' and 'equality' inevitably to outside of the workplace and work process. This almost limits socialism to being a hobby.

Yet it has become increasingly clear that such an approach and view of science is inadequate. While some debate is possible over the idea that 'science *is* social relations', few would argue that other edge of the spectrum that implies science is *neutral*. Few, that is, outside of the Labour movement. For the Labour movement is one of the most backward areas in assimilating this new view of science and technology, although a few small cracks are beginning to appear in the edifice. The reason for this is because of the very centrality of the view. Here I will attempt to show, firstly, that this central view exists, and has existed consistently over the past eighty years to the present, and, secondly, how it has influenced policy formulation and presentation. In order to do this I intend to concentrate, as Michels did in *Political Parties*, on the 'worst case': to look at the internal politics of the Labour Party and Labour movement to show that the attitudes and ideas of 'managing capitalism' originated within the movement itself, inevitably flowing from the 'image' of science and technology. There is, of course, a problem in that the imagery was so universal and so accepted that there was often no need to make it explicit, and it therefore can only be illustrated second-hand.

To do this, it is necessary to provide both a context, and to state some general axioms that apply. Firstly, this shares similarities with Gary Werskey's pioneering work *Visible College*, which investigated the impact of socialism on scientists. He studied the work of Bernal, Haldane, Needham, Hogben and Levy, and their impact on British socialism, in particular on the Communist Party of Great Britain (CPGB). Here is the mirror-image; the impact of attitudes towards science on socialists. This relates back to Werskey's identification of *Bernalism* and its consequences. Secondly, it is important to keep in mind the uniqueness of the British political scene in Western Europe, and to extrapolate with care either to or from other European countries. Thirdly, I would argue that to explain the failures of the Labour Party purely in terms of the 'insincerity' or betrayal of its past leaders is too simplistic and too easy. But once this is accepted, then there is the problem of explaining why so many have failed, as catalogued by Miliband's *Parliamentary Socialism*. The answer lies — albeit partly — in the image of science, scientists and expertise, and the self-imposed constraints this imposed upon political action. This is only compounded when the attributes of science are given to those fields clearly outside of its normal definition, such as economics and so on.

The Labour Party has always been portrayed as a broad church. Certainly, at its origins at the end of the 19th century, it fused together elements from Methodism and Marxism, with Fabian and trade union additions. All of these various strains contained similar images of science. Marx himself offered no critique of technology. Within the context of capitalism it was indeed a power hostile to labour. As he wrote in the *Grundrisse*, "it requires no great penetration to grasp that, where for example free labour or wage labour arising out of the dissolution of bondage is the point of departure, there machines can only arise in antithesis to living labour, as property alien to it and as a power hostile to it".

However, within the context of a socialist society the *same* technology would assume more benevolent forms: 'But it is just as easy to perceive that machines will not cease to be agencies of social production when they become for example property of the associated workers. In the first case, however, their distribution i.e. that they do not belong to the worker, is just as much a condition of the mode of production founded on wage labour. In the second case, the changed distribution would start from a changed foundation of production, a new foundation first created by the process of history'.

Thus, the taking over of society by the producers — socialism — at times means for Marx only an external change in political and economic management, a change that would leave intact the structure of work, and would simply reform its more 'inhuman' aspects. This idea is clearly expressed in the famous passage from *Capital*, volume 3, where, speaking of socialist society, Marx writes, 'In fact, the realm of freedom actually begins only where labour which is determined by necessity and mundane considerations ceases; thus in the very nature of things it lies beyond the sphere of actual material production...Freedom in this field can only consist in socialised man, the associated producers rationally regulating their intercourse with nature, bringing it under their common control, instead of being ruled by it...and achieving this with the least expenditure of energy and under conditions most favourable to, and worthy of, their human nature. But it nonetheless remains a realm of necessity. Beyond it begins...the true realm of freedom, which however can blossom forth only with this realm of necessity as its basis. The shortening of the working day is its basic prerequisite'.

Underlying the idea that freedom is to be found outside of work is Marx's failure to clearly see science and technology's role within capitalist society as part of the historical social project. For Marx, science, 'the process of nature', is somehow 'plucked' from outside society and history, and then transformed within society into a productive force. This faulty analysis led Marx and British Marxists to misunderstand the nature of technological development. The progress of technology was *inevitable* and therefore *rational*. Although it reduced the worker to a 'mere movement', it hastened the demise of capitalism as the development of the productive force of labour threatens capitalist relationships. Science and technology are therefore a 'good thing'.

The Fabians had much of their early thinking encapsulated by Sidney and Beatrice Webb, who shared images with Marx of science and technology and a hatred of society's 'drones'. Turgot's powerful idea of progress rolled through the Victorian world picking up an expression in terms of natural science and evolution. This was certainly true of the Webbs. As Sidney wrote in 1889, "Owing mainly to the efforts of Comte, Darwin and Herbert Spencer we can no longer think of the ideal society as an unchanging state. The social ideal from being static has become dynamic. The necessity of the constant growth and development of the social organism has become axiomatic. No philosopher now looks for anything but the gradual evolution of the new order from the old, without break of continuity or abrupt change of the entire social tissue at any point during the process".

This was a far seeing anticipation of the infamous phrase used by him in his presidential address to the Labour Party in 1923, when he spoke of "the inevitability of gradualness", a phrase for all its brevity loaded with the concepts of evolution and progress. While the Fabians might have demurred from accepting the Second International's stages of history theory in full, they, like the Bolsheviks, failed to break with the technological determinism which was such an integral part of the whole package, and which bound them to an inherently progressive view of science and technology. This meant science and technology was controllable in quantity, not quality. More science was a good thing for both the Fabians and the Bolsheviks. For the former, it speeded up the conveyor that was carrying through the 'inevitability of gradualness' — capitalism to socialism — while, for the latter, it advanced the date when the crisis would be precipitated as revolution.

But to return to an early period. If Labour's Marxists and Fabians were united, many historians of the Labour Party would expect to see disagreements between this position and that advocated by the trade union/methodist factions in the broad church. Here, Labour movement hagiography might turn to Labour's first leader, Keir Hardie. Yet there are indications that this disagreement was not to be found. Hardie, in 1893, proposed in the House of Commons a *Mines Nationalisation Bill*. In the preamble it stated 'whereas the present system of working mines as private concerns leads to great waste of our mineral supplies, and to strikes and lock-outs thereby imposing great hardship on the mining community and trades dependent on mineral supply for their continuance; and whereas the nationalisation of the minerals and mines would secure the economical working of the same, the just treatment and consequent contentment of the mining population, and a continuous and cheap supply of coal and other minerals'. A justification that emphasises improved management and efficiency at the expense of justice for the miners.

The first record I have been able to locate as to scientific advisors to the Labour Party was the establishment of an advisory committee in 1918 to the Labour Party's National Executive Committee (NEC). It was firmly based on a view that social change would follow automatically from acquiring 'the facts'. The membership was to be drawn from sympathetic intellectuals, sympathetic civil servants, and labour leaders, in that order.

The problems of the late twenties and early thirties, and the tragedy of Ramsay MacDonald, can also be treated in this way. As he said in his speech to the TUC Annual Conference in 1931, 'Nothing gives me greater regret than to disagree with old industrial friends, but I really find it absolutely impossible to overlook dread realities, as I am afraid you are doing'. The logical flow of policy from 'the facts' was an axiom of many of those recruits to the Labour Party who joined following World War One, and who wanted a vehicle to espouse efficiency and scientific planning. Oswald Mosley's political peregrinations can be explained as the search for such a vehicle. MacDonald himself in his pamphlet *Socialism for Businessmen* (1925) showed how far the facts were meant to convince. As early as 1919, Sir Richard Gregory, the editor of Britain's leading scientific journal, *Nature*, welcomed the possibility of a Labour Government because, 'the causes of scientific education and scientific research stand to profit enormously'. Obviously, the NEC's advisors had done part of their task very well. MacDonald's view might be seen in the letter from him that Gregor read to the Conference on *Science and Labour* in London in May 1924, in the presence of Sidney Webb. It read, in part, that he 'wished...to impress upon the public the necessity of treating political questions in a scientific spirit, and not merely in a short-vision, partisan frame of mind. Until we regard administration and legislation in precisely the same manner as a scientific worker approaches his work in a laboratory, we shall never be able to get results of a permanent character, nor shall we secure respect from our public institutions'.

MacDonald's fate can also be explained using this model. He was quite a prolific writer, and in his writings he revealed that for him the sole instrument of social change was to be the increasing technical capacity of industry. MacDonald looked backwards to classical political economy, spiced with ideas drawn from his friend J.A. Hobson, and from positivism. The result was a series of pamphlets and books showing a hard technological determinism expressed in the language of Carlyle, Ruskin and Sir Walter Scott. MacDonald had taken two key ideas from positivism, firstly, 'that social change was to come about by the unfolding of industry itself according to the laws of history', and secondly, 'that science was to play a vital role in society as the principle of social organisation'. The resultant determinism in the face of stubborn facts led inevitably to 1931, as his image of science and technology paralysed him in the face of scientific expertise. For MacDonald, politics in the last analysis was science. While, theoretically, MacDonald's Government could have taken a Keynesian route out of the crisis, it was not available in practice. The choice was public works versus deflation. For the former, there was no theoretical underpinning until the publication, in 1936, of Keynes' *General Theory of Employment, Interest and Money*. In the absence of this underpinning, MacDonald faced the cruellest of choices, desert the Labour Movement or reject his own image of science. In some ways, MacDonald deserves a better press, for he was at least more honest than those ministers who, under trade union pressure, reversed their support of MacDonald in the five days before the crisis broke. They ran away from themselves. They accepted the logic of the experts. They offered no alternative, and fled the field.

After the formation of the National Government, in 1931, the political struggle moved outside of Parliament. The 1930s was the heyday of *Bernalism*, which crossed the ideological divide between Communist and Labour quite happily as the 'social-fascist' period terminated and the Popular Front period began. For Bernal, scientific theories were neutral precisely to the extent that their practical value could be demonstrated in production. Science was also inevitably progressive, and only in a socialist society can it achieve its full potential, it inexorably leads mankind towards socialism — despite itself, if necessary. Thus, for Bernal, the problem was to 'free' science. With adequate funds, good management and co-ordination, the best scientists would produce first-class science. This was the message of Bernal's *The Social Function of Science* (1939). The message had come earlier in terms of the promise of a 'free' science in the anonymous *Britain without Capitalists* (1936). This was written by a 'group of economists, scientists, and technicians', and had the subtitle, 'A study of what industry in a Soviet Britain could achieve'. The Labour Party's own contribution was not to look at science itself but, instead, to investigate neglected areas of research and development as in *Labour's Plan for Oil from Coal*.

The War demonstrated again the importance of science, and Labour prepared itself for the post-war period with the clandestine establishment of the '1944 Association', or a Business Men's Labour Group, composed 'exclusively of men engaged in industry and commerce as employers, executives or proprietors'. The membership was open to those, 'who while not necessarily accepting all the tenets of the Labour Party, recognise the essential importance of applying the principles of technical efficiency and social justice in industry and the economic life of the Nation'. Its membership was both select and secret, and a number of these went on as Labour nominations to the Boards of the newly nationalised industries. The Group exchanged ideas and advice with many prominent Labour MPs, including Gaitskell, Brown, Wilson, Bevan, Jenkins, Jay, Callaghan, Attlee and Cripps.

Elsewhere, within the Labour Party Research Department, work commenced on Science Policy which ran, with some interruptions, almost continually from 1945 to the early sixties. Those involved included Bronowski, Ritchie Calder, and Robens. In the fifties, Bernal's 'single most important political act at home...was his continuing participation in a ginger group of scientists bent on changing the Labour Party's perspective on science and technology. Their meetings were regularly attended by Hugh Gaitskell, James Callaghan, Alf (later Lord) Robens, and, eventually, Harold Wilson and Richard Crossman. Out of these discussions arose a new commitment on the part of Labour to modernise its own political image and fight the 1964 General Election on the basis of its ability to bring a "white-hot" technological revolution to Britain'.

Not that much changing was necessary. The 1945 Manifesto, *Let Us Face The Future*, was an offer of efficiency, skilled administration, community and progress. 'The Labour Party intends to link the skill of British craftsmen and designers to the skill of British scientists in the service of fellow men...Each industry must have applied to it the test of national service. If it serves the Nation, well and good; if it is insufficient and falls down on its job, the Nation must see that things are put right'. In eleven pages the word 'efficiency' was used on twenty-one occasions.

Equally, Labour's future leader didn't require much convincing. In his book *A New Deal for Coal* (1945), Harold Wilson had come out firmly in favour of nationalising the coal industry. 'There is no single unfavourable factor confronting the future of the basic British industries which is more alarming than the price of domestic coal', he wrote. As to the details, 'it is difficult and presumptuous for any layman or economist to attempt to form an opinion'. The problem lay not with the management for, 'management (of the mines —

GF) is in general capable and on the whole willing to undertake the technical programme necessary', but with the owners, for 'control is exercised by the board of directors who are in the mass ultra-conservative, old-fashioned, amateur, out of touch with modern mining development — frequently out of touch with the mines they control — and above all completely inhibited against investing in the mines the capital necessary for the technical development of the industry'. Here Wilson is not even freeing Bernal's technology from the fetters of capitalism, rather he is freeing managers from the fetters of their boards, with technology left to the technologists. Emmanuel Shinwell's vision was little different, and probably explains the rapid evaporation of the euphoria that surrounded the nationalisation of the coal industry in the pit villages of Britain.

The failure of the 'white-heat of the technological revolution' to become anything more than a slogan that rapidly fell out of use after 1964 did not lead to any fundamental shift in the view of science and technology. The failure was seen as entirely external, although talk about science and technology was limited for a long time. The 1944 Association had collapsed in the mid-sixties, and the early seventies saw the establishment of the '1972 Industry Group', with the encouragement of Tony Benn. To join the new group required membership of the Labour Party. The Group shunned publicity, and had over a hundred members ten years later. Its most prominent member was Lord Wilfred Brown, also prominent as Mr Wilfred Brown in the 1944 Association. In 1976, it had a series of meetings to advise Harold Wilson on industrial policy.

In November 1981 the Home Policy Committee of the NEC recommended the establishment of a new study group 'to develop policies in the field of science and technology — subjects which have been neglected in the Party's policy-making for a number of years'. It was stated that the group would 'play an important part in developing our industrial policy'. 'One of the areas selected for specific emphasis should be the relation between technology policy and the wider industrial policy question of industrial regeneration'. The membership included trade union representatives from the Post Office Engineers (POEU), the Scientific, Technical and Managerial Workers (AUEW), and the University Teachers (AUT). Representatives from the PLP included Tam Dalyell, Geoffrey Robinson (1982 onwards), and Lord Gregson (member of 1972 Industry Group). There were also assorted experts from various universities and research institutes.

The interim report to the Labour Party Conference in 1982 stated a number of reasons for Britain's decline as a manufacturing power, and considered possible future directions. There were complaints that there was a 'lack of appropriate investment in science and technology in this country', and the fact that 'this simply underlines the need for socialist planning to overcome the barriers to faster progress thrown up by private enterprise'. All harking back to *Bernalism*, if not before.

However, there were a few cracks in the edifice; 'a key objective is the establishment of a democratic framework for science and technology in which government, management, trade unions, and the scientific community itself jointly influence the general direction of research and development'. This has been read by some commentators on the left as portraying a 'capitalist utopia of a common national interest'. It certainly is ambiguous. Nevertheless, some of the committee intended it to be read in quite the opposite sense of implying a pluralism of interests rather than a communality of interest. The issue of the male domination of science is raised, and it is stated that 'it must be opened up to women in both education and work'. Yet the whole report faces two ways, for while it is recognised that 'just providing more science and technology will not solve all our problems...(and) science and technology must therefore be redirected towards the solution of social problems and need as identified within the party's policies as a whole. This means we must see all technologies not as ends in themselves, but in terms of the needs they serve'. It is counterbalanced by the 'white-heat' imagery of, 'Never has scientific and technical potential been as great as it is today; and yet, equally, never has the failure to harness this potential in pursuit of our basic social goals been so manifestly evident'.

It might be argued that the Labour Party has taken three steps forward. If so, it has taken two steps back. Tony Benn said, 'technology is neutral. It is a question of what you use it for', and Tam Dalyell, Labour's shadow spokesman on science until his removal for his opposition to the Falklands War, managed to write a book, *A Science Policy for Britain*, that does not mention socialism or democracy at all, consisting as it does of a catalogue of what particular areas and institutions are being neglected. Neil Kinnock, in a clarion call after he became Leader of the Labour Party, stated that 'democratic socialism must appeal as a source of *efficiency* and justice'. The image of science remains the same.

ENDpapers 23, Winter 1992-93

64. One More Heave for South Africa

My first political commitment was to the struggle against apartheid. The late sixties saw Nelson Mandela in his second decade of imprisonment on Robben Island and me at Reading University where I marched with about a dozen others to protest against the South African Government's deep and open racism, and picketed the local branch of Barclays Bank.

It was more than 20 years before the South African regime was forced to bend in the face of the opposition orchestrated by Anti-Apartheid and the African National Congress. Barclays finally withdrew and sanctions started to bite as the boom economy of the early eighties slid into the recession of the early nineties. Even the Americans became serious about strong-arming South Africa back into the twentieth century, particularly once its job as the bastion of anti-communism in southern Africa became redundant. Finally Mandela came out into the sunshine and preached forgiveness at Wembley. It seemed that the battle had been won. Anti-Apartheid groups celebrated and embraced wider concerns: racism, refugees, immigrants and intolerance.

Last month I went to the centre of the Left's 'evil empire' for the first time, representing the Social Group in the European Parliament at the ANC's solidarity conference in Johannesburg. Almost 900 delegates were given a clear message. The battle may have been won but the war isn't over. It's not the final victory, only the beginning of the end. The danger is that our commitment may falter and we may relax before they cross the line. It would be a tragedy to lose the race after coming so far.

The ANC and the National Party have not yet agreed a date for elections for the first-ever one person one vote parliament, let alone how they are going to be conducted. The National Party is trying desperately to hold on to power by writing the rules to suit itself. The ANC in response wants to use its international support for leverage in the negotiations. At the conference it was announced that sanctions should remain until a date was agreed and only then be relaxed in all areas except arms sales and nuclear technology.

The National Party is trying to overload the ANC's resources by talking about the need to register all South Africa's 21 million voters, millions of whom have no documents at all and millions of whom are illiterate. This is from a Government that conducts the census of its black population by aerial photography. In this election, which will be conducted using a mixture of regional and national proportional representation, with a cut-off point designed to ensure the election of Inkatha, it will be simplest to ensure that nobody votes twice by marking voters at the ballot box rather than by trying the impossible job of registration.

In a mock election recently conducted by the South African Council of Churches among the local black leadership in Johannesburg, 26 out of 70 ballot papers were inadvertently spoiled. The churches are doing tremendous work in this area, but they must have the resources.

Collaboration between political forces in South Africa is necessary and will be welcome after the election, but this must flow from a position of strength. The ANC has estimated that it needs 48 million dollars for the election. The Labour and trade union movement must give one more heave for South Africa and help to provide the political solidarity to tip the negotiations in favour of the ANC, as well as people to help train ANC workers for the election. It must make available financial resources for the campaign. Anything else could see Yugoslavia re-run in southern Africa.

Tribune, 19 March 1993

65. Review

Head to Head by Lestor Thurow

Europe, not Japan or the United States, will win next century's global competition. The *Pax Europa* will succeed the *Pax Americana* and thus will Europe write the rules of world trade to suit itself. America is sliding from dominance to impotance as American companies retreat to the last industrial redoubts where they can still command a fifteen percent return on investment.

Individual capitalism can no longer compete with the corporatist variety found in Germany and Japan. Industry is no longer drawn to the comparative advantage of abundant natural resources, but instead to pools of man-made skills. American — and British — Governments neither provide the education and training in depth nor the infrastructural foundations necessary for the post electro-mechanical society. The future is being written in Japan's schools and Germany's technical colleges, where mass skills and group work playing long are destined to replace de-skilling married to individual genius and quick profits.

Subtitled *The Coming Economic Battle Among Japan, Europe and America*, this book contains the message of the Clinton campaign. Unless America changes rapidly they are in for a bumpy ride down.

They have sold the family silver and are now in danger of pawning the bedclothes. Lestor Thurow, Dean of MIT's Sloan School of Management, believes the only way for the US to remain a major industrial player is to switch resources away from the military into re-skilling the whole workforce and providing the infrastructural foundations for a new industrial revolution.

Japan is showing the way forward. The research cartels of Japanese companies that carry Research and Development swiftly to the fringes of the market leave American and European companies, hobbled by ideology and competition rules respectively that inhibit co-operation, far behind. Equally Japan's emphasis on process rather than product innovation means that they strip sales away from the investor by providing a cheaper version of the product. *Head to Head* says that the system has failed in the United States and Britain. Thatcherism and Reaganism have failed. Neither military nor financial power lead to industrial power, instead they flow from it.

The future, however, is European, says Thurow. What will put a German-led Europe past the tape in front of Japan is the greater size of the European 'domestic' market and the economic motor of East German refurbishment, the brain drain of low wage skilled workers from central and Eastern Europe, and the broad science and technology base.

An optimistic and hopeful vision, but one that does not instantly emerge from the current debate on the future of Europe being conducted either in the House of Commons or in Brussels and Strasbourg. There the images of bureaucracy, waste and sloth replace jobs, growth and tomorrow.

In Britain within the Labour Party there are even those who, clutching the comfort blanket of Little Englandism, cast doubt on whether we should be full members of the post-Maastricht Community. Thurow's rhetoric echoes Jacques Delors' image, arguing that economic muscle will provide the strength to shape Europe in the image we want.

If a world of managed trading blocks is to emerge then Europe — and Britain — cannot afford to be the back marker. If America can't halt the slide down the industrial league tables then global strategists might start digging out from dusty library shelves John Maclean's *The Coming War With America* (1919).

New Statesman, 19 March 1993

66. Review

Science, Technology and Society in Postwar Japan by Shigeru Nakayama

Is there a distinct and unique Japanese science and technology? Nakayama's book is an attempt to provide an initial answer to that important question: it is a history of the underlying philosophy of science and technology policy. The book is a preliminary summary volume setting the terms of reference for a group research project funded in Japan by the Toyota Foundation, which will lead to the publication of a series of twenty-four volumes in Japanese over the coming decade.

Nakayama attempts to get behind MITI to look for solutions and here he continues work initially published in *Nihon no gijutsuryoku* (Japanese Technological Power) by Asahi Shinbun-sha in 1986 and *Kagaku to shakai no gendaishi* (The Contemporary History of Science and Society) by Iwanami Shoten in 1981. Nakayama has pioneered the externalist religion of the history of science and technology in Japan, having initially worked with Thomas Kuhn, the author of *The Structure of Scientific Revolutions*, the book that was to do for this field what *De Revolutionibus Orbium Celestium* did for cosmology and *The Origin of Species* for palaeontology.

Nakayama puts his background to good use by explaining how it was that 'New Deal' American advisers imported democracy and technocracy, co-operation and intervention into Japanese science and technology policy. It was within the GHQ in the Science & Technology Divisions of the Economic and Science Section that the impulse came. A crucial role was played by Harry Kelly, a former senior scientist with the Radiation Laboratory at MIT, who wanted to use science for the reconstruction of the economy. He suppressed academic science and the Imperial Academy of Japan in favour of applied science for the immediate objective of economic recovery.

It was not just the Imperial Academy that was suppressed, so were other elements of Japanese science and technology. The horrors of Unit 731, coldly and clinically represented in the results of biological and chemical warfare experiments on prisoners of war, did not stop the Americans utilising the results or their perpetrators. It did lead to the occupation forces destroying scientific equipment, including four cyclotrons, and to the development of the *Shinkansen*. With the forced dissolution of the Department of Aeronautical Engineering at Tokyo Imperial

University, its young graduates dispersed into railway engineering and the automobile industry. Yet science for recovery was not just imposed by the Americans. It was positively embraced by the newly liberated Japanese Left, shot through with Engelsian scientism. The Japanese Communist Party and its front organisation *Minshushugi Kagakusha Kyokai* (*Minka*) were schooled on *The Social Function of Science*, the handbook for a scientific utopia by British communist scientist J.D. Bernal; this was translated into Japanese in 1951 and, amongst other ideas, introduced the concept of research associations to the Japanese.

Kelly and *Minka* collaborated to establish the Japan Science Council (JSC) and to allocate the central research budget through elected representatives of the various branches of science. Neither was entirely clear on the distinction between technocracy and democracy. At one extreme within *Minka* was the *Chigaku Dentai Kenkyukai* (The Society for Group Research in Earth Sciences), not merely a scientific organisation, but a crusading body determined to propagate the ideology and methodology of field geology. With its *jinkai senjutsu* (human sea strategy), it distributed its government research funds equally among the members of the profession.

The other side showed in 1952, when *Minka's* leadership promulgated the idea of *kokuminteki kagaku*, literally 'national science', with a distinct *narodniki* overtone mixed with pacifism. Attempts were made to promote this within the JSC, but *Minka* could not carry its own members, let alone others, and the elected delegates became more or less technocratic as *Minka's* line failed to hold.

Yet elements of all these ideas continued across the following decades. Both 'back to the people' and *jinkai senjutsu* showed themselves in the Citizens' Movement against Industrial Pollution. After the mass mercury poisoning of Minamata, the search for *kogai* (environmental pollution) began, with advice provided by *Jishu Koza* magazine and Red experts like Jun Ui cross-questioning the experts of *Showa Denko* as they tried to minimise their pollution of the Agano river near Niigata, in a way similar to the role played by representatives from the British Society for Social Responsibility in Science in the Windscale Enquiry.

The democratic side showed itself in education policies that led to cheap, low-key mass science education, with a rapid response capability to industrialisation that pushed up the annual intake of science students in national universities from 22,000 in 1957 to 51,140 in 1963. The science taught was everyday, normal science with all the Kuhnian overtones. Japanese science, therefore, was neither the elite science of the UK (Nobel Prize Science), nor the capital-intensive big science of the US, but market- and product-orientated 'Kentucky Fried' Science. It wisely shied clear of costly basic research that had only a remote and diffuse economic return to society, was forbidden to engage in military R & D, and invested moderately in the pseudo-civilian technologies of nuclear power and space.

Nakayama continues through the 1960s and 1970s, tracing the revolt against science as the counter-culture and Minamata bit home; the student revolt led by *Zenkyoto* (The Student Struggle Committee) and the positive response in the most conservative disciplines of forestry and medicine; and the rise of Jun Ui's ecology school from his base in the Engineering Department at *Todai* with its *han-daigaku koza* (anti-university seminars), which lasted nearly two decades.

He finishes with the fax as the ultimate communication technology for the Japanese language, a feeling that the distinctiveness of Japanese science requires further investigation and a hope that Toyota will produce at least some of the twenty-volume expansion of *Science, Technology and Society in Postwar Japan* in English.

Japan Forum, April 1993

67. Our Europe, Not Theirs

After the county council elections, our next two electoral tests will be the local and European polls in 12 months. If the wilted green shoots of economic recovery fail to revive (and maybe even if they do), the Tories are in for another drubbing.

The county elections confirmed a new electoral geography. We saw a triad of bilateral battles: Conservative-Labour fights in the smaller cities and towns; Tory-Liberal combat in rural England; Labour-Liberal contests in the declining inner cities, with Plaid Cymru and the Scottish Nationalists acting as surrogates for the Liberals in Wales and Scotland. So, next May, we may well see the Tories reduced to a third force, Labour with substantial gains, and the Liberals advancing slowly against Labour and spectacularly against the Conservatives.

Tory defeats will be greater as voters wake up to the undemocratisation of politics, with gangs of Tory appointees running services, such as the National Health Service, that used to be under a degree of democratic control. Next year is also the year of the European Parliamentary elections, the first and only complete national test of John Smith's Labour Party before the general election. By June 13, 1994 we will know if the road to power is open. Labour will be fighting 84 seats (six up on last time) and trying to improve on the superb 1989 results when we gained 13 seats giving us 45. What messages do we need for these campaigns? Clearly, the voters are increasingly dissatisfied with Europe. They believe that Europe dithers while Bosnia burns, yet manages simultaneously to be a busybody intruding where it is neither wanted nor needed, providing excuses for a Government that wants to increase VAT and the ammunition for endless jokes about cucumbers and Euro-sausages.

We must emphasise that we want our Europe, not theirs. Europe has been shaped by the overwhelmingly Right-wing Council of Ministers and the Right-wing Commission. Socialists have won battles in both institutions. Without François Mitterrand we would have no social chapter worth speaking of, even at a European level. Without Felipé Gonzalez we would have no cohesion fund for the poorer Community countries, and substantially smaller social and regional funds. Without Jacques Delors we would have no development of an economic recovery package. Nevertheless we haven't won the war.

The campaign requires a core set of economic proposals to address the issues of jobs, growth and recovery to get millions of Europeans back to work. These proposals need to link an interventionist industrial policy with training and retraining through an enlarged European Social Fund, and defence conversion to free the skill teams from over-elaborate, over-designed military technologies to battle, instead, with Japanese and American new civilian technologies. We need increased resources for regional development, and new ways of cutting the work-cake, earlier retirement and job-sharing, a shorter working week and working year and time off for training.

Collective decision should enable people to control their own lives. Long-term Labour councils can get dangerously out of touch with their electorate, resulting in the flight to the Liberals in our large cities. We have to oppose corruption wherever it is found. Labour must talk about accountability and democracy, locally and nationally, and mean it.

If we do all of these successfully, putting the work into key marginals, the Liberal tide against Labour could start to ebb. Next June, more than 50 Labour MEPs, plus a handful of Liberals, could be elected and John Major could start serving out his notice at Number 10.

Tribune, 28 May 1993

68. Review

Europe and America in the 1990s by John Peterson

John Palmer, *The Guardian*'s European editor and well known left federalist, published in 1989 *Europe Without America*. This book celebrated the widening gap between Europe and the United States. The end of the Cold War and emerging industrial union — the Single European Market — was unlocking the Alliance and driving it apart, as diverging economic interests took precedence over waning security imperatives.

Palmer cheered while others wept. John Peterson was clearly tearful, for *Europe and America in the 1990s* tries to put Humpty-Dumpty together again with a call for a New Transatlanticism. He recognises the emergence of global regionalism with the Europe, Japan and United States triad leading the way. He knows the American security umbrella over Japan and Europe is no longer necessary. It's stopped raining. Bill Clinton's latest defense cuts and his neo-isolationist tendencies show he and the American population know as well.

However, the Atlantacist tendency within the Labour Party hasn't got the message yet. Peterson knows, to paraphrase Bismark, any new alliance will still have a horse and a rider. He still wants Europe to carry America's burden, when its not clear we even want to go the same way.

The world went from Soviet-American stand-off, a momento of American hegemony, until the Gulf War demonstrated their bankruptcy. The war against Iraq represented the privatisation of conflict. The US fought and Japan and the other allies paid the bills. The American Treasury made a profit, at the cost of totally compromising notions of US independence and revealing a new totally multi-polar world.

In this new period Europe must act to secure its own best interests. These don't coincide with searching for excuses to maintain relations whose time is past. The United States exploits its privileged position *vis à vis* Japan and Europe to play the two off against one another. Industrial societies carefully multisource raw materials. Europe — and Japan — need to break their sole dependence for industrial, economic, political and security co-operation with the US.

We need to simultaneously compete and co-operate with our two potential post-war partners. All the more important as Japan's post-war political dinosaur — The Liberal Democratic Party — seems to be in its death-throws.

Peterson echoes his own quoted anonymous DGI official who admits: "it is very difficult to construct a convincing argument for collaborating in the technological areas with the US and not doing it with the Japanese... In practise you try and work it so you collaborate with the US and not the Japanese."

Europe and American in the 1990s is designed as an undergraduate text and source for specialists in international relations. It fails on two levels. Firstly, while it describes, it fails adequately to explain. It misses the pressures in Europe that want to pass beyond pooling resources and sovereignty, to pooling accountability. It notes current European dependence but doesn't see the forces moving to break from the past. In the USA it barely notices the new isolationism of the America-first-and-last-and-always rhetoric, hiding fear for the future under loud rock music slogans. Peterson thus also fails to predict. Secondly, the addendum to each chapter which tests the analysis against perspectives of neo-realism interdependence theories, liberal trade theory and reformism is entirely unconvincing. Despite its age, *Europe Without America* is both a better book and makes better politics.

Tribune, 6 August 1993

69. Review

Hope Dies Last by Alexander Dubcek

On August 19 1968 I was travelling back from Istanbul to Austria by train after spending the Summer hitch-hiking around Turkey. The journey was routed through Bulgaria and Yugoslavia. Bulgarian officialdom was never renowned for its cordiality. On this occasion it reached new depths. A motley collection of leftist students, imbued with the spirit of '68, were locked in compartments with armed soldiers patrolling the corridor during the transit.

When we finally reached Salzburg on the morning of the 21st the reason for Bulgarian cordiality became clear. The troops of the Soviet Union, Poland, the German Democratic Republic, Hungary and Bulgaria had the previous evening invaded Czechoslovakia in order to 'save the Revolution'. I marched in a small demonstration to fruitlessly protest against Soviet brutality and for Alexander Dubcek's politics outside of the Soviet Consulate.

Hope Dies Last is the assisted autobiography of the architect of that invasion that did so much to destroy any illusions about the Soviet Union amongst a generation that had been too young for the vicious repression of East Germany and Hungary.

Alexander Dubcek was a Communicant of the Communist religion. His Slovak Father, Stefan, emigrated from the Austro-Hungarian Empire to the United States in 1912, became an American citizen and was jailed for his pacifism during the First World War. As a result he returned home to Czechoslovakia in 1921 and joined the newly formed Czechoslovak Communist Party. He became involved with *International Workers' Relief*, the aid organisation that provided the Soviet Union with money, goods, and technical and medical services. One spin-off was *Interhelpo* a co-operative of several hundred Czechoslovakian workers and their families who emigrated to the Soviet Union in 1925 to build the new Jerusalem.

Dubcek, aged four, and his family arrived in Kirghizia on the Soviet-Chinese border and started to construct the future in the middle of nowhere. The ending of the days of hope saw the dawn of the terror. Heaven became hell, and by 1938, despite his communism, Stefan chose a return to crisis-torn Czechoslovakia rather than imposed Soviet citizenship.

With Hitler's war came resistance. Alexander and his brother Julius fought. Julius died in the Slovak National uprising of 1944. In 1949 Dubcek became a full-time *apparachnik* moving, partly because of his Slovak background, rapidly up the hierarchy. Via a spell at the Higher Political School of the Soviet Communist Party Central Committee in Moscow in 1955 for high-flying communists, he was catapulted into the Czechoslovak Central Committee in June 1958. From there he battled with Novotny as Krushchev's revisionism spread and won, freeing Czech lands and Slovakia from the suffocating orthodoxy of communist theology with the *Action Programme* agreed in April 1968. This programme was designed to overcome the stagnation of the Czechoslovak economy. It was the document that triggered the avalanche of events that culminated in the Invasion, as the other European Communist leaders felt the chill wind of change coming from the West.

Husak played Judas and sold Dubcek out. He was rapidly driven from power, and spent twenty years as a forestry worker under continuous surveillance and suspicion. In November 1989 he was resurrected to stand shoulder to shoulder with Vaclav Havel in Wenceslas Square, cheering the end of the Soviet Empire. By September 1992 Dubcek was dead. Before his death, in a car crash, he had sadly seen the end of the new beginning with the tension between Slovakian social-democracy and Czech free-market enthusiasms tearing the country in two.

Alexander Dubcek was a courageous man, playing a key role in hastening the collapse of Communism in Europe. He paid a price for all the people of Central and Eastern Europe and the Soviet Union.

It is a pity fate didn't give him more time to finish his autobiography. It's all too clean and sanitised. Dubcek, like Gorbachev, didn't end up at the head of his nation's Communist Party by accident. This was the result of brutal in-fighting within the Party machine. Dubcek wasn't standing on the sidelines. Yet the only hint we get of his involvement in realpolitik is when he records that he split Novotny from his henchman Hendrych by offering the latter one of Novotny's own posts. Otherwise, it seems history just conscripted him. It would be much more revealing to have seen what social and economic forces drove an intelligent, cultured communist to apostasy.

Tribune, 27 August 1993

70. Sheron Gags Swales Boo-Boys

Sheffield Utd...0   Man City...1

Manchester City's second away win of the season will inevitably mute the 'Swales out' chants.

After two disappointing games earlier in the week against Wimbledon and Reading, Maine Road chief Peter Swales and manager Brian Horton can relax a little. With Terry Venables and Alan Sugar hogging the headlines, Swales is off the front and back pages.

Like it or not, if the team can keep this up, Frannie Lee's takeover bid could be dead in the water. At the final whistle City fans at Bramall Lane sang 'Blue Moon' rather than barrack the chairman.

The all-important goal came after 56 minutes. Alfons Groenendijk fed Niall Quinn a long ball ten yards out on the right of the area. Goalkeeper Simon Tracey could not hold Quinn's shot and Mike Sheron applied the finishing touch to make it six games without a win for Sheffield United. Although I come from near Swindon, I have stood at the Kippax End at Maine Road and supported Manchester City since I moved to the North in the 1970s. This season I moved to the family stand with my 12-year old daughter Elise.

Originally, I watched both United and City — but I haven't been to Old Trafford since the Reds were a Second Division side. Mike Summerbee, whom I had watched at Swindon, won me over to City playing alongside Lee and Colin Bell in that fine, crowd-pulling side. It is fair to describe City as a club with a great deal of unfulfilled promise. Despite living in the shadows of United, once a City man always a City man.

City gave Steven Lomas his debut, with Garry Flitcroft and David White the latest in a long line of casualties, and he showed nice touches and seemed confident. He almost scored ten minutes from time with a lob that was scooped over the bar by the goalkeeper.

Groenendijk should have buried his effort after 31 minutes when Sheron flicked the ball on — but he shot far too close to talented Tracey.

The United goalkeeper, in his first League game for a year, then did well to smother a Sheron shot. And Alan Kernaghan, City's recent £1.5 million acquisition from Middlesbrough, almost caught out Tracey with an adventurous lob.

Sunday Express, 26 September 1993